Valley Forge to Monmouth

Valley Forge to Monmouth

Six Transformative Months of the American Revolution

JIM STEMPEL

McFarland & Company, Inc., Publishers

Jefferson, North Carolina

LIBRARY OF CONGRESS CATALOGUING-IN-PUBLICATION DATA

Names: Stempel, Jim, 1948– author.
Title: Valley Forge to Monmouth : six transformative months
of the American Revolution / Jim Stempel.
Other titles: Six transformative months of the American Revolution
Description: Jefferson, North Carolina : McFarland & Company, Inc.,
Publishers, 2021 | Includes bibliographical references and index.
Identifiers: LCCN 2020041940 | ISBN 9781476682679 (paperback : acid free paper) ∞
ISBN 9781476640938 (ebook)
Subjects: LCSH: United States—History—Revolution, 1775-1783—Campaigns. |
Lafayette, Marie Joseph Paul Yves Roch Gilbert Du Motier, marquis de,
1757-1834. | Washington, George, 1732-1799. | Valley Forge (Pa.)—
History—18th century. | Pennsylvania—History—Revolution,
1775-1783. | Monmouth, Battle of, Freehold, N.J., 1778. | New
Jersey—History—Revolution, 1775-1783.
Classification: LCC E234 .S836 2021 | DDC 973.3/3—dc23
LC record available at https://lccn.loc.gov/2020041940

BRITISH LIBRARY CATALOGUING DATA ARE AVAILABLE

ISBN (print) 978-1-4766-8267-9
ISBN (ebook) 978-1-4766-4093-8

On the cover: Soldiers standing in snow-covered military camp,
Valley Forge, Pa. (artwork from 1920); General Washington at the Battle
of Monmouth (artwork circa December 4, 1856)

Printed in the United States of America

McFarland & Company, Inc., Publishers
Box 611, Jefferson, North Carolina 28640
www.mcfarlandpub.com

Table of Contents

Table of Contents

Preface

Carl Jung, the great psychoanalyst and explorer of the human soul, once asked, "Who has fully realized that history is not contained in thick books but lives in our very blood," a cautionary reminder that we are all products of the past, whether we are aware of that fact or not. History, then, at least from Jung's point of view, was a living, shaping, vital essence in our lives, the cultural equivalent of DNA. Yet today in the United States—as it has been for at least thirty years—a firm grasp of the nation's history remains, for many in the general public, sadly lacking. Virtually every historical survey—from the Heritage Foundation, to the American Council of Trustees and Alumni, to the American Revolution Center of Philadelphia, to the Woodrow Wilson National Fellowship Foundation, to the Intercollegiate Studies Institute—demonstrates that the American people have in recent decades become woefully uninformed regarding their own history, and hence, from Jung's perspective, painfully ignorant of their own nature. On this critical point Jung is hardly alone. "Neither the life of an individual nor the history of a society can be understood without understanding both," insisted American sociologist C. Wright Mills, and today the American populace appears to be suffering from a profound ignorance of their historical origins, an affliction that is decidedly unhealthy.

The flow of history has created the world we now experience—the language, concepts, clothing, values, art forms, etc., that we all use every day, often without a second thought as to their origins. It seems the history of the United States has faded into a vague blob of misconceptions, confusions, and misrepresentations, and no aspect of that history has been more prone to these tribulations than the Revolutionary period, when the American nation first came into being. To comprehend the ongoing American experiment in democracy it is of course crucial to have at least a basic understanding of its beginnings, times when the motivations, ideals, prejudices, misconceptions, and even the meaning of some words differed somewhat from our own today. This book is an attempt to bring a piece of that Revolutionary era to light, to offer the modern reader an accurate look at the nation's early history, not as vainglorious myth, but as a factual narrative from which we might judge for ourselves the motivations, success, and failures of our predecessors.

It seems almost impossible today to grasp those years of the American Revolution, and what those times meant for the people who lived them. Something entirely new seemed to be in the air, a sense of positive transformation and excitement, the sensation of *sui generis* (something unequaled), as if the winds of change were in the process of reconfiguring the entire world. It was a time of great anticipation as a tide of new ideas—of liberty, equality, and independence—swept whole generations of American men and women up in their heady currents. Today those currents seem virtually lost, buried under years of neglect, myth, and historical inaccuracies to the point that our American origins seem these days only slightly less distant than the Mesozoic Era when dinosaurs roamed the earth.

It is generally accepted that the American Revolution began on April 17, 1775, when shots were exchanged between British regulars and American militia at Concord Bridge, near Boston, but that is correct only in a military sense. The American Revolution involved a transformation of status and concomitant worldview, from that of serf or peasant—a status that had prevailed on the European Continent since the Dark Ages—to that of free citizen, endowed with enumerated constitutional rights. That transformation had begun almost 150 years before the first shots were fired, evolving to maturity in the town councils, assemblies, and legislative bodies that oversaw the daily lives of the colonists, and it was that evolution in thought and status that ushered forth an entire encyclopedia of revolutionary *ideas*, most of these based upon literature written and circulated during the Enlightenment. These deliberative bodies therefore served as incubators for not only democracy, but the democratic mind, a nascent consciousness that was then in its most formative stages on the North American Continent. In that sense, the colonists had become free, self-governing, and prosperous citizens long before the violence at Concord Bridge. The Revolution, then, might best be understood as a natural progression in the development of political and social thought, not simply as a war that ultimately produced independence from Great Britain and a new, constitutional government. In that sense, the American Revolution represented a huge leap forward for humankind into the emerging space of individual rights and freedoms, a development that shook the foundation of the old monarchical order to its core, and over time reframed human aspirations across the globe.

This book is about a six-month period during that Revolutionary War, a period when the men who marched in the ranks and the officers who led them all went through a remarkable transformation which began in the cold and famine of Valley Forge, only to end some six months later in battle at Monmouth Courthouse. Properly understood, the bitter

Valley Forge encampment and the stunning battlefield execution exhibited by the Continentals at Monmouth appear inextricably linked, events that can only be understood as an organic whole, and a transformation that cannot be sensibly captured in the mere logistics, tactics, and strategies of Eighteenth-Century warfare. It is my hope to pass on to the reader a rudimentary grasp of this remarkable period, such that they might appreciate both the factual and emotional forging the American nation underwent during those six incredible months. Along the way, then, I'm confident they will come a bit closer to those primal experiences that—as Jung suggested—have shaped not only the American nation, but the world at large, and that, whether we are conscious of them or not, remain alive and dynamic in us all to this day.

These are the times that try men's souls.
—*Thomas Paine*, The Crisis

Prologue

The men were freezing, exhausted, starving. Regardless of their physical condition, however, they began gazing skyward, staring into the heavens, craning their necks for a better look. Some were standing, some kneeling, still others pointing in wonder as the night sky slowly changed from black to scarlet, then eventually to a canopy of what seemed like pulsating vermilion. Many who were watching were stunned beyond speech, some literally awestruck, while others were too numb to even fathom just what they were experiencing. It was the Northern Lights dancing in the night sky, the aurora borealis, an event most had never seen or imagined before, emerging now in dazzling splendor in the darkness above the frozen Pennsylvania landscape. One man who witnessed the event later wrote, "At one time the whole visible heavens appeared for some time as if covered with crimson velvet."[1] Was the blazing sky above them a sign of impending good fortune, or an omen of approaching doom? No one had the slightest idea.

It was early December 1777 on a hill not far from the Schuylkill River (pronounced Scoo-kill; Dutch for "hidden river") some thirteen miles west of Philadelphia. The freezing men were part of the Continental Army of the United States, weary and worn from years of marching, fighting, scanty rations, and fruitless defeat. That night as they gazed into the heavens in awe, they couldn't help but wonder if the spectacle they were witnessing was a sign from God and, if so, just what such a sign might portend.

Not far away the Redcoats had assumed a strong defensive position on Chestnut Hill after marching out of their winter quarters in Philadelphia just a few days earlier. Marching up the Gulph Road along the southern bank of the river, they had stampeded local militia all the way west to Swedes' Ford near modern Norristown before falling back upon Chestnut Hill near the village of White Marsh. Indeed, the Continentals had been in the process of crossing the river themselves at Matson's Ford as the militia came tumbling back into view that day, and with the British so near, the Americans were forced to hastily scramble back up the same hill from

5

whence they had come. There they had dug in on good ground, anticipating a British advance, but for two days now the Redcoats had not budged.

Doctor Albigence Waldo, a surgeon with the Connecticut Line, watched all of this closely, and later described in his diary the position the British had taken. "The Enemy forming a Line from towards our right to the extremity of our left upon an opposite long height to ours in a Wood. Our men were under Arms all Day and this Night, also, as our Wise General was determined not to be attack'd Napping."

Far more worried about the lack of provisions than the British, however, most of the freezing men had had precious little to eat for days. Hungry himself, Doctor Waldo added this comment to his diary: "All at our Several Posts. Provisions & Whiskey very scarce. Were Soldiers to have plenty of Food & Rum, I believe they would storm Tophet."[2] Private Joseph Plumb Martin, also enduring the cold and hunger with the Connecticut Line high above Matson's Ford, endorsed Waldo's observations. "About this time the whole British army left the city, came out, and encamped, or rather lay, on Chestnut Hill in our immediate neighborhood. We hourly expected an attack from them; we had a commanding position and were very sensible of it. We were kept constantly on the alert, and wished nothing more than to have them engage us, for we were sure of giving them a drubbing, being in excellent fighting trim, as we were starved and as cross as ill-natured as curs."[3]

Continental regiments continued to be shifted here and there to meet potential British threats, but the Redcoats eventually thought better of an attack against such a formidable position and slipped quietly back to Philadelphia. Doctor Waldo was on hand when "Intelligence came that the Enemy had made a precipitate retreat and was safely got into the city. We were all Chagrin'd at this, as we were more willing to Chase them in Rear, than meet such Sulkey Dogs in Front. We were now remanded back with several draughts of Rum in our frozen bellies, which made us so glad we all fell asleep in our open huts, nor experienced Coldness of the night 'till we found ourselves much stiffened by it in the Morning."[4] Hunger, the lack of shoes, clothing, blankets, and food, became once again the men's principal concerns. Private Martin described the desperate situation the army now faced. "Starvation seemed to be entailed upon the army and every animal connected with it. The oxen, brought from New England for draught, all died, and the southern horses fared no better; even the wild animals that had any concern with us suffered."[5]

The American War for Independence, which had begun at Concord Bridge near Boston in April 1775 with such high hopes, had now dragged on for more than two and a half difficult, discouraging years, and, for the men of the Continental Army, victories had proved difficult to come by. During the summer of 1777 General William Howe, commander of the British troops in New York City, had loaded his army onto ships and shifted his focus toward the Mid-Atlantic colonies. In late August the fleet anchored at the northern terminus of the Chesapeake Bay at Head of Elk in Maryland (modern Elkton), where Howe began a campaign aimed at capturing the American capital of Philadelphia. General George Washington, in command of American forces, attempted to block the British advance at Brandywine Creek in Southern Pennsylvania, but was routed from the field when the Redcoats found and turned his right flank. Brandywine proved another dismal Continental defeat, and a defeat that forced Congress to flee Philadelphia for York, in the interior of Pennsylvania.

Tumbling back from defeat, the Continentals regrouped north of Philadelphia in the area around Skippack, Pennsylvania, and on October 4 launched an attack of their own back down the Skippack Road aimed at the

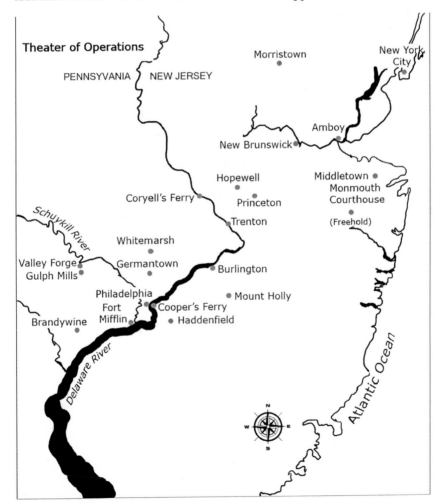

Theater of Operations

British near Germantown, a small conclave of German immigrants, just north of Philadelphia. The assault planned by Washington that day was elaborate—perhaps *too* elaborate—calling for the coordination of numerous columns converging simultaneously on the Redcoats, but a pea soup fog magnified by clouds of sulfurous gun smoke wreaked havoc on the timing of the American columns, and the battle wound up a confused, staccato effort of piecemeal attacks. Nevertheless, the Americans fought well, giving as well as they received that day, and while the Continentals withdrew after about three hours of intense combat, both officers and men felt a renewed sense of confidence as a result of their performance. Still, while the Americans had fought hard, they continued to fight in a disorganized, undisciplined fashion that in the long run would never succeed against one of the finest equipped, trained, and disciplined armies in the world—the red uniformed army of Great Britain.

After the clash at Germantown, the British Army settled comfortably into winter quarters in the American capital, emerging but occasionally on foraging expeditions, while the Continentals wandered the countryside rather like an orphan in search of sustenance, clothing, shoes, and sanctuary from the cold. Unfortunately, none of those critical elements had yet materialized; thus the army continued to shiver, starve, and grumble on the hills above Matson's Ford as they watched the British slip away from Chestnut Hill. Once it had been confirmed that the Redcoats had withdrawn from their position, however, the business at hand changed from potential combat to the needs of the army, most importantly, where the army might be quartered for the winter. The strength of Washington's army at the time numbered approximately 11,030, this consisting of 8,313 Continentals and 2,717 militia.[6] Just how to house, clothe, and feed such a number of men—already exhausted, starving, and bereft of winter gear—somewhere in the Pennsylvania countryside was at the time a question far easier asked than answered. Washington had been listening to recommendations from his officers since late October, but the general remained very tight-lipped about any final decision he might have made.

Complicating Washington's decision was the fact that Congress had fled Philadelphia for York, just slightly over 100 miles west of Philadelphia, while the Pennsylvania Legislature had also packed its bags, departing for Lancaster, a mere 70 miles from the British. The approaches to both these towns had therefore to be covered by the American Army, and any position east of the Schuylkill appeared to be inadequate for that purpose. It was also important to position the army's winter quarters so that the troops could still pose a threat to any British foraging activities in eastern Pennsylvania, while not wintering so close to Philadelphia as to invite attack. So, on December 11 Doctor Waldo tells us that "At four o'clock the Whole Army were Order'd to March to Swedes Ford on the River Schuylkill, about 9 miles

N.W. of Chestnut Hill, and 6 from White Marsh our present Encampment." The sick were all loaded into wagons and sent off for Reading, and the march began the following morning, the army along with all of it artillery, wagons, and baggage marching for the high ground overlooking Swede's Ford where that night they "encamped in a Semi circle nigh the Ford."

Doctor Waldo, like most of his companions, was suffering severely from the lack of adequate nourishment and struggled all the way to the new encampment, and his diary reflects his state of distress: "I am prodigious Sick & cannot get any thing comfortable," he wrote. "What in the name of Providence am I to do with a fit of Sickness in this place where nothing appears pleasing to the Sicken'd Eye & nauseating Stomach."[7]

Regardless of the men's condition, the army had to move on, so they were all up early the next morning and formed by regiments to cross over to the southern or western bank of the river. To accomplish this, and to avoid forcing the troops to wade through cold water up to their waists—which could easily have ended the lives of many, considering their compromised physical condition—36 Conestoga wagons were driven into the river, and a rickety bridge of rails then built between the wagons by the Corps of Artificers (engineers). Below this ramshackle affair an even more wobbly raft bridge was constructed, lashed firmly to the opposing banks. These arrangements hardly recalled Xerxes' forces crossing the Dardanelles in 480 BC on an enormous pontoon bridge constructed with precision by expert Persian engineers, but for the ragtag American Army of 1777, they would have to do. It was to prove a difficult passage. "Sun Set—We were order'd to march over the River—It snows—I'm Sick—Eat nothing—No Whiskey—No Forage—Lord—Lord—Lord. The Army were 'till Sun Rise crossing the River—some at the Waggon Bridge & some at the Raft Bridge below. Cold & Uncomfortable."[8]

From the southern bank of Swede's Ford, the army marched another three miles south east to present day Gulph Mills, a location where a grist mill had been built years earlier. In December 1777 the area was sparsely populated, and the troops were greeted by little more than a cold, barren, and uninviting open field atop a windswept hill. On this stark landscape the army began to encamp, its condition steadily deteriorating. Waldo, now ill and physically struggling, on December 14 scratched these bitter notes in his diary: "The Army which has been surprisingly healthy hitherto, now begins to grow sickly from the continued fatigues they have suffered this Campaign. I am Sick—discontented—and out of humor. Poor food—hard lodging—Cold Weather—fatigue—Nasty Cloaths—Nasty Cookery—Vomit half my time—smoak'd out of my senses—the Devil's in't—I can't Endure it—Why are we sent here to starve and Freeze."[9] The good doctor's despair was hardly unique. Most of the soldiers were beyond miserable. Private Martin added his note of personal despair to the general chorus.

"And after a few days more maneuvering we at last settled down at a place called 'the Gulf' and here we encamped some time, and here we had liked to have encamped forever—for starvation here *rioted* in its glory."[10]

The army lay about Gulph Mills for several days, freezing and starving, often grouped about open fires fueled with green wood that whipped funnels of smoke into their faces whenever the wind blew, which often it did. Somewhat remarkably, Congress had on November 1 decreed the 18th of December to be set aside as a national day of thanksgiving to honor the American victory over the British at Saratoga, New York, in October, but for the famished soldiers at Gulph Mills, the notion of a thanksgiving seemed little more than a very poor joke. Colonel Henry Dearborn complained:

> Weather still Remains uncomfortable—this is Thanksgiving Day thro the whole Continent of America—but god knows We have very Little to keep it with this being the third Day we have been without flouer or bread—& are Living on a high uncultivated hill, in huts & tents Laying on the cold Ground, upon the whole I think all we have to be thankful for is that we are alive & not in the Grave with many of our friends—we had for thanksgiving breakfast some Exceeding Poor beef which was boil'd & Now warm'd in an old short handled frying Pan in which we are Obliged to Eat it having no other Platter.[11]

Private Joseph Plumb Martin recalled that thanksgiving day with bitter sarcasm.

> While we lay here there was a Continental Thanksgiving ordered by Congress; we had nothing to eat for two or three days previous, except what the trees of the fields and forests afforded us. But we now have what Congress said, a sumptuous Thanksgiving to close the year of high living we had now nearly seen brought to a close. Well, to add something extraordinary to our present stock of provisions, our country, ever mindful of its suffering army, opened her sympathizing heart so wide, upon this occasion, as to give us something to make the world stare ... it gave each and every man *half a gill* [an eighth of a pint] of rice and a *tablespoonful* of vinegar![12]

That these bitter sentiments came not from the fainthearted, but rather from tough, veteran troops with long records of service, only serves to underscore just how grim the situation at Gulph Mills had become. George Washington, leader of the Continental Army since he had taken command of what one British general had derisively called "a rabble in arms"[13] at Cambridge, Massachusetts, in 1775, knew only too well the desperate conditions his men were facing. But Washington was hardly a magician. He was dependent upon an irresolute and irresponsible Congress to provision his army, and a quartermaster corps that appeared feckless to the point of corruption.

On December 17, the day before the "National Thanksgiving," he addressed the army, knowing all the while the prospect of additionally hard times that was now staring them all in the face. He extolled the troops for their efforts, and explained the reason for crossing the Schuylkill and taking up a position west of the river. Then he continued:

> With activity and diligence Hutts may be erected that will be warm and dry. In these the troops will be compact, more secure against surprise than if in a divided state and at hand to protect the country. These cogent reasons have determined the General to take post in the neighborhood of this Camp; and influenced by them, he persuades himself that the Officers and Soldiers, with one heart, and one mind, will resolve to surmount every difficulty, with a fortitude & patience becoming their profession and the sacred cause in which they are engaged. He himself will share in the hardship, and partake of every inconvenience.[14]

Little did the general realize at the time, however, just how trying those hardships would be.

Over the next few days the conditions at Gulph Mills hardly improved. In fact, they deteriorated precipitously. Many of the men had not eaten in days, upwards of 2,000 were without shoes, while blankets, even shirts, had worn down or rotted away to almost nothing. "The army was now not only starved but naked," Private Martin tells us.

> The greatest part were not only shirtless and barefoot, but destitute of all other clothing, especially blankets. I procured a small piece of raw cowhide and made myself a pair of moccasins, which kept my feet (while they lasted) from the frozen ground, although, as I well remember, the hard edges so galled my ankles, while on the march, that it was with much difficulty and pain that I could wear them afterwards; but the only alternative I had was to endure this inconvenience or to go barefoot, as hundreds of my companions had to, till they might be tracked by their blood upon the rough frozen ground. But hunger, nakedness and sore shins were not the only difficulties we had at that time to encounter; we had hard duty to perform and little or no strength to perform it with.[15]

Meanwhile, General Washington was in search of a more defensible position where the army might construct winter quarters, since the camp at Gulph Mills seemed far too open, and therefore potentially prone to attack. This he found just a few miles up the road on a high, open, windswept plateau of almost 2,000 acres surrounded by woods and small farms. The location allowed for defense—the Schuylkill River covering its left and rear, while a long, snaking stream called Valley Creek protected its right. The heights discouraged attack, yet the plateau was near enough the road leading west to York and Lancaster to protect that avenue from British adventures. There was wood enough for campfires and the construction of huts; nevertheless the place had a desolate sense about it that even Washington could not ignore, describing it as "a dreary kind of place and uncomfortably provided."[16] But the army, already suffering and exhausted, could not march terribly far, Washington knew, and the Lancaster Pike had to be defended. So on to the heights beyond Gulph Mills it would have to move.

Several other sensible arrangements were made. The cavalry would be shifted east to Trenton in New Jersey for the winter, and a detachment of infantry sent to Wilmington, Delaware, where they might be better provisioned while still presenting a credible threat to the British, wintering in Philadelphia. Other smaller detachments would also be dispatched south and west of the encampment to screen the army and forage. It was hardly the best plan, or even a particularly good plan, but in many ways, it was the *only* plan.

Hence, the orders were issued, and on December 19 the Continental Army began struggling toward the plateau that would become its home for the next six months. That morning the weather turned decidedly foul— "Wind cold & piercing. Snow begins"—complicating the pace and laying a carpet of fresh snow upon which the men's bloody footprints marked the route north.[17] The army, untrained in even the basics of maneuver, moved off in single file, the only method of marching they knew. Of the men that tramped through the cold and snow that day, many were bereft of anything resembling an overcoat, and a good number still had no shoes or shirts to speak of.[18]

They were headed toward a plateau previously called Mount Joy Forge, the forge structure built in the middle years of the 18th century on property originally titled as the Manor of Mount Joy, and granted by William Penn to his daughter, Letitia, in 1701. Even before the forge had been constructed a school later referred to as Letitia Penn Schoolhouse had been built on the grounds, and not long thereafter a full ironworks, grist, and sawmill were built, transforming the area into a small hub of colonial activity. Later purchased in 1757 by farmer John Potts, the forge, buildings, and acreage surrounding were in 1777 little more than a typical swath of Southern Pennsylvania countryside, marked by rolling hills, open farmland, and dense woods.[19] It would be by its new name, however, that the area would be forever seared into the American consciousness as the location of an epic tale of hardship, disease, misery, death, and struggle, yet ultimately of positive transformation. For its new name was Valley Forge.

ONE

Washington

Fire Cake & Water

It is difficult today for us to grasp, let alone fully digest, the enormity of the task that lay before George Washington and his Continental Army as they stumbled onto the snowy plateau at Valley Forge that December 19, 1777. The mission, of course, was to construct cantonments, that is, suitable winter quarters for the army, but that statement fails to capture in any objective sense the sheer scale of the project that awaited them. So, some comparisons might prove helpful. For instance, before 1790 there had been no official national census, but individual jurisdictions had performed a census by order of the British Board of Trade, generally conducted every ten years. These figures were later compiled and printed by the United States Census Bureau in 1909, and the closest year to 1777 in that printing was 1780, near enough for our purposes. In 1780 the four largest cities in the United States listed were Philadelphia (population 30,000), Boston (population 20,000), New York (population 18,000), and Charleston, South Carolina (population 10,000).[1]

So, in a very real sense, the undertaking facing those 11,000 or so members of the Continental Army was to construct what would be the fourth largest city in the United States of America. Keep in mind, this project was not going to take place along the coast where the builders could be readily supplied by sea, but in the wilds of Pennsylvania, in the dead of winter, with virtually no supplies, food, or the requisite tools on hand, and little in the way of plans or knowhow, and all to be accomplished by a workforce that was already exhausted and starving. Moreover, this city could not take decades or years or even months to build. No, it would have to be constructed virtually overnight. To understand the undertaking from this perspective, then— and even this leaves out many of the difficulties—is to grasp how frightfully close to fantasy the construction of the Valley Forge encampment must have seemed to virtually any sentient onlooker at the time. Nonetheless, despite the almost incredible nature of the undertaking, that encampment soon became a reality. In that sense, it might be best to appreciate what occurred

13

that winter at Valley Forge, not so much in terms of the physical processes that were involved, no matter how staggering, but rather as an example of the virtually astonishing capacity of the human spirit to at times triumph over even the most frightful of material limitations. Mind over matter; I'm not sure how else Valley Forge can be explained.

That the men who stumbled into camp that first night were closing on the limits of their physical endurance is beyond question. Here, as but one example, are the comments of Joseph Plumb Martin: "We arrived at the Valley Forge in the evening. It was dark; there was no water to be found and I was perishing of thirst. I searched for water till I was weary and came to my tent without finding any. Fatigue and thirst, joined with hunger, almost made me desperate."[2] Doctor Waldo seconds Martin's grim assessment of those first few days, jotting this note in his diary: "Skin & eyes almost spoil'd with continual smoke. A general cry thro' the Camp this Evening among the Soldiers, 'No Meat! No Meat!' the Distant vales Echo'd back the melancholy sound—'No Meat! No Meat!'"[3] The men were starving, and clearly at the breaking point. Make no mistake about it; this demand for food surely carried the unnerving sense of mutiny about it.

No one understood the mutinous menace then echoing off the nearby hills more clearly than the man who had led them there, General George Washington. While maintaining a calm, reserved air, Washington, the realist, knew just how desperate the situation had become, and shortly after arriving he made his thoughts clear in a letter to Henry Laurens, then President of Congress. "I am now convinced beyond doubt," he wrote, "that unless some great and capital change suddenly takes place in that line [in terms of the commissary] this Army must inevitably be reduced to one or other of these three things. Starve—dissolve—or disperse, in order to obtain subsistence in the best manner they can. Rest assured, Sir, this is not an exaggerated picture."[4]

When starving soldiers begin clamoring for food, riot is generally near at hand, and the fact that the army did not mutiny during those first few days of the Valley Forge encampment is a testament to their personal devotion to the cause for which they were fighting, not to mention the faith they had in their leader. Washington and his men would be tested at Valley Forge as never before. Yet—despite the suffering, illness, and numerous deaths—the fact that the army would not only survive, but emerge the following spring better for their shared ordeal can in large measure be attributed to Washington's ceaseless efforts on his army's behalf, and the admiration the men held him in because of those efforts.

Indeed, the men's intense belief in Washington may well have been the most important factor in the army's weathering of the Valley Forge ordeal, yet today even a sense of that devotion seems difficult for most modern readers to fathom. Because no contemporary military or political leader has ever achieved the level of public respect that Washington earned during the 18th century, it is easy to understand why many today find it difficult to understand the profound influence he had on those around him—we simply have no model with which to make the comparison. But the intense loyalty and admiration he engendered in the soldiery certainly seems to have been the principal factor that held the army together, not only during that long winter, but throughout the entire course of the war. To fully appreciate the Valley Forge encampment, then, and the Revolution as a matter of course, it is essential to have at least a basic understanding of the general who led them.

George Washington was born on February 11, 1731, in Westmoreland County, Virginia, to Augustine and Mary Ball Washington. The marriage was Mary's first, Augustine's second, and George was their first child together. George was raised in a family of reasonable means, although hardly considered gentry. He grew up on farms in the Tidewater Region of Virginia, then along the Rappahannock River near Fredericksburg. Schooled irregularly due to economic hardships, he never received the formal education other young men of "quality" experienced, a deficiency that seemed over the years to grate at times on his sense of self-confidence. His father died when George was eleven years old, and his half-brother, Lawrence—from an earlier marriage, and whom George looked up to—then inherited one of the family plantations on the Potomac River, known as Epsewasson. Lawrence later renamed the estate Mount Vernon in honor of his British commanding officer, and George inherited the estate some years later after Lawrence's passing.

Today Washington is perhaps best known by his portraits. Generally painted in his later years, they seem to show a stern, distant, aging patriarch, aloof and never smiling. But that image fails to capture even a sense of the real Washington who, as a young man, first cut his teeth in Virginia's wilderness, then later developed a deep affection for his wife and stepchildren. Except for the cities that hugged the coast, America was then a frontier society, and George Washington possessed the physical size and imposing features that made him stand out in a frontier world where endurance, strength, and natural intelligence mattered a great deal. Historian Joseph J. Ellis crafts a striking image of the young Washington, suggesting,

> a very tall young man, at least six feet two inches, which made him a head higher than the average male of his time. He had an athlete's body, well proportioned and trim at about 175 bounds with very strong thighs and legs, which allowed him to grip a horse's flanks tightly and hold his seat in the saddle with uncommon ease. His eyes were grayish blue and widely set. His hair was hazel brown, destined to darken over the years, and usually tied in a cue in the back. He had disproportionately large hands and feet, which contributed to his awkward appearance when stationary, but once in motion on the dance floor or in a foxhunt the natural grace of his movements overwhelmed the initial impression.

Washington was powerful and athletic, Ellis tells us, "the epitome of the man's man: physically strong, mentally enigmatic, emotionally restrained."[5]

Although schooled only sporadically, Washington received tutoring in mathematics, trigonometry, surveying, and map making, and it was in the profession of surveyor that Washington first struck out on his own in 1749. As a result of his work in the wilds of Western Virginia—at the tender age of only twenty-one—he was appointed adjutant of the Northern District of Virginia, a military position he coveted. This new post opened a wide range of new possibilities. In 1753, for instance, Washington was selected by Governor Dinwiddie to deliver a letter to the French commander in the Ohio Territory, far west of the Blue Ridge. The journey took Washington through tedium and travails, and his account of the trek was later published, giving the youthful Washington name recognition in both America and England alike.

Despite warnings from British authorities, the French nonetheless continued their incursions into the Ohio Territory, and Dinwiddie was again forced to send Washington off on a mission to provide protection to a British fort, then under construction. Things went horribly awry, however, when Washington's party surprised a small group of French soldiers along the way. Washington led a surprise attack which quickly spun horribly out of control. Most of the Frenchmen were killed, either by the troops under Washington's command or his Indian allies, and the incident soon sparked an international crisis between England and France. Meanwhile, receiving news of Washington's fatal attack, French troops swarmed after Washington, and he was forced to fall back upon a rough defensive position he had earlier prepared and named Fort Necessity. There his command was rapidly surrounded and attacked by the enraged French. Surrendering after a nearly hopeless defense, Washington was spared but forced to sign an incriminating document of surrender.

This incident temporarily ended Washington's military adventures, but he returned to the service in 1755 as a senior aide to General Edward Braddock in another westward expedition, designed again to drive the French out of the Ohio Territory. Braddock, ignoring Washington's advice on how to advance troops through the backwoods of Virginia, marched his column westward in customary European style, only then to be ambushed by the French and their Indian allies as the British attempted to cross the Monongahela River, south of present day Pittsburgh. The British column was mauled, and Braddock grievously wounded in the action. Washington, however, responded coolly, handling the troops with skill while managing a difficult retreat under fire, for which he was later highly commended. For his actions that day Governor Dinwiddie rewarded Washington with a new commission, this as Colonel of the Virginia Regiment, charged with protecting the frontier. In this Washington excelled, handling a regiment of approximately 1,000

This illustration, engraved by W. Warner from the original by Colonel John Trumbull, depicts Washington in full military uniform, gripping a telescope as an aide-de-camp holds his horse nearby (Library of Congress Prints and Photographs Division)

men while fighting numerous skirmishes and battles. He gained considerable experience in the art of handling and disciplining troops, and his reputation as an able military officer was substantially augmented once more as a result.

In 1759 Washington left the military service and married Martha Dandridge Custis, one of the wealthiest widows in Virginia by previous marriage. The two moved to Mount Vernon along with Martha's two children, Patsy and Jacky, and there Washington assumed the lifestyle of a wealthy planter. By marriage Washington inherited a great deal of money, farms, along with the slaves that lived on the land. He was soon elected to Virginia's House of Burgesses from Frederick County, and over time became known as a reasonably adept politician.

It was during his Mount Vernon years that Washington seems to have delved deeply into Enlightenment thought and politics, both of which eventually had a profound influence on his thinking and behavior. That his understanding and belief in Enlightenment theory never extended to his slaves or the institution of slavery itself until his death, however, is a fact for which Washington has been justly criticized, and which haunts his legacy to this day.

During the early 1770s Washington strongly sympathized with the colonies in their growing dispute with the English crown, and he was elected to the Continental Congress as a delegate from Virginia. As war loomed more ominously on the horizon, Washington appeared at the Second Continental Congress in full military garb, silently but obviously lobbying for command of any potential American forces. In 1775 Congress commissioned him commander of the American militias then gathered at Boston, in open rebellion against the king's troops. He accepted the commission, and except for the reimbursement of expenses, declined payment for his services.

George Washington was at the time the best-known military man in the colonies, but the task he had undertaken was without question far beyond the limited experiences he had acquired as commander of a regiment consisting of only one thousand men. He was now in command of an army, but it was an army in name only. The troops gathered at Boston were little more than a collection of ragtag militias, with no central doctrine, drill, supply apparatus, common uniform, tactics, or name, and George Washington quickly grasped just how inept, undisciplined, and undersupplied this army was. But by guile, a willingness to listen to subordinate officers, and a determination that would prove indefatigable, the Americans succeeded when Henry Knox, then in command of a battery of artillery, returned from an epic trip to Fort Ticonderoga in the dead of winter with an ample supply of heavy guns. Those guns were promptly deployed one night on the heights overlooking Boston harbor. Looking up the next morning, the British were astonished to find their position in the city suddenly and entirely untenable and promptly fled by sea for more hospitable climes.

The Americans responded to this stunning victory with visions of a short and easy revolution, but those visions were fool's gold. The next venue turned out to be New York City, an important port that Congress wanted defended to the last. Unfortunately, with no American navy to speak of, the city was virtually indefensible. The Redcoats then reappeared off shore with a massive invasion fleet that was capable of overwhelming virtually any and all resistance the Americans might offer. Moreover, the British had at the time the largest and most powerful navy in the world, and any land force attempting to defend Manhattan Island or its environs would be at the mercy of British ships simply sailing up any one of the numerous rivers that flowed north past the city and disembarking troops, in the process cutting off and trapping any American defenders below. Nevertheless, Washington attempted a defense as ordered, was routed from Long Island when the British turned his left flank then beaten repeatedly until a flight from New York to New Jersey became a necessity.

Beaten and demoralized, the American Army began a long, disconcerting trek across New Jersey, dogged, for some reason, rather slowly by the British, until finally crossing the Delaware River into Pennsylvania in December 1776. By then Washington's force—which had once numbered almost 20,000—had shriveled to about 3,000 weary men, and the Revolution seemed little more than a lost cause. On December 18, for instance, Washington complained to his brother, Samuel, "If every nerve is not straind to recruit the New Army with all possible Expedition I think the game is pretty near up."[6] Realizing that many enlistments would soon expire, Washington then struck upon the boldest plan of his military career, crossing back over the Delaware on Christmas night and attacking a Hessian garrison at Trenton the following morning. The attack proved a complete surprise and stunning success. Several days later, Washington again crossed the Delaware into New Jersey, fought the British at Trenton once more, then slipped away during the night and attacked the Redcoats at Princeton the following morning, scoring yet another small but resounding triumph.

The British then abandoned New Jersey, withdrawing into New York City until the summer of 1777 when General Howe loaded his army onto naval vessels and set sail for the head of Chesapeake Bay, disembarking near modern Elkton. Washington responded by pushing his army from Northern New Jersey to Pennsylvania in hopes of defending Philadelphia— then the American capital—but, in a string of unfavorable contests, was unable to stop the Redcoats from seizing the city.

Thus, had the winter of 1777 descended on Washington and his Continental Army; temperatures had plummeted, snow had begun to fall, and the Continentals—bereft of food, clothing, and suitable quarters—stumbled their way onto the snow-covered plateau at Valley Forge. Once again, the Revolution appeared "pretty near up."[7]

As George Washington surveyed the open acres of Valley Forge the dismal morning of December 20, 1777, surely the range of obstacles that confronted him must have appeared nearly insurmountable. There was no shelter, food, clothes, or supplies, and there was no realistic hope that any of those deficiencies would be remedied anytime soon. But at least one small item made an appearance in the plus column that morning; the snowfall that had hindered yesterday's march had mercifully ceased. Still, there was no shelter for the men, and many had spent the entire night huddled before open campfires, desperately trying to stay warm.

In such dire straits there are only two choices, press on or quit, and Washington was not one to give up. So "General Order 20" was issued that day which was both confident and straight to the point. In part it read:

> The Major Generals accompanied by the Engineers are to view the ground attentively, and fix upon the proper spot and mode for hutting so as to render the camp as strong and inaccessible as possible—The Engineers after this are to mark the ground out, and direct the field officers appointed to superintend the builds for each brigade where they are placed.
>
> The soldiers in cutting their firewood are to save such parts of each tree, as will do for building, reserving sixteen or eighteen feet of the trunk, for logs to rear their huts with—In doing this each regiment is to reap the benefit of their own labour.
>
> All those, who in consequence of the orders of the 18th instant, have turned their thoughts to an easy, expeditious method of covering the huts, are requested to communicate their plans to Major Generals Sullivan, Greene, or Lord Sterling, who will cause the experiments to be made, and assign the profer'd reward to the best projector.[8]

There it was in plain English. There would be no time for complaining, carping, or self-pity, only for getting on with the tasks at hand. Still—and surely Washington realized this as his orders were posted and read aloud that day—all this would be far easier ordered than accomplished. After all, orders were not food, shoes, shelter, or blankets no matter how well conceived. Joseph Plumb Martin, for instance, recounts those first few days at Valley Forge, and his account seems far less optimistic than General Order 20. "I lay here two nights and one day and had not a morsel of anything to eat all the time, save half of a small pumpkin, which I cooked by placing it upon a rock, the skin side upper-most, and making a fire upon it. By the time it was heat through I devoured it with as keen an appetite as I should a pie made of it at some other time."[9]

Doctor Waldo fared no better than had Martin. Indeed, there was so little food that often all the men had to eat was a chunk of dough cooked over a rock which they mockingly called a fire cake, this washed down with a gulp or two of poor water. "What have you for your Dinners Boys?" Doctor Waldo inquired. "'Nothing but Fire Cake & Water, Sir.' At night, 'Gentlemen the Supper is ready. What is your Supper Lads? 'Fire Cake & Water, Sir.'" Waldo, like the other soldiers, had at best a tent to stay in while huts enough for all 11,000 men were being constructed, hence his first few days at the Valley Forge encampment were cold, uncomfortable, and unhealthy. He noted the dreadful circumstances emphatically in his diary: "Lay excessive Cold & uncomfortable last Night—my eyes are started out from their Orbits like a Rabbit's eyes, occassion'd by a great Cold & Smoke."

"What have you got for Breakfast, Lads? 'Fire Cake & Water, Sir.' The Lord send our Commissary of Purchases may live [on] Fire Cake & Water, 'till their glutted Gutts are turned to Pasteboard." Later, the good doctor, while contemplating his current fate, struck upon a more philosophical tone. "Ye, who eat Punkin pie and Roast Turkies—and yet curse Fortune using you ill—curse her no more—lest she reduce your allowance to a bit of Fire Cake & Water, and in cold weather too."[10]

So, it would be Fire Cake & Water for some time to come, the men still huddled around campfires at night in a desperate attempt to keep from freezing to death. On the 22nd the weather remained cold, but word was received of a British movement out of Philadelphia, in all probability a hunt for provisions. Continental troops were ordered out to confront them, but due to the troops' exhausted condition and the lack of essential supplies, they could not even leave camp. While George Washington may have had high hopes for the future efforts of his army, other officers were less sanguine, and confided as much in print: "Our officers are moved by this Army's plight. Today we were advised that unless some vigorous exertions and better regulations are made this Army will have to dissolve. The Divisions ordered out last night could not go because of the lack of Provisions."[11] On the 23rd of December 2,898 men were reported as unfit for duty due to lack of shoes or blankets, or illness, and the army's entire supply of food had dwindled to a mere 25 barrels of flour, with no meat, and no hope of resupply anytime soon.[12]

Christmas day arrived, a bit warmer but raining, a joyous occasion in previous years, but not so much this time around. "We have Not so mery a Crismus as I have seen,"[13] was the gloomy diary notation from Colonel Dearborn, while Doctor Waldo added his own lament to the general chorus. "*December 25, Christmas.*—We are still in Tents—when we ought to be in huts—poor Sick, suffer much in Tents this cold Weather."[14] That night the rain turned over to snow, and by dawn some four inches of that frozen inconvenience had blanketed the muddy encampment, adding a freezing exclamation point to an already depressing scene.[15]

Nevertheless, animated by need, aspiration, spirit, or whatever unknown factors animate the human soul in such dismal times, the very next day, December 26, the soldiers of the Continental Army stumbled out of their tents and went to work, cutting down trees and dragging them back to camp through the snow with their bare hands. They would construct the fourth largest city in the United States of America, if that's what it took, for Colonel Dearborn tells us that on the morning of the 26th "The whole army are busy building huts."[16]

Two

Lafayette

Scarcely More Cheerful Than Dungeons

If the soldiers at Valley Forge were hoping for better weather after Christmas in order to get on with their work, they were both promptly and bitterly disappointed. On December 27 the ground was covered in deep snow, and the temperature plummeted. On the 28th the wind blew lightly out of the northeast, but four more inches of fresh snow fell, and the temperature remained very low. The next day dawned clear and blue, but the morning hours remained bitterly cold. Then around noon snow began to fall again and continued falling throughout the day. The nearby Schuylkill River froze solid with ice an inch and a half thick.[1]

Despite the turn of bad weather, work continued, not only on huts for the men, but on extensive redoubts and other defensive measures that had to be completed in order to secure the encampment. Previously, while still camped at Gulph Mills, General Washington had issued very specific directions as to how and where the huts were to be built.[2] Huts were to be uniform, and Washington directed that squads of twelve men were to be formed, each tasked with building its own hut. The general directed that the huts themselves were to be sixteen feet long, fourteen feet wide, and six and one-half feet high. They were to be constructed from logs cut from the nearby forest, then dragged to the encampment, properly hewed and, once firmly in place, carefully chinked with clay for insulating purposes. Each hut was to have a fireplace built in the rear, this of wood and clay. The huts were to be arranged along company lanes, the front door of each facing out toward the street. Then, behind the soldiers' huts, officers' huts were to be constructed, each occupied by the officers of two companies, or field officers, brigade staff, or generals where appropriate. While Washington was meticulous regarding the overall design of the huts, roofing components were left open to the creativity of the soldiers. "Wood shakes, turf and dirt and or a combination of all three" were used, but wood shingles ultimately proved to be the most waterproof.[3]

None of this work was easy. Due to the lack of sturdy draft animals, the men, still ill-fed and exhausted, had, by-and-large, to drag the cut trees back to the encampment through the mud and snow by hand. The individual logs then had to be hewed to specification, a task difficult enough with proper tools and seasoned wood, but doubly difficult with green wood and tools in such short supply. There were no nails to speak of, so men had to improvise securing each log in place as best they could, generally fashioning wooden pegs for the task. Nevertheless, the first hut was up and finished on December 21, and by the 29th roughly 900 were in some state of construction.[4]

While Washington's vision of the encampment called for a precise conformity, the structural reality that slowly emerged that winter varied considerably from the specified standard. Huts were of different shapes and sizes, some dug a few feet into the ground—presumably to use fewer logs while exposing less exterior wall to the wind—while others had chimneys on the sides or corners. The floors were of dirt, often covered with straw, but there was little if any light or ventilation throughout the structures, and they ultimately proved breeding grounds for disease.

Whatever their downsides—and there were many—the huts were at least warmer than tents, and offered shelter from winter winds, rains, and driving snows. Haste, not conformity, was what animated the men, and slowly but surely the small city—if not precisely as Washington had envisioned it—began to take shape. Ultimately the camp would form a rough triangle housing 11,000 men, the sides of which measured approximately seven miles in length, over time approaching in size the fourth largest city in the country.[5] The huts were arranged principally along the exterior of the encampment, close to the camp's defenses, while a Grande Parade ground occupied a small valley in the center. On December 29, however, that city was far from finished, and Doctor Waldo, whose hut had not yet been completed, added yet another dreary note to his diary: "Cold Weather. Hutts go on moderately—very cold lying in Tents—beyond what one can think."[6]

Albigence Waldo, whose diary is one of the more detailed, informative, and charming that has survived the centuries, was born on February 27, 1750, in Pomfret, Connecticut, to Abigail and Zachariah Waldo. Little is known of his youth, other than the fact that his medical teacher was Doctor John Spaulding of Canterbury, and that he was married in November of 1772. He then emerges during the American Revolution, first as a clerk in Captain Samuel McClelland's Company, later after being commissioned a surgeon's mate and assigned to the Eighth Connecticut Regiment. Suffering from ill health, he was briefly discharged from the service, but returned and was commissioned chief surgeon of the ship *Oliver Cromwell* by the Connecticut Committee of War in 1776. Then in January 1777 Waldo was commissioned a surgeon and attached to Huntington's Brigade of the First Connecticut Infantry. That brigade was then ordered to join the main

Continental Army in September 1777, and Waldo saw duty at the Battle of Germantown where his unit was involved in severe fighting.[7]

Meanwhile, Private Martin, who was last heard from while cooking half a small pumpkin on a rock for dinner, had been selected for a different duty. He was born November 21, 1760, in Becket, Massachusetts, to Ebenezer and Susanna Martin. Joseph's father, a minister in the Congregational Church, had difficulties in maintaining employment, and young Joseph was subsequently raised from the age of seven on by his grandparents, Joseph and Rebecca Plumb of Milford, Connecticut. The Plumbs were well-to-do farmers, and Joseph lived the typical life of a New England farm boy. In 1776, at the age of fifteen, Joseph enlisted as a private with the Connecticut state troops for a period of six months, writing later that he wanted "to take a priming before I took upon me the whole coat of paint for a soldier." He served out his enlistment, wintered at home, then enlisted once again come spring 1777 in the Continental Army, a private in the Eighth Connecticut Continental Regiment. Martin then saw action during the New York Campaign, handled assignments in and around New York City, and later was actively involved in the battle at Germantown.[8] At the age of only seventeen, Joseph Plumb Martin had already become a grizzled veteran in the cause of American independence.

Fortunately for Martin, as the fates would have it, two days after his arrival at Valley Forge, he was told to be ready for a two-day mission, its nature, for him at least, unclear. Martin, still starving and exhausted, was virtually undone by the news. "I never heard a summons to duty with so much disgust before or since as I did that," he writes. "How could I endure two days more fatigue without nourishment of some sort I could not tell." The next morning, Joseph, along with a number of equally confused and fatigued mates, was ordered to report to the quarter master general, a good three-mile hike from Valley Forge. There they were provided short rations of beef and bread, enough for two days, and while those provisions were meager, they were at least superior to no rations at all—precisely what they had been trying to live on for days. The troops were then formed into squads; Martin's consisting of a lieutenant, two noncommissioned officers, and eighteen privates. The squad promptly marched off westward, quartered overnight in a large farmhouse, then departed early the following morning, marching steadily until arriving in Downingtown, a small village about twenty miles west of Valley Forge.

Quartered in a small house in the center of town, the squad was then advised that they would winter there in Downingtown, performing as foragers for the main army. "We were immediately furnished with rations of good and wholesome beef and flour, built us up some berths to sleep in, and filled them with straw, and felt as happy as any other pigs that were no better off than ourselves." Martin would winter in comparative comfort compared to those he had left behind at Valley Forge, and our narrative will check on him occasionally as both necessity and curiosity dictate.[9]

Back at Valley Forge, the huts continued to go up gradually, snow and cold impeding steady progress. Some provisions had managed to make their way into camp down the frozen, rutted road from Reading, and the food was distributed as fairly as possible among the men. As the New Year drew nearer, Doctor Waldo applied to his superior, Doctor Cochran, for a furlough to return home to Connecticut. His request was granted with this caveat: "We shall soon have regimental Hospitals erected—and general Ones to receive the superabundant Sick from them;—if you will tarry till such regulations are made—you will have an honourable furlow, and even now—I will, if you desire it—recommend you to his Excellency [General Washington] for one—but desire you would stay a little longer—and in the mean time, recommend to me some young Surgeon for a Regiment, and I will immediately appoint him to a chief Surgeoncy from your recommendation."

Thinking this request entirely reasonable, Doctor Waldo agreed, writing: "I concluded to stay—& immediately set about fixing accommodations for the Sick &c. &c."[10]

Watching all of this unfold—the snow, cold, lack of food and provisions, huts arising, sickness, and deaths—in a state of almost perpetual astonishment was twenty-year-old Marie-Joseph Paul Yves Roch Gilbert du Motier, Marquis de Lafayette, soon to be known in America as simply Lafayette. That a twenty-year-old French major general had been accepted into Washington's staff and military family is surely a curious fact that requires some explanation.

Lafayette was born on September 6, 1757, into one of the most wealthy and aristocratic families in all of France. His family had a long and admired history in French military affairs, and his father had been a colonel of grenadiers, killed at the battle of Minden fighting the British when Lafayette was only two.[11] After his father's death, Lafayette became the Lord of Chavaniac, but his mother left for Paris, perhaps demoralized by the death of her husband, leaving Lafayette behind to be raised by his grandmother. When he turned eleven, however, Lafayette was summoned to Paris to live with his mother where he was enrolled in college, soon also in the school for Musketeers.[12] When his mother and grandmother died in 1770, Lafayette inherited a bountiful yearly income from his estate. At the age of fourteen, he was commissioned an officer in the Musketeers, a largely ceremonial position, and continued with his education. Then at the age of only fourteen, he met his future wife, Marie Adrienne Francoise, who was two years younger than he at the time. The two married two years later, however, and moved to Versailles where Lafayette continued his education, while being simultaneously commissioned a lieutenant in the Dragoons.[13] Then in 1775, while training with the Dragoons, Lafayette became deeply involved in discussions about the American War for Independence then raging against the British Empire, and the thought of fighting on the American side—against the hated British whom his father had been fighting at the time of his death—fired the young man's ambition like nothing before. When he turned eighteen he was promoted to captain in the Dragoons, a daughter, Henriette, was born, and Lafayette seems to have decided at that point that he had to cross the ocean and fight for the American cause.

His family, however, was resolutely against his departing for North America, and forbade the venture. Unable to book passage, Lafayette simply purchased the ship *Victore* with his own funds and set sail for Charleston, S.C, on April 20, 1776, having been promised the rank of major general in the Continental Line by the American diplomat, Silas Deane.[14] Intelligent, slender, ambitious, gracious to a fault, and utterly infatuated with the rightness of the American cause, as the *Victore* bobbed across a grey sea some ten days out of Charleston, on June 7 he poured out his heartfelt (and hopelessly idealistic) convictions in a letter to his wife. "Whilst defending the liberty I adore, I shall enjoy perfect freedom myself: I but offer my service to that interesting republic from motives of the purest kind, unmixed with ambition or private views; her happiness and my glory are my only incentives to the task.... The happiness of America is intimately connected with the happiness of all mankind; she will become the safe and respected asylum of virtue, integrity, toleration, equality and tranquil happiness."[15]

On June 13, 1777, Lafayette finally landed on North Island, near present day Georgetown, South Carolina. From there he was canoed upstream to the home of Major Benjamin Huger, who took Lafayette on a two week tour of Charleston, a city he found utterly enchanting.[16] But there was little time to waste, so soon thereafter he began the arduous nine hundred mile journey north on horseback to present himself to the American Congress in Philadelphia. He arrived in the American capital in July, and initially had a disappointing hearing before Congress. The problem was that both Congress and the Continental Army had been flooded with requests from foreign born officers, most of them often assuming smug and superior attitudes. No less than George Washington himself had complained bitterly about the situation, writing to Congressman Richard Henry Lee in July:

These men have no attachment to the County, further than Interest binds them—they have no influence—and are ignorant of the language they are to receive and give orders in, consequently great trouble or much confusion must follow: but this is not the worst, they have not the smallest chance to recruit others, and our Officers thinks it exceedingly hard, after they have toiled in this Service, & probably sustain many losses to have strangers put over them, whose merit perhaps is not equal to their own;but whose effrontery will take no denial.[17]

Fortunately for Lafayette, he had arrived with an entirely different attitude than most of the French officers who had preceded him, and confided as much in his papers: "The Americans were displeased with the pretentions and disgusted with the conduct of many Frenchmen."[18] But he had come a long way to serve, and was not about to be rebuffed without contesting the initial decision. Subsequently, he sent this short note back to Congress, and waited for a reply. "After the sacrifices I have made, I have the right to exact two favors: one is, to serve at my own expense,—the other is, to serve at first as volunteer."[19] Impressed by the young Frenchman's obvious humility and willingness to pay his own way, Lafayette was called back to Congress where he was soon accepted into the army as a volunteer and given a ceremonial commission as major general.

LA FAYETTE IN 1777.[2]
From a French Print.

A contemporary pen and pencil illustration of the Marquis de Lafayette done by Benson J. Lossing. Lossing's work was later compiled in the *Pictorial Field-Book of the Revolution* in 1860. Like most of Lossing's work, the illustration is signed personally by the Marquis.

The young Frenchman was thrilled by his acceptance, but hardly as thrilled as the day, soon thereafter—August 5, 1777—when he first met General Washington. Washington had come to Philadelphia that day riding at the head of the Continental Army. Washington realized that General Howe had moved his British army south by ship, as previously discussed, but was still unsure where Howe intended to land and disembark his troops. Despite having met both the kings of France and England and having been raised among nobles schooled in the ways of the court his entire life, Lafayette was awed by his first sight of the American commander-in-chief. He recalled later standing in the crowd as the general approached: "Although he was surrounded by officers and citizens," wrote Lafayette, "it was impossible to mistake for a moment his majestic figure and deportment; nor was he less distinguished by the noble affability of his manor."[20]

Lafayette was introduced to Washington, and the two almost immediately struck a mutual friendship that would last throughout their lives. Shortly thereafter Washington invited the young French general out to view the American troops. While Lafayette had recently joined the Freemasons—an organization devoted to republican (democratic) principles—and he had developed a passionate zeal for the ideals of the Revolution, the grim reality of the American struggle against Britain was yet to dawn upon him. That was very soon to change. For this, he tells us, is what he beheld that day as the American troops passed in review: "About eleven thousand men, ill armed, and still worse clothed, presented a strange spectacle to the eye of the young Frenchman: their clothes were partly-colored, and many of them were almost naked; the best clad wore *hunting shirts,* large grey linen coats which were much used in Carolina."[21]

Lafayette's astonishment must have been obvious, for it is said that Washington apologized in some manner, acknowledging that the American troops were hardly up to the European standards he was sure Lafayette was accustomed to. Washington, used to the haughtiness of most French officers, was probably pleased beyond measure when the young Frenchman replied: "It is to learn, and not to teach, that I come hither."[22] With those words, along with many spirited actions, Lafayette soon became a special part of George Washington's military family. As Washington biographer Ron Chernow notes, "Washington found irresistible this young Frenchman who saw him in such Olympian terms, but Lafayette was also canny and hardworking and constantly honed his military skills: 'I read, study, I examine, I listen, I reflect.... I do not talk too much—to avoid saying foolish things—nor risk acting in a foolhardy way.' Lafayette opened an emotional spout deep inside the formal Washington. Although he seldom showed such favoritism, Washington made no effort to mask his fondness for Lafayette."[23]

In late August Washington finally got word that the British fleet had made its way into the Chesapeake and was headed for the upper reaches of the Bay. Lafayette rode at Washington's side as the Continental Army marched through Philadelphia to confront the British landing and, along with General Greene and Alexander Hamilton, journeyed south with him in late August to the small Maryland village of Head of Elk. Their aim was to reconnoiter the situation, but the trip uncovered nothing of substance, and was probably more dangerous than it was worth—the three were forced to remain overnight in the abandoned home of a Tory due to heavy thunderstorms. According to Lafayette, the following morning when "at daybreak he [Washington] quitted the farm, he acknowledged that any one traitor might have caused him ruin."[24] While Washington later tried to shrug off the danger he faced that night as routine, there was no denying the fact that he had taken an unnecessarily foolish chance.

Later in September, Lafayette acquitted himself remarkably well during the American defeat at Brandywine, considering the fact that it was his first experience of combat. Desperately trying to rally American troops late in the day after the Continental lines had collapsed, he suffered a nasty wound to his leg. "During the American retreat, Lafayette showed his usual valor, jumping into the fray to rally his men. Shot in the left calf, he didn't grasp the severity of the wound until his boot was soaked with blood and had to be lifted off the battlefield."[25] In his *Memoirs* Lafayette later recalled the chaotic American collapse and retreat, and he paints a vivid picture of that terrible night. "In the midst of that dreadful confusion, and during the darkness of that night, it was impossible to recover; but at Chester, twelve miles from the field of battle, they met with a bridge which it was necessary to cross; M.de Lafayette occupied himself with arresting the fugitives [rallying the defeated troops]; some degree of order was reestablished; the generals and the commander-in-chief arrived, and he had the leisure to have his wound dressed."[26]

Removed first to Philadelphia, then by boat up the Delaware River to Bristol, Lafayette was finally taken to Bethlehem where he was cared for by the Moravian community. There he would remain, bedridden for a month and a half, recovering from his wound. "Confined to his bed for six weeks," he tells us, "M. de Lafayette suffered from his wound, but still more severely from his inactivity. The good Moravian brothers loved him, and deplored his warlike folly."[27]

In November, however, he returned to his warlike folly and, despite the fact that he could not pull a boot up over his wounded calf, departed with General Greene on an expedition into New Jersey. While the British had successfully taken Philadelphia, the banks of the Delaware River below the city were still occupied by American forts at several locations, interfering with the Redcoats' waterborne supply line that ran out to the Atlantic. So, in November Cornwallis, with about 5,000 troops, crossed over the river and began operations in New Jersey, opposite Philadelphia. Washington then countered by sending Greene, commanding a force comparable to Cornwallis's, across the river, first to perform a reconnaissance, and secondly to engage Cornwallis, should the situation warrant a clash.

Greene gave Lafayette about 350 men and asked him to find and reconnoiter the British activities nearby. Lafayette promptly located the Redcoats outside of Gloucester, a small village on the Delaware. The young Frenchman successfully scouted the British position, exposing himself to enemy fire on a number of occasions, before deciding to drive in the advanced British pickets. With a mere 350 men, Lafayette launched an immediate attack, catching the Redcoats by complete surprise. Here he describes the assault: "Having only three hundred and fifty men, most of them militia, he [Lafayette] suddenly attacked the enemy, who gave way before him. Lord Cornwallis came up with his grenadiers; but, supposing himself to be engaged with the corps of General Greene, he allowed himself to be driven back to the neighborhood of Gloucester, with a loss of about sixty men." During this attack Lafayette suffered only one killed and five wounded, and the audacity and skill of his assault was much admired on the American side. Indeed, so impressed was Congress with Lafayette's handling of the situation at Gloucester that on December 1, his volunteer grade and ceremonial status were altered, and he was officially commissioned a major general in the Continental Army. The young Frenchman now "succeeded Stephens in the command of the Virginians,"[28] and his enthusiasm proved boundless.

Since Lafayette's commissioning, of course, the army had shifted to Valley Forge for the winter, and Lafayette had been fully accepted into the commander-in-chief's military family. Washington had moved sometime after the initial occupation of the Valley Forge site into a small stone farmhouse owned by Isaac Potts, taking with him those officers he needed regularly at hand, Lafayette included among them. Although the general had initially wanted to live and suffer under the same conditions as his men, he soon discovered that he could not attend sensibly to the needs of the army while living and working in an exposed tent, and subsequently made the move to more adequate quarters.

Lafayette, meanwhile, in an apparent demonstration of republican zeal, had decided to adopt the manner of an American soldier, even to welcome the privations the men were then suffering at Valley Forge. "He [Lafayette] adopted in every respect the American dress, habits, and food," he explains. "He wished to be more simple, frugal, and austere than the Americans themselves. Brought up in the lap of luxury, he suddenly changed his whole manner of living, and his constitution bent itself to privation as well as fatigue."[29] Of course, there was no gainsaying the grim conditions of the camp in general. "The unfortunate soldiers were in want of everything," Lafayette observed, "they had neither coats, hats, shirts, nor shoes; their feet and legs froze till they became black, and it was often necessary to amputate them. From want of money, they could neither obtain provisions nor any means of transport; the colonels were often reduced to two rations, and sometimes even one."[30] Penning a letter to his wife on January 6 from the bleak, freezing camp at Valley Forge, he wrote: "It is in a camp, in the centre of woods, fifteen hundred leagues from you, that I find myself enclosed in the midst of winter. It is not very long since we were only separated from the enemy by a small river; we are at present stationed seven leagues from them, and it is on this spot the American army will pass the whole winter, in small barracks, which are scarcely more cheerful than dungeons."[31]

But privation or good fortune are notions often cast in the mind of the beholder, and for those who had marched, starved, and suffered for so many months, the meager rations and small huts they now occupied seemed, for many, not privations, but blessings. Doctor Waldo, for instance, celebrated the New Year in good form, enjoying a letter from his wife, while finally settling into his new abode. "*New Year.*—I am alive. I am well," he wrote. "Hutts go on briskly, and our Camp begins to appear like a spacious City. We got some Spirits and finish'd the Year with a good Drink & Thankfull hearts in our new Hutt, which stands on an Eminence that overlooks the Briagade, & sight of the Front Line."[32]

The dreadful winter of 1777 was now a thing of the past. Unfortunately, the even more dreadful winter of 1778 was now at hand.

THREE

Washington

What a frail-dying creature is Man

While Doctor Waldo may have felt snug and thankful in his new hut, the list of difficulties at Valley Forge continued unchanged. During the first several days of 1778, for instance, there was no meat to be had, and supplies of that essential commodity continued to arrive on an irregular basis throughout the entire month. On the 28th the army's entire herd of beef cattle consisted of only ninety head, and many of those were starving themselves, hence unfit for consumption. Over two hundred artillery horses had already died of starvation, and there was virtually no feed for those few that remained alive. Dead horses, unburied, soon became a serious health issue in the camp.[1] Mother Nature, always fickle, failed to lend a helping hand. The first day of the New Year was clear but quite cold, and snow continued to blanket the earth. Snow fell again on the 2nd, and by the 3rd it lay heavy across the entire encampment. In the basement of the nearby Deweese House, ovens had been built to serve as a bakery, but there was virtually no flour to bake into bread. The official ration for each enlisted man was set at "a pound of bread, a pound of either meat or stockfish, a pint of milk, a quart of beer, peas, beans, and butter," but with no provisions to draw upon, the official ration remained pointless to the point of satire for virtually the entire duration of the encampment.[2]

On a more positive note, the force at Valley Forge consisted of infantry regiments from almost all the states, with Native Americans and some 300 African Americans serving alongside the more numerous soldiers of European descent. In that sense, the Continental Army at Valley Forge represented the only desegregated army the United States would field until the 20th century. Indeed, several notable African Americans were present in camp, namely Windsor Fry, Shadrack Battles, and the heralded Salem Poor who had previously distinguished himself at the Battle of Bunker Hill. The misery in camp, then, while intense and unrelenting, was shared equally by men not only of varied religions, ethnic groups, and geographic regions, but of firm and equal dedication.[3]

Despite all these glaring deficiencies, many men tried to maintain positive attitudes, and continued working diligently on their huts. Among them was Doctor Waldo, who noted in his diary: "Our Hutt, or rather our Hermits Cell, goes on briskly, having a short allowance of Bread this morning we divided it with great precision, eat our Breakfast with thankful hearts for the little we had, took care of the sick, according to our dayly practice, and went to Work on our little humble Cottage." The very next day he added: "Properly accouter'd I went to work at Masonry, None of my Mess were to dictate me, and before Night (being found with Mortar & Stone) I almost completed a genteel Chimney to my Magnificent Hutt, however, as we had short allowances of food & no Grogg, my back ached before Night."[4]

Meanwhile, General Washington had now to face two additional problems of some consequence. The first was the virtual dissolution of his officer corps due to a staggering number of requests for furlough, or outright resignation. The second was the discovery of a group of politicians and high-level officers apparently intriguing behind his back. First, the fleeing officers.

The problem for most officers was not an issue of loyalty, but rather the inferior pay scale under which they were forced to serve. Following in the European tradition, American officers were required to furnish their own food, equipment, and provisions, these to be paid for out of their pockets. For European armies, which had always drawn their officer corps from the wealthy aristocracy, this was rarely a problem, but in the United States, where there was no established aristocracy, and where officers were generally selected and advanced on merit alone, this system proved an ongoing difficulty. At Valley Forge—where there was little food to purchase, even had the officers money enough to procure it—this system almost immediately produced a situation where many of the junior officers literally faced starvation, and were subsequently forced to petition for furlough, or offer their resignations if a furlough was not forthcoming. "The failure to pay on schedule and the depreciation of money thus hit the officers especially hard. Further, the characteristics of maturity and civilian standing which caused individuals to be commissioned in the first place meant that they were especially likely to have heavy responsibilities at home."[5] This situation naturally began to spin almost completely out of control. Waldo noted: "So much talk about discharges among the Officers—& so many are discharged—his Excellency lately expressed his fears of being left Alone with the Soldiers only."[6]

Doctor Waldo, an officer himself, was painfully familiar with the situation, and offers this sympathetic explanation: "Yesterday upwards of fifty Officers in Gen Greene's Division resigned their Commissions—Six or Seven of our Regiment are doing the like to-day. All this is occasion'd by Officers Families being so much neglected at home on account of Provisions. Their Wages will not by considerable, purchase a few trifling

Comfortables here in Camp, & maintain their families at home, while such extravagant prices are demanded for the common necessaries of Life— What then have they to purchase Cloaths and other necessaries with?"

Waldo continues: "The present Circumstances of the Soldier is better by far than the Officers—for the family of the Soldier is provided for at the public expense if the Articles they want are above the common price—but the Officer's family, are obliged not only to beg in the most humble manner for the necessaries of Life,—but also to pay for them afterwards at the most exorbitant rates—and even in this manner, many of them who depend entirely on their Money, cannot procure half the material comforts that are wanted in a family."[7]

So, for many officers it was a question of starving at Valley Forge as their families likewise starved at home or resigning their commissions and returning home to try and help their wives and children. Many, rather naturally, opted for the latter, perhaps with the hope of returning to the army once spring arrived. Washington grasped the difficult situation his officers were in, but when these men departed, their duties still had to be performed, and those responsibilities fell increasingly upon Washington himself and his small staff. He responded by making furloughs increasingly difficult to secure, but the overall problem would not be addressed until spring, when Congress finally provided half pay for seven years for those officers who served for the duration of the war—a respectable incentive— along with increased pay scales for the entire army.[8] Until Congress acted there was little Washington could do except hold on to as many officers as possible, and lament the situation, which, for instance, he did in a letter to General George Weedon. "It is a matter of no small grief to me," he wrote, "to find such an unconquerable desire in the Officers of this Army to be absent. I must attempt (for it can be no more than an attempt) to do all of these duties myself, and perform the part of a Brigadier—a Colonel—&c."[9]

To address this ongoing problem, on January 2 this order was issued: "The Commander in Chief, to prevent unnecessary applications for furloughs, informs the Officers that none will be granted by him unless the Officers who apply for same produce certificates from the Major Genls of the Division to which they belong, that the state of their Regiments will admit to their absence from Camp."[10]

That order slowed the flood of officers that were either turning in their resignations or seeking furloughs, but the second problem, which had been simmering for weeks, appeared equally as ominous for the fate of the army. A group of officers and politicians in Congress appeared to be intriguing behind Washington's back with the object of replacing him with General Horatio Gates, the "Hero of Saratoga." Lafayette tells us, for instance, that "In addition to the difficulties that lasted during the whole of the war, the winter of

Valley-Forge recalls others still more painful," the principal difficulty of which was a dispute that over time came to be known as the Conway Cabal.[11] The genesis of this scheming was Washington's failed attempt at defending the American capital, the subsequent flight of Congress to York, and the current state of the war itself, which for many seemed dire. The principal intriguer at the time appeared to be Horatio Gates, whose career had received a meteoric boost as a result of his victory at Saratoga where his troops had forced the complete surrender of an entire British army. This was heady stuff for Gates, and grist for those in Congress dissatisfied with Washington as commander-in-chief.

This disaffection had come to Washington's attention in late October when an aide-de-camp for Gates, Major James Wilkinson, then on his way to Congress to report news of the great victory at Saratoga, told an aide at Lord Stirling's headquarters about certain disparaging remarks about General Washington. These insults were supposedly contained in a letter Thomas Conway, then a general himself in the Continental Army under Washington, had written to Gates. Stirling passed the information on to Washington, and the commander-in-chief responded to Conway on November 5, intimating that he had seen the actual letter. "Sir, a letter which I received last Night contained the following paragraph. In a letter from Genl Conway to Genl Gates he says—'Heaven has been determined to save your Country, or a weak General and bad Councellors would have ruined it.'"[12]

Thomas Conway was a recent arrival from Europe, an officer who had served in the French Army, and had received a major general's commission from Congress in the spring of 1777. He had apparently performed decently at the Battle of Brandywine, but at Germantown serious questions had arisen about his efforts and his politicking for higher rank at Congress had already come to Washington's attention. Ron Chernow, one of Washington's biographers, offers this insight regarding Conway: "Born in Ireland, he had been an officer in the French Army but, unlike Lafayette, was a self-aggrandizing fortune hunter. For him, the Continental Army was a convenient rung to grasp in climbing up the military hierarchy in France."[13] In October Washington had written to Congress expressing his disapproval that any higher rank be awarded Conway, and the commander-in-chief's letter of November 5 to Conway was meant to serve as a shot across the Irishman's bow.

But Conway, unflappably boorish, was not about to back down, and he responded immediately, stating among other things:

> I will venture to say that in my Whole Letter the paragraph of Which you are pleas'd to send me a copy can not be found. My opinion of you sir without flattery or envy is as follows: you are a Brave man, an honest man, a patriot, and a Man of great sense. Your modesty is such, that although your advice in council is commonly sound and proper, you have often been influenc'd by men who Were not equal to you in point of experience, Knowledge or judgement.[14]

This contained a rather obvious backhanded insult, suggesting that Washington did not have the intellectual gravitas required to make sound judgments on his own. Conway's letter might have been brushed-off as nothing more than self-serving rubbish, had it not come on the heels of the deteriorating relationship Washington was then experiencing with Horatio Gates, the very man to whom Conway's initial letter had been directed.

Ever since his victory at Saratoga, Gates—a former officer in the British Army—had adopted a rather imperious attitude toward the commander-in-chief, notifying Congress directly of his success on the battlefield, for instance, rather than through the proper channels; a snub that ruffled Washington's feathers. He also refused to return troops Washington had sent north for the sole purpose of confronting the British near Saratoga, this, despite the fact that General Gates remained subordinate to Washington's command. Gates then traveled to York in order to "report" to Congress, and in Washington's mind, all of this very quickly took on the appearance of conspiracy.

Lafayette, personally close to Washington and aware of both the exchange of letters and devolving relationships, explains the evolving situation at the time. "Gates was at Yorktown [York, Pennsylvania], where he inspired respect by his manners, promises, and European acquirements. Amongst the deputies who united themselves to him, may be numbered the Lees, Virginians, enemies of Washington, and the two Adams. Mifflin, quarter-master-general, aided him with his talents and brilliant eloquence. They required a name to bring forward in the plot, and they selected Conway, who fancied himself the chief of a party."[15]

In early December Congress's Board of War then created the position of inspector general, and Thomas Conway was not only given the position, but advanced to the grade of major general as a consequence, this over Washington's previous objections. Washington was unaware of the appointment, however, until Conway showed up one day at Valley Forge, intent on flaunting his new authority. Stunned, the commander-in-chief refused to allow Conway to inspect anything until so instructed by Congress, and a bitter Conway stormed off in a huff. It was at this point that Washington became convinced that Gates, Conway, and a few other members of Congress were trying to tar his reputation while scheming to replace him with either Gates or Charles Lee, another ex-British officer who had been captured by the British, and was then awaiting exchange. Then the plot thickened even more. Historian John Buchanan explains: "The appointment and promotion [of Conway] were not meant to embarrass or antagonize Washington, but of course they did, and then in the same bumbling way Congress reorganized the Board of War, made Gates its president and selected Washington's enemy Thomas Mifflin to serve on it along with Colonel Timothy Pickering, who was critical of the senior commanders and aides-de-camp surrounding Washington."[16]

Washington, while also trying to put out a hundred different fires at Valley Forge, became convinced at this point that a plot was afoot to defame and unseat him. And why not? It was a fact well known that his defense of New York had failed, as had his defense of Philadelphia. His victories leading the Continental Army paled in comparison to his defeats, and it can be assumed that Washington, a man of some pride, personally felt the sting of these failures. Just as jackals surround wounded prey, knaves, scoundrels, and scheming politicians throughout the ages have always circled when opponents appear wounded, and the Congress at York contained any number of men who fancied themselves superior to the commander-in-chief. Washington's correspondence with Gates and Conway became increasingly hostile, while on more than one occasion he received word from friends that some in Congress were scheming against him. Keeping his cool, but obviously frustrated, in a letter to William Gordon on January 23, Washington intimated that he might be willing to step aside, should Congress find someone far better suited for the job.

> So soon then as the public gets dissatisfied with my services, or a person is found better qualified to answer her expectation, I shall quit the helm with as much satisfaction, and retire to a private station with as much content, as ever the wearied pilgrim felt upon his safe arrival in the Holy-land, or haven of hope; and shall wish most devoutly, that those who come after may meet with more prosperous gales than I have done.[17]

When word of this got out, the public response so overwhelmingly favored the commander-in-chief that any movement against him seemed immediately, and obviously, doomed. Fortunately, in the end the "cabal" proved to be more hot air than serious plot and by late January it had essentially run out of steam. Whether there ever was, in fact, an actual scheme to replace Washington has never been verified, but that did not stop him from believing that one had existed. Indeed, in a letter written to Patrick Henry in March of 1778, Washington explained his suspicions.

> I cannot precisely mark the extent of their views, but it appeared in general, that General Gates was to be exalted, on the ruin of my reputation and influence. This I am authorised to say from undeniable facts, in my own possession, from publications , the evident scope of which, could not be mistaken, and from private detractions industriously circulated. Genl Mifflin it is commonly supposed, bore the second part in the Cabal; and Genl Conway, I know, was a very active, and malignat partizan but I have Good reasons to believe that their machinations have recoiled most Sensibly upon themselves.[18]

Meanwhile, just outside the door of the commander's headquarters, the wretched conditions at Valley Forge continued virtually unabated. Disease, far more than the enemy, was beginning to take a heavy toll, and there was little in the way of medical resources to stop or contain it. Field hospitals had been established at Reading, Ephrata, Easton, Lititz, and Yellow

Springs—all small towns a good distance from the main encampment—but getting the men transferred from Valley Forge to any of the field hospitals proved a difficult process, what with the muddy roads now frozen, a critical lack of blankets, and a dearth of horses to pull the wagons.[19] "We sincerely feel for the unhappy condition of our poor fellows in the Hospitals," a doctor wrote, "and wish our powers to relieve them were equal to our inclinations. It is but a melancholy Truth that our Hospital Stores are exceeding scanty and deficient in every instance. Our difficulties and distress are certainly great and such as wound the feelings of Humanity. Our sick are naked, our well naked, our unfortunate men in captivity naked!"[20]

The British, in the meantime, were enjoying their stay in Philadelphia, well supplied while ensconced in agreeable quarters. Henry Lee was at the time a young American cavalry officer serving at an outpost some six miles from Valley Forge. He would soon be known as "Light-Horse Harry," eventually the father of Robert E. Lee, the famed, Confederate general, and in his memoirs Lee explains the current situation: "While Washington was engaged, without cessation, to perfect his army in the art of war, and to place it out of the reach of that contagious malady so fatal to man, Sir William [Howe] was indulging, with his brave troops, in all the sweets of luxury and pleasure to be drawn from the wealthy and populous city of Philadelphia."[21]

While it is true Howe had no intention of attempting a major assault in the dead of winter against the Continental camp at Valley Forge, British patrols routinely tested the outer ring of American videttes and sentry posts, and during the early morning hours of January 20, a substantial cavalry column descended on the one containing Henry Lee. Years earlier Lee, along with a few dragoons from his Legion, had embarrassed the British on more than one occasion with lighting like raids in New Jersey, these few incidents providing the young cavalry officer with a burst of sudden fame. Now the Redcoats intended a little payback. Charles Royster, Lee's biographer, explains: "Lee, two officers, and five dragoons barricaded themselves in a house and defended it for twenty-five minutes against the attacks of a force variously estimated at 70 or 130 or 200 of the enemy. After killing three and wounding five of the British, Lee and his party, by shouting, made the British believe that the American infantry was coming." The British cavalry fled the scene, dragging off only a few American sentries as prisoners.[22]

The American camp celebrated gleefully over Lee's clever defense, the good news making its way all the way up the chain of command to the commander-in-chief himself. "Today his Excellency return'd the warmest thanks to Capt Lee and his Officers and Men of Lee's Legion for the Victory which their superior bravery & address gained over a party of the Enemy's Dragoons…. After a violent attack of 25 minutes, finding so gallant a resistance, & fearing that their retreat would be cut off, they disgracefully turned tail & made for Philada.... An English Officer who lay in the House (being on parole and on his way to Philada) speaks in raptures of the bravery and proclaims it thro' the City."[23]

Henry Lee that day had a narrow escape from death, but many more American soldiers that winter would fare less fortunately. Frigid temperatures, a lack of food, clothes, blankets, and a shortage of anything remotely approaching proper medical care would continue to take a heavy toll on the men for weeks to come. Black, frost-bitten limbs were being amputated, bodies loaded into wagons for transfer or burial, the grim ritual of the dead and dying repeated time and again across a brutal landscape of freezing men and decaying carrion.

Doctor Waldo no doubt attended to as much of this gloomy business as anyone, past or present, and, as a result, there are times when his diary observations seem as much the work of philosopher as that of chronicler, doctor, or soldier. In early January he received a notice to attend a soldier in difficulty, and it is easy to imagine him pulling his collar close while heading across the snowy ground into the cold, unwelcoming hospital tent where the poor man now lay. The doctor's subsequent thoughts remind us that death, not cabals or shortages or inadequate shelter, no matter how grievous those issues might be, is what war is ultimately about, and his simple words capture the horror and futility of Valley Forge far better than any modern chronicler ever could. Gazing down upon the soldier, he penned this thoughtful meditation, a brief homage to our shared humanity which seems fitting, not only for those terrible days at Valley Forge, but for the ages:

I was call'd to relieve a soldier tho't to be dying—he expir'd before I reach'd the hutt. He was an Indian—an excellent Soldier—and an obedient good natured fellow. He engaged for money doubtless as others do;—but he has serv'd his country faithfully— he has fought for those very people who disinherited his forefathers—having finished his pilgrimage, he was discharged from the War of Life & Death. His memory ought to be respected, more than those rich ones who supply the world with nothing better than Money and Vice. There the poor fellow lies not Superior now to a clod of earth— his Mouth Wide open—his Eyes staring. Was he affrighted at the scene of Death—or the consequences of it?—doubtless both;—but he has doubtless acted agreeable to the dictates of Nature in the course of his whole life—why should he then be afraid of the consequences of Death. Where then is his immaterial part taken its flight—undoubtedly the scene Changes, and admits him into another State, there fixes him forever,— but what is that state—is it happy or miserable. He has been an honest fellow—has done his duty to his Maker and his fellow creatures as far as his Inclinations and Abilities would permit of,—therefore we'll suppose him happier now than ever.
What a frail-dying creature is Man.[24]

Four

Lafayette

I am at a loss how to act

It is often assumed that the officers at Valley Forge—particularly the general officers—lived in relative comfort while the soldiers they commanded shivered away in huts, starving for want of food, warmth, and medical care. But this was hardly the case. While it's true that several generals at the division level found small farmhouses on the outskirts of the encampment to rent for the winter, most officers, including brigadiers, were as desperate for clothes and food as the men they led. This notation, taken from the General Orders dated January 10, offers a telling example: "Today a Frenchman came into Camp imagining to find an Army with fine uniforms, glittering Arms, flowing Standards, &c. Instead he saw grouped a few poorly clad Militia, for the most part still without shoes. Passing thro' Camp he saw soldiers having for Cloaks or Great Coats, coarse woolen blankets like those provided in the French Hospitals, from whence they also have come. These were our General Officers."[1] These general officers, men of some pride, distinction, and accomplishment, were on the 10th day of January wrapped, not in fine warm coats, but blankets, recently supplied from France—so much for the good life of a Continental officer.

Clothing the army—including its corps of officers—along with the supply of food, forage, and medical supplies were Washington's primary concerns throughout the entire Valley Forge encampment. Writing to the President of Congress in early January, for instance, he insisted the commissary again be effectively reorganized. He noted that, while the army's foragers had gone out and secured some needed articles of clothing by means of seizure, he grasped rather clearly the fact that seizures would never, in the long run, do anything but cause the disaffection of the very people the army was fighting for:

It will never answer to procure supplies of clothing or provision by coercive measures. The small seizures made of the former a few days ago, in consequence of the most pressing and absolute necessity, when that, or to dissolve, was the alternative, excited

41

the greatest alarm and uneasiness even among our best and warmest friends. Such procedures may give a momentary relief; but, if repeated, will prove of the most pernicious consequence. Besides spreading disaffection, jealousy, and fear in the people, they never fail, even in the most veteran troops under the most rigid and exact discipline, to raise in the soldiery a disposition to licentiousness, to plunder and robbery, difficult to suppress afterwards, and which has proved not only ruinous to the inhabitants, but, in many instances, to armies themselves.[2]

Washington seemed caught between the proverbial rock and hard place; he could not seize the clothing his soldiers desperately needed, but at the same time the army's own commissary had proven time and again its inadequacy in this regard. He subsequently sent letters off to virtually everyone he could think of who might in some way help remedy the situation, like this letter to Governor Wharton of Pennsylvania: "From the quantity of raw materials and the number of workmen among your people, who being principled against Arms, remain at home and manufacture, I should suppose you have it more in your power to cover your Troops well than any other State.... I am therefore in hopes that the exertions of the States aided by foreign importations, will contribute to cloath our Troops more comfortably and plentifully than they have heretofore been."[3]

Other than a fortunate few, those officers who had not been furloughed lived in huts and suffered along with their men, but many had already fled Valley Forge for the reasons detailed in the preceding chapter. Their absence was deeply felt at headquarters. "At one time in February there were only three major generals in camp, several brigades were without brigadiers, and many regiments had no officers present above the rank of captain."[4]

What sort of men were Washington's top lieutenants? Doctor Waldo had naturally either met personally, or become acquainted with, many of them and, as a result, had developed a sense of each man's character, and his opinions are worthy of consideration:

The Marquis De la Fayette, a Volunteer in Our Army—& he who gave three Ships to Congress, is very agreeable in his person and great in his Character; being made a Major General—Brigadier Conway, an Irish Colonel From France, took umbrage thereat, and resigned—but is now made Inspector General of the Army—he is a great Character—he wore a Commission in the French Service when he was but ten years old. Major General Lord Stirling, is a man of a very noble presence,—and the most martial Appearance of any General in the Service—he much resembles the Marquis of Granby—by his bald head—& the make of his face—and figure of his Body—He is mild in his private Conversation, and vociferous in the Field;—but he has always been unfortunate in Actions.

Count Pulaski—General of the Horse is a Man of hardly middling Stature—sharp Countenance—and lively air;—He contended a long time with his Uncle the present king of Poland for the Crown—but being overcome he fled to France—and has now joined the American Army, where he is greatly respected & admired for his Martial Skill, Courage & Intrepidity. Gen Greene & Gen Sullivan are greatly esteemed. Baron De Kalb, a Major General is another remarkable Character, and a Gentleman much esteemed.[5]

Back amongst the huts, numerous forms of disease and infection continued to rage, and in early January a particularly uncomfortable ailment surfaced among the troops. General George Weeden of Virginia, a brigadier in Nathanael Greene's Division, kept an orderly book for the duration of his stay at Valley Forge, and a glance at his book for January 8 notes: "Being informed that many men are render'd unfit for duty by the itch, the Commander in Chief orders and directs the Regimental Surgeons to look attentively into this matter and as soon as the men who are infected with this disorder are properly disposed in Hutts they are to be anointed for it."[6] In our modern world, it might be assumed that the "Itch" referred to was in all probability a product of lice, or the simple fact that, due to harsh weather and the lack of clothing, most Revolutionary soldiers had probably not bathed or changed their clothes for weeks or even months. But the Itch mentioned (or Etch, as it is at times referred to) was actually scabies, a serious although nonfatal disease caused by the infection of the itch mite, and a condition well known at the time. It was generally understood that proper hygiene and health practices prevented the Itch, but in the 18th century those practices, particularly while serving in the army or navy, were difficult to observe. Numerous remedies were practiced at the time, many of them little more than homemade concoctions, but the principal ingredient in almost all of them was sulfur in ointment form. This was generally understood to allay if not entirely defeat the itch, and no doubt the Revolutionary surgeons had specific ointments known to work on the infection.[7]

So, it is reasonable to presume that at the main encampment most of the men suffering from the itch received some form of effective treatment, but for those stationed at the outlying posts, creativity ruled the day, and a brief examination of these novel arts provides a fascinating look into 18th century medicine. To accomplish this, and to get an interesting and somewhat amusing look at the forms of medicinal concoctions this creative alchemy often achieved, a glance some twenty miles west of Valley Forge to where, it can be recalled, Private Martin was that January engaged in foraging activity, will provide a ready example. It seems that, much like the troops at Valley Forge, Martin and a few of his mates had become consumed by the itch that January. "I had it to such a degree," he complained, "that by the time I got into winter quarters I could scarcely lift my hands to my head. Some of our foraging party had acquaintances in the artillery and by their means we procured sulphur enough to cure all that belonged in our detachment. Accordingly, we made preparations for a general attack upon it."

Martin continues his medicinal tale:

The first night one half of the party commenced the action by mixing a sufficient quantity of brimstone and tallow, which was the only grease we could get, at the same time not forgetting to mix a plenty of hot whiskey toddy, making up a hot blazing fire and laying down an oxhide upon the hearth. Thus prepared with arms and ammunition, we began the operation by plying each other's outsides with brimstone and tallow and inside with hot whiskey sling…. Two of the assailants were so overcome, not by the enemy, but by their too great exertions in the action, that they lay all night naked upon the field. The rest of us got to our berths somehow, as well as we could; but we killed the itch and we were satisfied, for it had almost killed us.[8]

Meanwhile, as the men attempted to recover from the itch, hearsay of a curious new endeavor began swirling around the main encampment. "Rumors late today that Congress has appointed the Marquis de la Fayette, Genl Conway and Brigadier Genl Stark to conduct an eruption into Canada. This comes from the Board of War, of which Genl Gates is the President, and was made without the knowledge of his Excellency."[9] And then this:

The Canadian expedition proposed by the Congress is not viewed favorably here. A certain quantity of strength and treasure would be employ'd which might better be applied elsewhere. It will be impossible to hold our conquests in Canada while the Enemy continues superior by sea. The proposed organization of this force does not give satisfaction. It is feared that the ambition & intriguing spirit of Genl Conway will be subversive to the public good, while he will proceed securely behind the shield of his commanding Officer, the Marquis de la Fayette, taking to himself the merit of everything praiseworthy and attributing every misfortune to the ostensible head.[10]

On January 22, the Board of War, Horatio Gates now at the helm, resolved that a new expedition to invade Canada ought to be launched. A similar adventure had been tried in the fall of 1775, organized and led at that time by Benedict Arnold, the talented Daniel Morgan driving the lead elements through Maine's frozen wilderness, the object of the expedition being Quebec. Exhausted and half-starved, the American troops finally arrived on the outskirts of Quebec in December, and an ill-coordinated attack was launched against the city on December 31. Unfortunately, bad weather and poor coordination doomed that assault. Arnold was badly wounded, another commanding officer shot dead in the initial surge, and Morgan was finally surrounded and forced to surrender on the city's snowy streets. Ultimately that effort gained nothing at all, while costing the Americans dearly in terms of men, money, wasted capital, and provisions.

Unfortunately for the American cause, it would take another two years before Horatio Gates would be able to demonstrate to everyone's complete satisfaction his glaring lack of strategic thinking and tactical skill. It would not be until 1780, while then in command of the Southern Army, that Gates would march a physically depleted command composed primarily of militia literally into the teeth of Lord Charles Cornwallis's British Army on the road to Camden, South Carolina, and watch the following morning as his militia fled at the mere sight of British bayonets. Caught in the surge of American fugitives, Gates leaped to his horse and rode for three days, finally halting in Hillsborough, North Carolina, some 180 miles from the disaster his incompetence had created. Gate's flight hardly went unnoticed, however, prompting Alexander Hamilton to quip: "Was there ever an instance of a general running away as Gates had done from his whole army? And was there ever so precipitous a flight? One hundred and eighty miles in three days and a half! It does admirable credit to the activity of a man at his time of life. But it disgraces the general and the soldier."[11] Nevertheless, during the Valley Forge winter of 1777–78 General Gates was still regarded by many in Congress as Washington's better, quite possibly by Gates himself.

Considering the dreadful state of American military affairs at the time, the very notion of another foray into Canada, this undertaken once again in the dead of winter, and all under the direction and supervision of a twenty-year-old novice French general, seems today difficult to fathom. So difficult, in fact, that it appears to have the distinct scent of intrigue about it, far more so than anything credibly strategic. Consider, for instance, the fact that Gates' friend and confident Thomas Conway had been selected to join the expedition as second in command, and that initially Lafayette's command, the so called "Northern Department," was to be entirely separate from Washington, thus elevating the young Frenchman, on paper at least, to an almost equal status with Washington himself.

Was this a serious military plan, or simply more shenanigans from the cabal of Gates, Conway, Mifflin, et al.? Is it possible, for instance, that this was merely a scheme to separate Washington from his young general; to diminish the commander-in-chief's power by creating and staffing other departments, and to curry favor with the French? After all, it was the French who, after Saratoga, were known to be contemplating entering the war on the side of the Americans, and who might, as a result of Lafayette's elevation, prefer Gates over Washington as a commander-in-chief. These are all distinct possibilities, especially when considering the failed Conway Cabal. Unfortunately, Gates' strategic grasp would later prove so disappointing that it is impossible to determine with any degree of certainty whether the proposed Canadian expedition for the winter of 1778 was intrigue, or merely another example of Gates' uncommon capacity for strategic folly.

At any rate, the orders for Lafayette arrived in a package at Valley Forge in late January, previously unbeknownst to Washington himself. In his memoirs Lafayette explains that the orders had the whiff of intrigue about them from the start, an odor not unlike the seductive scent of ambition. "Hoping to intoxicate and govern so young a commander [as himself] the war office," he explains, "without consulting the commander-in-chief, wrote to him [Lafayette] to go and await his further instructions at Albany." According to Lafayette, he immediately refused the orders, unless he remained under the direct command of General Washington, as an officer temporarily detached, and was assured that all of his correspondence would pass through Washington's headquarters, while any correspondence sent to him by Congress would be duplicates only. He then rode off to York to confront Congress with yet further demands, insisting that he have "a statement of the means to be employed, the certainty of not deceiving the Canadians, and augmentation of generals, and rank for several Frenchmen." The Marquis insisted, he claimed, that "At Gates own house he [Lafayette] braved the whole party, and threw them into confusion by making them drink the health of their general [Washington, that is]."[12]

Congress, apparently at the urging of Henry Laurens, acquiesced to all of Lafayette's demands, and shortly thereafter the Frenchman received his final orders. "His instructions from the war-office promised that 2,500 men should be assembled at Albany, and a large corps of militia at Coos; that he should have two millions in paper money, some hard specie, and all means supplied for crossing lake Champlain upon the ice, whence, after having burnt the English flotilla, he was to proceed to Montreal, and act there as circumstances might require."

Leaving York behind, Lafayette started off for Albany, New York, a straight-line distance of some 300 miles, but undoubtedly much more difficult and circuitous on the limited, frozen roads and snowy landscape of 1778. "Repassing then, not without some danger," he tells us, "the Susquehannah, which was filled with floating masses of ice, M. de Lafayette set out for Albany, and, in spite of obstacles offered by ice and snow, rapidly traversed an extent of four hundred miles."[13] Stopping briefly in Flemming Town (modern Flemington, N. J.), he took the time to write Washington on February 9, his language already suggestive of pessimism. "I go on very slowly some times pierced by rain, sometimes covered with snow, and not thinking many handsome thoughts about the projected *incursion* into Canada—if success were to be had it would surprise me in a more agreable manner, by that very reason that I do'nt expect very shining ones—Lake Champlain is very cold for producing the least bit of laurels, and if I am neither drawned [drowned] neither starv'd I'll be as proud as if I had gained two battles."[14]

Nevertheless, despite the bad weather and question marks surrounding the proposed Canadian incursion, Lafayette seems to have been charmed by his lengthy trek across the American countryside, the journey producing many agreeable encounters with simple, ordinary people. Here he recounts the trek in his own inimitable style: "Whilst traveling thus on horseback," he wrote, he [Lafayette] became thoroughly acquainted with the simplicity and purity of the inhabitants, their patriarchal mode of life, and their republican ideas. Devoted to their house-hold cares, the women are happy, and afford to their husbands the calmest and truest felicity. To unmarried women alone is love spoken of, and their modesty enhances the charm of their innocent coquetry.... In America, a girl marries her lover, and it would be like having two lovers at the same time if she were to break that valid agreement; because both parties know equally how and in what manner they are bound to each other. In the bosom of their own families, the men occupy themselves with their private affairs, or assemble together to regulate those of the state. They talk politics over their glasses, and become animated by patriotism rather than strong liquor.

The trip for Lafayette finally ended in Albany, where the Marquis found things not quite up to his expectations. "M. de Lafayette, on arriving at Albany, experienced some disappointments," he states, which, as we shall soon see, serves as considerable understatement.[15]

In fact, the list of unfulfilled expectations was extensive. "Instead of 2,500 men, there were not 1,200," he complained. "Stark's militia had not even received a summons. Clothes, provisions, magazines, sledges, all were insufficient for that glacial expedition. By making better preparations, and appointing the general earlier, success would probably have been secured."[16] But those arrangements hadn't been made, and by February 23 Lafayette already had the feeling that the proposed expedition was little more than a ruse, and said as much in a letter to Washington. "There are things, I dare say, in which I am deceived.... I am Sure a cloud is drawn before my eyes—however there are points I can not be deceived upon—the want of money the dissatisfaction among the soldiers, the disinclination of every one (except the Canadians who mean to stay at home) on this expedition, are conspicuous and as clear as possible—however I am sure I will become very ridiculous, and laughed at."

The young general, now in a situation well beyond his depth, went on to express despair at having no one around like Washington whom he could trust or get guidance from, writing out all his concerns in his still limited grasp of English: "I should be very happy if you was here to give me some advises—but I have not any body to consult with—I would beg you would give me the line of conduct you advise me to take on every point—I am at a loss how to act, and indeed I don't know what I am here myself."[17]

In the meantime, as Lafayette despaired at Albany as to what would become of him, on the last day of January conditions at Valley Forge continued in their typical, downward spiral:

Pouring rain all day.
The Committee on Conference met today. When shall the Army's plight be altered? When shall indecision, indifference or merely *embarrass du choix*, which prevents action, be changed?

The malignant factions working against his Excellency's interests in York Town continue their scheming. The Genl remains indifferent to their insinuations, impervious to their scheming and unswerving in his loyalties and devotion.

This Army is short of salt. Genl Forman is somewhere in Jersey making experiments in the manufacture of this necessary and essential article in sufficient quantity.

This morning a gallon of spirits was drawn for each Officer's mess, in all Brigades, Against these raw and bitter days.[18]

Amid this pervasive gloom, there was at least one piece of cheery news. Doctor Waldo rejoiced that he "Unexpectedly got a Furlow. Set out for home."[19] He would spend quite a few days riding through muck and mire to return to his beloved family in Connecticut. Waldo would return to Valley Forge later in the year, but recurring illness would limit his effectiveness.

Lafayette remained in the Northern Department until the end of March, at which time he finally returned to Valley Forge, through no fault of his own, having accomplished almost nothing. Still, even if nothing of great substance had been accomplished, at least some valuable lessons had been learned. The young Frenchman had received, first-hand, schooling in just how deceitful some American military officers and politicians could be—an instruction of some importance. The Marquis would also go on to experience the great, green wilderness of North America, something most Europeans could only conjure in their fantasies.

Because several of the Native American tribes of Northern New York and Canada had been allied to the British, they began a campaign of bloodshed and carnage across much of the frontier. Lafayette, at Albany, was then confronted by this campaign, and responded sensibly. "M. de Lafayette, conscious that he could not protect such an immense extent of frontier, prepared quarters in every direction, and announced the speedy arrival of troops in all the counties; and this stratagem stopped the depredations of the savages, who do not usually attack those places in which they expect to find much resistance. But he kept the Albany troops close together, satisfied them a little as to payment, provisioned the forts, which had been hitherto neglected, and arrested a plot of which the particulars have never been precisely known."[20]

An assembly of the marauding tribes was then called, this to take place at Johnson's Town on the Mohawk River, and Lafayette, knowing that many of these same tribes had at one time favored the French over the English, "repaired thither in a sledge to shew himself in person to those nations whom the English had eneavoured to prejudice against him." For such a young officer, born to French royalty, and now perfectly aware of the carnage the local tribes were capable of inflicting, his willingness to travel miles across a frozen landscape to meet with them seems today a decision of no little courage. Drawn through the forest all the way to the Mohawk River, at Johnson's Town Lafayette stepped from his sled and glanced about in wonderment. This is what he saw: "Five hundred men, women, and children, covered with various coloured paints and feathers, with their ears cut open, their noses ornamented with rings, and their half-naked bodies marked with different figures. Their old men, whilst smoking, talked politics extremely well. Their object seemed to be to promote a balance of power."

Lafayette must have made a good impression—perhaps, as with Washington, his sincerity may have carried the day—for they gave him the name *Kayewla* or *Fearsome Horseman*, and after the distribution of some coins and medals, a treaty was agreed to in the hopes of circumventing future marauding attacks. Lafayette explains that "the course of the evil was at least arrested for the present," and that "whenever there was any dealings with these tribes, recourse was always had to the credit of M. de Lafayette, whose *necklaces* and *words* were equally respected."[21]

Lafayette would go on to lead an extraordinary life, indeed a life so full of action and drama that it reads far more like a tale of theatrical fiction created for the Hollywood screen, rather than the real-life story of a nonfictional character. A central player in three revolutions—one in the United States and two in France—reaching national acclaim on two continents, yet ultimately declared a traitor and imprisoned for some five years, he and his family would nevertheless endure. He was restored to prominence in France, and ultimately returned across the Atlantic to tour the United States, where he was adored. Thus his "Canadian Incursion," while surely interesting in terms of the American Revolution, forms an intriguing but slim chapter in a life where many more fascinating chapters were waiting to be lived, just off the North American stage.

FIVE

Steuben

Now Sir I am an American

While living conditions in early February became even more desperate, inaugurating the most critical period of the entire Valley Forge encampment, two arrivals nevertheless gave General Washington some reason for hope. On February 1, for instance, Washington penned a letter to his stepson, John Parke Custis, in response to correspondence he had recently received. "Your mamma is not yet arrived," he wrote, "but if she left Mount Vernon on the twenty sixth ultimo, as intended, may, I think, be expected every hour."[1]

Martha Washington had traveled to stay with her husband at virtually every winter camp the army had occupied throughout the war. No "wilting flower" when it came to the needs of her husband or the camp in general, she was hugely respected by the men of the army, and desperately appreciated by her husband. George Washington, a stoic soul with legendary self-control, was then carrying the weight of the Revolution on his shoulders, and Martha represented the love, comfort, and companionship he desperately needed at the time. She finally arrived on the road from Lancaster on February 10, having experienced a difficult trip on the frozen roads, in particular, like Lafayette, crossing over the ice-clogged Susquehanna.[2] She immediately moved into the already populated Potts headquarters house (where at times up to thirty staff and servants lived), went right to work, but could hardly fail to notice the tension her husband and his staff were under. "The General is well but much worn with fatigue and anxiety," she confided to a friend. "I never knew him to be so anxious as now."[3]

While the arrival of Martha may have calmed Washington's nerves to a degree, her presence could not alter the grim facts. Just three days before her arrival, for instance, he had written to Peter Colt, Deputy Commissary General, in hopes of procuring much needed food for the army, the tone of his letter as severe as any he had ever penned.

50

The present situation of the army is the most melancholy that can be conceived. Our supplies of provisions of the flesh kind for some time past have been very deficient and irregular. A prospect now opens of absolute want, such as will make it impossible to keep the army much longer from dissolution, unless vigorous and effectual measures be pursued to prevent it—Jersey, Pennsylvania, and Maryland are now intirely exhausted. All the Beef and Pork already collected in them, or that can be collected, will not by any means support the army one month longer.... To the Eastward only, can we turn our eyes with any reasonable hope of timely and adequate succor. If every possible exertion is not made use of there, to send us immediate and ample supplies of cattle, with pain I speak the alarming truth, no human efforts can keep the army from speedily disbanding.[4]

This additional notation made in the General Orders, dated February 11, addressed the ongoing problem: "The Commissary's Department has been all along in a very defective and deplorable situation. Unless a very considerable alteration shortly takes place, we see no prospect of adequate supplies for the succeeding Campaign. To attempt supplying this Army from hand to mouth scarcely ever having more than two or three days provisions beforehand, and sometimes being as much in arrears, is a dangerous and visionary experiment."[5] Under a barrage of constant criticism, Thomas Mifflin, previously in charge of the Commissary, had resigned his position, but a replacement had yet to be picked; thus the endless problems continued with no end in sight.

Officers had fled Valley Forge for the sake of self-preservation, and individual infantrymen likewise soon began to desert in droves. The Continental Army, which had marched single file into Valley Forge in December, had already shrunk precipitously, yet, despite the decrease in size, the Commissary could not even come close to meeting its physical requirements. The brutal living conditions at camp made it impossible to attract any new recruits, yet a new campaigning season would arrive for sure come spring, now only two months away.

Thomas Paine, the author of the fiery and inspirational pamphlets *Common Sense* and *The Crisis*, had visited Valley Forge when the army first arrived, and had been impressed with the industry he saw. Now Washington repeatedly had both pamphlets read to the troops in an attempt to bolster their dedication and morale. "These are the times that try men's souls. The summer soldier and the sunshine patriot will, in this crisis, shrink from the service of their country; but he that stands by it now, deserves the love and thanks of man and woman."[6] Although those words were written in the winter of 1776, never had they been more stirring or appropriate than during the brutal Valley Forge winter of 1778. There is no objective evidence, however, that they had any emotive effect on the men, now stupefied from want of food, clothes, shelter, and warmth for months ongoing.

It was during this period of unprecedented difficulty that the second important arrival made his way into camp, this on February 23.

Appearing on horseback, he was trailed by a small staff of two, Captains Pierre Duponceau and Louis Ponthière.[7] Washington was aware of his imminent arrival and, crossing the small bridge that had been constructed over the Schuylkill near his headquarters, rode out with members of his own staff to meet and accompany him back into camp. The new arrival was Friedrich Wilhelm Ludolf Gerhard Augustin von Steuben, to be known in Revolutionary lore forever after as simply Baron von Steuben. Having received a letter from the Baron several weeks earlier, and also having gotten positive feedback regarding Steuben from numerous people he trusted at York, Washington had high hopes this new arrival might perform a critical task the Continental Army was in desperate need of. That need was not in leadership or logistics, but rather in basic training, something the Baron's background in the Prussian military—considered by many at the time the most professionally trained infantry force in the world—suggested he would be especially well qualified to perform.

While Washington had high hopes for the Baron, he also realized that the Prussian had just ridden up from York, where he had spent a considerable amount of time with numerous politicians and military officers such as Gates, Conway, and Mifflin, hence Steuben's true loyalties remained at the time— from Washington's perspective, at least—obscure at best. Only time would reveal the Baron's genuine sympathies, but Washington, having no reason to suspect him in league with his enemies at the moment, greeted him cordially, and had him moved into the small but comfortable farmhouse that General de Kalb—now departed on the Canadian incursion with Lafayette—had recently vacated. The Baron was thrilled with his quarters, and instantly took to Washington, the camp, and the American cause. From York, for instance, he had written to John Hancock in Boston, one of the baron's supporters, "Now Sir I am an American and an American for life; your Nation has become as dear to me as your Cause already was."[8] At the time of its creation this letter may well have been more practical politicking than genuine feelings, but over time that sentiment would become, for the Baron, demonstratively true.

Outgoing, well educated, and genuinely good natured, the Baron, although a stranger to the English language, soon came to feel at home. Particularly, he delighted in the company of Alexander Hamilton and John Laurens, two of Washington's most trusted aides, both of whom were fluent in French. Paul Lockhart, one of Steuben's biographers, explains: "Here were two impressionable young men who understood his speech and who hung on his every word as he regaled them with tales of bloody battles decided by massive cavalry charges and the point of the bayonet, of warrior-kings and glittering courts. He could converse with them on topics ranging from infantry tactics to the works of Seneca, Cervantes, and Voltaire.... He regarded the two aides as his intellectual and social equals, and felt completely at home joking informally with them and being on the receiving end of their good-natured barbs."[9]

Typically, Washington maintained an emotional distance from Steuben, but was seemingly impressed by both Hamilton's and Laurens's ready acceptance of the Prussian. As a result, Steuben became a frequent guest at Washington's dinner table, where no doubt the reticent commander-in-chief carefully evaluated him amidst the evening chatter. On February 27, for instance, only four days after the Baron's arrival, John Laurens wrote to his father in Congress: "The Baron de Steuben appears to be a man profound in the science of War, well disposed to render his best services to the United States.... He would be the properest man we could choose for the office of Inspector Genl, and there are several good assistants that might be given him. He seems to be perfectly aware of the disadvantage under which our Army has laboured from short enlistments and frequent changes. He seems to understand what our soldiers are capable of and not so staunch a systematist as to be averse to adapting established forms to stubborn circumstances. He will not give us the perfect instructions, absolutely speaking, but the best which we are in condition to receive."[10] Washington—still playing his cards very close to the vest—penned this brief note to Henry Laurens, also on the 27th: "Baron Steuben has arrived at camp. He appears to be much of a gentleman and as far as I have had an opportunity of judging, a man of military knowledge and acquainted with the World."[11]

Very soon, however, Steuben had gained enough of Washington's confidence to be given the freedom to roam the encampment as he pleased, with an eye toward uncovering any and all military deficiencies, hopefully with experience enough to suggest corrections. Steuben immediately hurled himself into the task with a sense of unbridled energy. But who, exactly, many wondered at the time, was this Prussian officer now roaming the American encampment as Ponthière and Duponceau trailed dutifully behind?

Friedrich Wilhelm Ludolf Gerhard Augustin von Steuben was born on September 17, 1730, in the German garrison town of Magdeburg, then located in the Kingdom of Prussia. "The baby's given name reflected the exalted station and honorable life into which he had been born. He was named for his godfathers: Ludolf von Lüderitz, royal forester in Magdeburg; Gerhard Cornelius von Walrave, colonel of artillery, a Catholic of Dutch birth who would shortly become the highest-ranking engineer officer in the entire army; and Augustin von Steuben, the infant's paternal grandfather and patriarch of the Steuben clan, a prominent theologian."[12] His fourth godfather, absent the day of his christening, was none other than Friedrich Wilhelm I, King of Prussia, a fact that announced the importance of young Friedrich's birth far more than any other.

The kingdom young Steuben had been born into was then a highly militarized state, perhaps the most martially oriented government since the days of Sparta in ancient Greece. Napoleon was said to have quipped that the Kingdom of Prussia appeared to have been hatched from a cannonball, while the French politician, Mirabeau observed that Prussia seemed to him far more an army with a state than a state with an army. Indeed, the Kingdom of Prussia existed to support its army as 80 percent of the national budget was set aside for military affairs. At the time of birth, every Prussian male was registered for conscription, and young Friedrich had been no exception.[13]

Friedrich's father, Wilhelm August von Steuben, had entered the cavalry as a cadet at the age of only sixteen, and it was assumed that Friedrich, a first child, would follow in his footsteps. Unfortunately, very little is known about Steuben's early years. He never wrote about them, and they may well have been chaotic, possibly troubled.[14] Additionally, many modern historians have cast doubt upon Steuben's noble birth, suggesting that his grandfather, Augustin von Steuben, had fudged his lineage, claiming to be a von Steuben, rather than the son of a nearby miller named Steube. More detailed research, however, has shown that this was not the case, and further that the King of Prussia would never have consented to godfather the son of anyone who did not have an impeccable lineage. As Lockhart emphatically states, "The details of his paternal grandfather's may be unclear, but they were *definitely* noble. Measured by any yardstick, Friedrich von Steuben was indeed a nobleman."[15] But "nobleman" in Prussia hardly meant either landed or wealthy as it did in other countries. In Prussia the idea of nobility rested entirely on bloodlines, and in terms of his ancestry, Friedrich qualified.

Steuben's early years were spent moving post-to-post, wherever his father was assigned, then reassigned, and during these early years his education was largely neglected. Much of that time was spent, first in Russia, later in Poland. Then, in 1746, at the age of sixteen, he joined the infantry as a cadet and—typical for the exacting Prussian Army—not until the age of twenty-two would he be commissioned a lieutenant. Unique to the Prussian system, officers were responsible for the care of their troops, and directly accountable for their training and performance on the parade ground. Prussian officers routinely drilled their own troops while officers in the other European armies did not, often finding these duties distasteful and beneath their social position. But close order drill was essential on the 18th century battlefield, where cohesiveness often led to victory. The British may have had larger armies across the globe at the time, along with a navy that ruled the waves, but the Prussian Army was considered in a class by itself when it came to individual training, cohesive maneuver, and fighting efficiency.

For the next ten years Steuben served as a garrison officer in Breslau, today a town in modern Poland. There he busied himself with routine duties, while in his spare time reading extensively across a wide swath of topics. He also learned French, a proficiency that was deemed essential for any officer in the Prussian Army aspiring to high command. In 1740 Steuben's godfather, Friedrich Wilhelm I, passed away, and his son, Friedrich Wilhelm II, ascended to the Prussian throne. This new Wilhelm was very soon to be known as Frederick the Great due to his military aggressiveness and skill on the field of battle, and he had big things in mind for the small state of Prussia. Looking outward in order to expand his territory, Wilhelm initiated a series of predatory actions, these in turn inciting seemingly half of Europe into an extended war against him in what came to be known as the Seven Years' War.

In this conflict Prussia was opposed by Russia, France, Sweden, and several other German states, and very quickly the conflict became a war for Prussia's very existence. It was during the Seven Years' War that Steuben experienced his first combat and was seriously wounded in the Prussian attack on Prague. He was subsequently involved in heavy fighting on a number of occasions, and reportedly handled his troops with courage and skill. In 1759 he was elevated to the position of a staff officer, and later—during the Prussians' furious defense of Berlin during the Battle of Kunersdorf—wounded again, as was King Wilhelm himself.

Steuben's proficiency and courage in battle had been noticed, however, and in 1761 he was promoted yet again, this time to the king's own staff, a post not only of high honor, but of merit, demonstrated time and again. Friedrich continued as a high-ranking staff officer for the duration of the war, was ultimately taken prisoner by the Russians at the battle of Treptow, but was treated well while in captivity due to his status. While in confinement in Russia Steuben's fluency in French came in handy, and he helped the Russians negotiate a peace treaty with Prussia, much to the satisfaction of King Wilhelm. When the Seven Years' War finally ended, Steuben returned home a hero, and was given an audience with the King as a reward for his extended service.

While Prussia had not been victorious during the Seven Years' War, it had at least been able to survive, which, considering the odds, ranked as no small accomplishment. This was achieved, by and large, as a result of the extraordinary precision with which the Prussian Army marched, deployed, maneuvered, and fought, and these feats could only be attributed to the endless training instilled by the army's corps of officers, Friedrich von Steuben among them. By war's end Steuben had become a known commodity in the upper echelons of the king's staff, and his star appeared clearly ascendant.

Soon thereafter Steuben, along with twelve other highly regarded Prussian officers, was selected to attend a new prestigious training class, taught by the king himself; surely a feather in his cap, and a sure sign of his enhanced standing. Unfortunately, after only one year, Steuben was dismissed. Although it appeared he was simply the victim of another scheming and resentful officer, the precise reasons for his dismissal were never made clear. Moreover, the Prussian Army was at the time downsizing, and soon thereafter Steuben found himself reduced in rank, and then dismissed from the army entirely. All of this, on top of his discharge from the staff school for reasons still unknown to him, proved a devastating blow for the young officer. He had no money, land, nor prospects. The son of a soldier, and a soldier all his life, Friedrich von Steuben had no idea where to turn. At the age of only thirty-one, he had tumbled unceremoniously out of the only profession he had ever known, and his future looked bleak indeed.

Over the ensuing years, Steuben was able to talk his way into a few petty assignments, finally landing a minor position at court in the small German principality of Hohenzollern-Hechingen. This lasted a few years, but barely paid his bills. On the bright side, however, with the help of several royals, he was accepted into the Order of Fidelity in 1769, a knightly society of long-standing prestige. Steuben was given the designation of *Freiherr,* a title that translated very roughly into baron in either French or English, and it was that title—von, or baron—that Steuben rightly used when first setting foot in the United States.[16]

Unfortunately for Steuben, the prince's funds in Hohenzollern-Hechingen dwindled away, and the Baron was once again on the hunt for a job, this time aspiring to a military position. But despite years of searching, and many promising possibilities, nothing ever materialized. Finally, broke and essentially out of options, he decided to travel to Paris in hopes of landing a commission in the Continental Army, which by then was fighting for independence on the other side of the Atlantic. Unfortunately, Steuben was a bit late in calling, for both General Washington and Congress had by then become fed-up with foreign born officers filling the halls of Congress with their supercilious chatter and uppity demands. Some, like Lafayette, de Kalb, and Pulaski, had proven themselves capable military officers, but the vast majority seemed to excel in haughtiness alone, producing more headaches than they were worth.

The baron's first meeting with the American diplomats—Silas Deane and Benjamin Franklin—did not go well, Franklin refusing to pay for Steuben's travel expenses, and the Baron departed, crestfallen. Shortly thereafter, while Steuben was hunting yet another European military position, a rumor was circulated suggesting that, while at court in Hohenzollern-Hechingen, the Baron had been involved in homosexual activity. This charge, in 18th century Europe, was potentially ruinous, and it virtually ended any hope he had of procuring a military position on the Continent.

Steuben returned to Paris in the summer of 1777, and met again with the American delegation, this time virtually hat-in-hand. Out of both money and prospects, he had little choice but to accept whatever the Americans might offer. Fortunately, he also had friends at hand who wanted to see him prosper, and the wealthy Frenchman Beaumarchais agreed to float a loan for his passage. But as far as rank and pay were concerned, the Americans remained inflexible: there would be no commission; Steuben would have to serve as a volunteer, with no guarantee of grade or salary. He would simply have to travel to Philadelphia and offer his services to Congress and hope for the best. To this humble offer, Steuben agreed.

One immediate problem facing Friedrich was that, while he had a wealth of training and experience, indeed a training and battlefield background far beyond almost all of the other European officers then in America, he had never risen above the rank of captain in the Prussian Army. This defect was immediately remedied by his European and American supporters who simply falsified his credentials. Several letters were prepared to be delivered to those individuals deemed critical in the United States, including Washington himself. "All three letters made roughly the same claims on Steuben's behalf. He was, they wrote, 'Lieutenant General in the Prussian army' and had 'seen more than Twenty Years Service under the King of Prussia,' 'whom he attended in all his Campaigns.' For a portion of that time he had served the king in person as 'Quarter Master General' and another portion as 'Aid de Camp' to the king."[17] Other fallacious qualifications and testimonials were created for Steuben to carry across the Atlantic and to present to Congress in the hopes of making an impression.

He arrived in New England in early December along with a small staff, also hand-picked by his European friends in order to bolster the aristocratic impression they had just fabricated on his behalf. Thus, had Steuben presented himself to General Washington via correspondence upon his arrival, and likewise to Congress in late December. Fortunately for all concerned, George Washington was at the time far more interested in results than credentials. Thus, for Steuben, it would not be the fictional persona created abroad for which he would be remembered in American history, but rather his skill, knowledge and, most importantly, the stunning results he produced.

In late February 1778, then, and only days after his arrival, Steuben was granted permission to roam the Valley Forge encampment at will, detailing any problems he might uncover. This he accomplished with great vigor. For the next few weeks the Baron seemed to be everywhere, poking, prodding, sticking his nose into every little nook and cranny, asking questions, taking notes. He spoke with privates and officers alike. No issue was either too large or too small for his inquiry. Importantly, while Steuben always presented himself in the exacting, impressive dress of a Prussian officer, his conversations with the troops were never imperious, but rather friendly and direct. As a result, the soldiers at Valley Forge began to take to the stocky Prussian stranger with the barrel chest and pleasant manner, for over time he seemed far more like them than most of the foreign-born officers they had previously encountered. Steuben inspected the huts, closely observed the guard details, made notes on the inadequate supply of food, etc., etc. These areas of concern were all within the accepted purview of a Prussian officer, but had been ignored, by and large, by American officers educated in the British system where these issues had been left to noncommissioned officers to handle.

Interestingly, while compiling his survey, Steuben seems to have developed a keen admiration for the soldiers he met at Valley Forge, an attitude few might have expected from a nobleman with links to the hard-nosed, hard-marching Prussian Army. Baron von Steuben seemed to grasp almost intuitively the profound difference between the European infantryman, and the soldiers he now encountered in the American encampment. In Europe most musket-wielding infantrymen were from the lowest rung on the social ladder, former serfs or peasants, customarily raised with a cultural deference to authority that made them obey orders without hesitation.

In the United States, however, the average infantryman was not a former serf or peasant, but a free citizen, raised in what had been an open and free-thinking society for almost 150 years. These men were not fighting because they had been dragooned into the fight by royal edict, but because they had made the willful decision to do so, and for the Baron this must have struck him—both immediately and powerfully—as something entirely novel. What he was now witnessing first-hand at Valley Forge was not only a different sort of war, but an entirely different category of people.

In reality, however, Steuben was a baron in name only; hence in many ways he was not terribly different from the men he was now attempting to communicate with—this as his aides stumbled and fumbled over confused translations. Neither he nor his family had ever had much in the way of wealth; his education had been limited; he had been raised in impoverished Russia and had for years struggled along on a meager lieutenant's pay. Indeed, when he departed France for the United States, he did so for a lack of finances and opportunities, and it seems that very soon after his arrival at Valley Forge, the Baron developed a deep respect for the American soldier. Indeed, the conditions at the American encampment were so frightful that he must have grasped instinctively the fact that these men were not fighting because they had been forced to do so, but rather because the war meant something deeply and personally important to them. Steuben readily admitted that "no European army could have been kept together under such dreadful deprivations,"[18] and yet at Valley Forge he regularly witnessed the enduring fact that American soldiers willfully braved them.

After a few weeks of detailed inquiry, Steuben had come to a troubling conclusion; to him the Continental Army appeared to be little more than a well-intentioned mob with muskets. Precious equipment was being squandered, lost, stolen, or simply absconded with by departing soldiers. Guard details were unprofessional and ill-disciplined, the food unhealthy and inadequate, the entire supply system a shambles. The army had no standard size for regiments, or even divisions for that matter, hence the tactical impossibility—in terms of firepower—of directing a coherent attack, or properly supporting one, once directed. There was no uniform drill or system of commands, not even a unified concept of battlefield maneuver throughout the entire stumbling mass. Individual soldiers did not know how to properly load, carry, or utilize their muskets. Bayonets, one of the two primary offensive weapons employed by all European infantrymen,

The excellent pen and pencil illustration of Baron von Steuben crafted by Benson J. Lossing. As with Lossing's other portraits, the picture is signed by the subject himself. From *The Pictorial Field-Book of the Revolution*, Vol. 2 by Benson J. Lossing.

were used in the Continental Army principally for roasting food over open campfires. The list went on and on, an almost catastrophic indictment of the army.

Steuben then met with Washington and a group of his most trusted officers to outline his observations, and the notes made from that meeting are instructive: "Our arms are in horrible condition, covered with rust, half of them without bayonets, many from which not a single shot can be fired. The pouches are quite as bad as the arms. A great many of the men have tin boxes instead of pouches, others have cowhorns; and muskets, carbines, fowling-pieces and rifles are to be seen in the same Company. His [Steuben's] descriptions of our dress is not easily repeated: our men are literally naked, some in the fullest extend of the word. Officers have mounted

Guard at the Grand parade in a sort of dressing-gown, made of old blankets or woolen bed covers."[19]

Washington is said to have digested all of this patiently, displaying no particular emotion either for, or against, the points the Baron enumerated. First and foremost, Steuben pointed out, the army had to be retrained, from the ground up, and this had to be done very quickly, before spring weather dried the roads. To this Washington heartily agreed, then provided Baron von Steuben his first clear directive: If the army had to be retrained from the ground up, then it would be Steuben's job to do it—immediately!

Six

Greene

No body ever heard of a quarter Master

While Friedrich von Steuben was frantically racking his brain, trying to improvise a system by which he, along with only two aides, might train the entire Continental Army, Washington turned to another, even more galling problem—his system of supply. Thomas Mifflin had resigned his position at the head of the commissary, yet for the better part of a month Congress dallied in appointing a replacement. In January Congress had dispatched a committee to Valley Forge to investigate and hopefully remedy the situation, and it did not take long for them to grasp the horrors then endemic in the current system of supply. What they discovered stunned them. Men, not horses or oxen, were being yoked to carts to perform the standard transport throughout the encampment, and that was just the tip of the iceberg. The committee quickly discerned that there was literally no transport system to speak of: "There was a never ending shortage of all the components of land transport: carts, wagons, sleighs, sledges, oxen, horses, harness, packsaddles, wagoners, carters, and forage."[1] Men in the encampment were not getting the food, shoes, or clothing they needed because there was literally no functioning organization in place to get those necessities to them. The appointment of a new Quarter Master General was immediately urged upon Congress by the committee, and the initial candidate for the position was General Philip Schuyler of New York. But Schuyler had too many enemies in Congress to pass muster in York, so the position remained open, and hence the problem continued to languish.

As a result of this enduring crisis Washington's army was melting away before his eyes. Resignations, furloughs, illness, desertions, and deaths were taking an increasing toll on the manpower rolls of the Continental Army. The monthly returns compiled by the various divisions then totaled and placed upon the commander-in-chief's desk told him everything he needed to know, and those numbers were increasingly grim. The returns for December, for instance, had numbered 12,501 men fit for duty.

In January that number dropped precipitously to 7,950 and decreased again in February to 6,264. The bleeding would continue into March, when the army's return decreased to 5,642, 45 percent of the original December manpower totals.[2] Should the loss of manpower continue, by spring Washington would have little more than a corporal's guard with which to confront the British, and once again the game would be near up.

Responding to this ongoing catastrophe, in early February General Washington, who had to have been pulling his hair out over the army's non-existent system of supply, decided to employ a new and desperate measure. Unable to count upon his own Commissary Department to accomplish anything of substance, he decided to send a few of his best officers off with orders to confiscate as much material as was possible in the surrounding states. General Anthony Wayne was ordered to New Jersey, Captain Henry Lee, Jr., to Delaware, and General Nathanael Greene sent to scour Pennsylvania for supplies of every variety. As an example, Washington's orders to Greene were clear:

> I do therefore Authorise impower & Command you forthwith to Carry off & secure all such Horses as are suitable for Cavalry or for Draft and all Cattle & Sheep fit for Slaughter together with every kind of Forage that may be found in possession of any of the Inhabitants within the Aforesaid Limits [between the Delaware and Schuylkill rivers] Causing Certificates to be given to each person for the number and value & quantity of the horses Cattle Sheep & Provender so taken.[3]

By February 1778, Nathanael Greene had become one of Washington's most trusted lieutenants, possibly the most trusted of all. Known as "The Fighting Quaker," Greene had grown up in a Rhode Island Quaker family, but had eschewed the Quakers' pacifist teachings. Now commanding a full division in the Continental Army, he set out at once for the area his orders prescribed and four days later replied to his commander-in-chief:

> I will do everything in my power here—but the face of the Country is strongly marked with poverty and distress—All the Cattle and most of the best Horses have been carried into the City—the few Whigs [rebels] that are here say there has been great numbers drove along for the Philadelphia market—We take all the Horses and Cattle, Hogs and Sheep fit for our use—but the Country has been so Gleaned that there is but little left in it.
>
> Capt. Lee this moment writes of the increasing distress of the Army for want of Provisions—God grant we may never be brought into such a wretched condition Again— General Wayne will cross over into the Jerseys from Willmington to execute the design of destroying the Hay and driveing in all the Stock from the Shores, which he proposes to forward on to Camp by the shortest and safest rout—But this will not afford an immediate relief—I shall send into Camp this Night every thing I can collect.[4]

On February 15 this distressed note was penned at camp, even as Greene, Wayne, and Lee made their way east in search of provisions: "Still no meat. Some Troops have not drawn supplies of this Article for four days.

Their patience and endurance are great, but the demands of nature must be satisfied. They must have instant relief or we shall have reason to apprehend the worst consequences.

"Forage is wanting. Our horses starve, as do their masters. If help does not arrive, and forage does not appear, we shall not have one horse left."[5]

When Congress balked at appointing Schuyler as the next Quartermaster General, both Washington and the committee began to focus their attention on Nathanael Greene, the only other man they all felt had the intelligence, character, knowhow, and discipline to handle the job. Greene, then one of only three division commanders in the Continental Army, initially resisted the appointment, however, sensing in it a lateral move into oblivion. He was a fighting soldier, after all, proud of having risen to the position he now held, and he did not want to be taken out of the order of battle. Like many of his generation, he was fighting for the cause of liberty and independence, of course, but he was also fighting for fame and glory, neither of which he expected to find purchasing onions, beef, cloth for uniforms, leather for shoes, or any of the other hundreds of items the army required daily. Even after taking the position, he would complain to Washington: "No body ever heard of a quarter Master in History."[6] But Frederick the Great, Baron von Steuben's onetime mentor, and then considered the reigning military genius of the day, was quoted insisting that an army marched on its belly, and throughout history surely more than one negligent military commander had met his doom by disregarding the physical needs of his army. If the American cause was to survive, a new, capable Quartermaster General would have to be put into place—and soon!

Nathanael Greene was born on July 27, 1742, in Potowomut, Rhode Island. His family had lived in Rhode Island for generations, and by the time of Nathanael's birth they had become financially prosperous, with interests in farming, ironworks, grist mills, and sawmills, along with other commercial endeavors. At the time the Quakers looked down upon the basic elements of a liberal education; thus as a youth Nathanael spent the majority of his time hard at work, on the farm, then later attending to the forge. Despite the endless tedium and lack of schooling, however, Greene soon developed a thirst for knowledge, and began in his teens to read virtually any book he could get his hands on. If he had a moment to himself, he snuck off to a small room to read without interruption, and as his knowledge and understanding of the world grew, his desire for learning blossomed exponentially. Despite the Quakers' disdain for advanced learning, after constant pleading, his father finally agreed to hire a tutor to provide Nathanael lessons in mathematics and Latin, and he continued to read across a wide range of subjects, including history, poetry, and eventually the military arts.

As Nathanael slowly educated himself, his mind developed accordingly, and in his early twenties he developed the depth of analysis that allowed for sophisticated thought and penetrating scrutiny, the accepted hallmarks of what modern psychologists today call critical thinking. As a result, he began to question the inherent ignorance of his upbringing, and the pervasive superstition of his family's faith. At the age of thirty, for instance, he wrote this letter to his friend, Samuel Ward, Jr.: "I lament the want of a liberal Education. I feel the mist [of] Ignorance to surround me, for my own part I was Educated a Quaker, and amongst the most Supersticious sort, that of its self is a sufficient Obstacle to cramp the best of Geniuses; much more mine. This constrained manner of Educating their Youth has prov'd a fine Nursery of Ignorance and Supersticon [sic] instead of piety; and has laid a foundation for Form instead of Worship."[7] His distance from the religion of his youth increased until on April 5, 1777, when he officially removed himself from the rolls of the Society of Friends.[8]

As Nathanael Greene began to distance himself intellectually from the roots of his Quaker religion, he naturally began to question its pacifist doctrine, but it was not until the pre–Revolutionary events of 1772 that the politics of revolution began to stir him. It was then when his family's small sloop *Fortune* was boarded by the British Navy in Narragansett Bay. The sloop, captained by Greene's cousin, Rufus, was in the process of slipping into port in order to avoid the duties imposed by the royal authorities, as was the custom with most New England merchants of the day. The vessel was boarded and its cargo seized as Rufus was physically abused by British naval officers. That incident infuriated Nathanael Greene, as it did many other Rhode Island merchants, and it appears to have been the flashpoint for his ever-evolving disdain of British rule.

Greene was a handsome man, but always a bit stout, asthmatic, and plagued since his youth by a bad knee that forced a noticeable limp. Despite these modest handicaps, in 1774 he married Catherine Littlefield, known as Caty, thirteen years younger than him, a stunning beauty who reportedly had the ability to captivate entire roomfuls of men with little more than a glance or smile. The couple moved into a home in Coventry, where shortly thereafter Greene helped to form and organize a militia unit that exists to this day, known as the Kentish Guards. Naturally expecting to be appointed one of the Guard's officers, he was stunned and humiliated when notified that he had not been accepted, possibly because of his limp, more probably due to the envy of other scheming officers.

Rather than slinking off and licking his wounds, however—as many others surely would have done—Nathanael Greene stayed on in the Guards as a mere private, marching with a musket in the ranks. It was a powerful display of dedication over ego, the very characteristic that would mark his later revolutionary service. Greene continued as a private in the Guards until the clash of Minutemen and British regulars at Lexington and Concord, these actions in turn developing into the fabled siege of Boston by militias from across New England. At the time Rhode Island responded by sending the Rhode Island Army of Observation, and, in an almost unimaginable inversion of status, Nathanael Greene was promoted from private to brigadier general, and given command of the entire Rhode Island contingent.[9] No one has ever bothered to explain Nathanael Greene's almost inexplicable elevation in rank, but it can be assumed that someone, somewhere, grasped the intelligence and leadership qualities Greene possessed, qualities that over time would turn him into Washington's most trusted right hand man, and one of the true heroes of the American Revolution.

Leaving the lovely Caty behind, Greene then marched off to Boston, where he promptly fell under the discerning gaze of General George Washington. Washington had a gifted eye for talent, and very soon the commander-in-chief began to rely heavily on the Rhode Island brigadier, whose troops appeared the best equipped and drilled of all the militias then in camp. It may be recalled that the British vacated Boston once the Continentals fortified Dorchester Heights with heavy artillery, recently brought overland from Fort Ticonderoga in Upstate New York. As the scene shifted from Boston to New York City, however, the Continental Army would not be nearly as fortunate. Nathanael Greene, grasping at once the impossible nature of defending Manhattan Island, was one of the few who argued for abandoning the city in the face of a foe that had enormous strategic advantages. But Congress, with no real grasp of either the strategic or tactical situation facing the overmatched Continentals, thought otherwise.

Hence the defense of New York rapidly devolved into a ruinous affair, Nathanael Greene inexplicably adding a disastrous flourish of his own by insisting upon the defense of Fort Washington, a position he had fortified on the east bank of the Hudson River. The fort had been established on high ground overlooking the river, very near modern Harlem Heights, for the hopeful purpose of defending the waterway from British ships hoping to sail north. It contained a vast array of supplies and Continental defenders, but with its back to the river, the installation was virtually indefensible against vastly superior British land and naval forces. Fort Washington was overrun in a day; Washington and Greene barely escaped capture by being hastily rowed back across the river to the western bank, from where George Washington watched—it is said with tears in his eyes—as his troops were wantonly bayoneted by British and Hessian infantry on the hills opposite. After a violent, fruitless defense, over 3,000 men and officers were forced to surrender, along with mounds of supplies, a horrible American defeat that only served to underscore the foolish decision that had led to the fort's demise in the first place. After the disaster at Fort Washington what remained of the American Army fled across the Hudson River into New Jersey. From there it embarked upon a long, desperate retreat across Jersey toward the Delaware River with a hopeful eye toward Pennsylvania, then looming as a potential sanctuary on that river's western shore.

The horrible loss of Fort Washington would dog Greene's reputation for years. John Marshall, for instance, who at the time was a young lieutenant in the Virginia Line, then later Chief Justice of the United States Supreme Court, and one of the most distinguished jurists in American history, years later penned this commentary:

> From too great a confidence in the strength of the post at Fort Washington, and a hope that by still further increasing the obstructions in the North River [Hudson River] the original object for which that place had been fortified might be obtained; from an unwillingness too, further to discourage the army by an evacuation of posts, General Greene had not withdrawn the garrison under the discretionary orders he had received on that subject; but still indulged a hope that the post might be maintained; or, if its situation should become desperate, that means might be found to transport the troops across the river to the Jersey shore, which was defended by Fort Lee.[10]

While the horrible defeat at Fort Washington could be attributed to Nathanael Greene's total misconception of the tactical situation he faced (and George Washington's hesitant, half-hearted approval of Greene's decision), neither his, nor Washington's, failure should in fairness be viewed as evidence of anything other than both men's glaring lack of military experience. The Continental Army was then, and would be for some time to come, an army of amateurs, from the lowliest private in the ranks up to and including the men who led them. They were all learning on the job, and mistakes, even horrific mistakes, were to be expected as a natural consequence of novice leadership at every level.

Fortunately, Greene had already made up for at least some of the tragedy he had engendered at Fort Washington by having the foresight to have had a string of depots erected across New Jersey. "He had ordered three months provisions for 20,000 men to be placed 'upon the Back Road to Philadelphia.' He established a chain of supply depots that was very well placed, lying west of the main road between New York City and Philadelphia.... Greene did not know (but perhaps guessed) that this supply line would be vital to cover Washington's retreat to the Delaware [River], should he choose that route. It is not an exaggeration to say that Greene's actions here (made without prior guidance from Washington) saved the army and the Revolution in December 1776."[11] This foresight was an example of Greene's ability to grasp the "big picture," where others fumbled over situational details, precisely the sort of mind that hopefully could take over the far-flung enterprise of logistics for the army, and at long last make it hum.

NATHANIEL GREENE,

Major General of the Armies of the United States of America,
In the War of the Revolution.

Engraved by J.B. Longacre, from a drawing by H. Bounetheau.

General Greene is presented here in a painting done by Henry Bounetheau and later engraved by J.B. Longacre. (His first name has often been misspelled as seen here.) As General Washington's most trusted lieutenant, in 1781 Greene was sent south to handle Continental forces in that region. From the Miriam and Ira D. Wallach Division of Art, Prints and Photographs, New York Public Library.

It was precisely because of this ability to think with a broad strategic lens that Washington turned to Greene in late February 1778, desperate to find a man of intelligence and character who would take the position of Quarter Master General. But for some few days Greene hesitated.

"For a length of time it was impossible to get any competent person to undertake the office, and it was only when General Washington was compelled to exclaim, 'Some one must make the sacrifice,' that Greene submitted to undertake it. But he subjoined two conditions; first, that he should not lose his right to command in action; and secondly, that he should have two assistants that would be agreeable to him."[12] To these conditions both Washington and Congress readily agreed and at last the commander-in-chief had his man.

On March 2 Greene accepted the position, with John Cox, a merchant from Philadelphia, and Charles Pettit as his specified assistants.[13] Perhaps Greene had been partially mollified by the arrival in camp of his wife Caty, along with the wives of several other generals. After the lady's appearance, the officers often joined them at night to chat and sing songs. These were hardly "festive" affairs, but coffee, tea, and various other light refreshments were somehow produced in quantities enough to lighten the gloom that had reigned in camp since late December.

General Greene went straight to work at his new post. He immediately wrote to Henry Laurens in Congress and asked for more money to pay wagon drivers at the going rate, an enduring problem that had greatly reduced the availability of capable wagoners. To this Congress initially hesitated, but finally agreed. Then Nathanael ordered the purchase of tents, horses, and the impressments of wagons, anywhere they could be found. "[He] drew up new procedures for hiring wagons and teams; arranged for supplies to travel on the Schuylkill River to reduce the need for animals to draw them. He urged Washington to enlist wagoners for the duration of the war."[14] New forage depots were erected, established agents told to get out and purchase every commodity the army needed. Amid weeks of constant work, a flurry of new procedures was put into place. Soon supplies by the wagonload began to flow into Valley Forge.

"Washington no longer suffered the vexatious delays which had resulted from the previous defects in this department. Although often driven to the most disagreeable of all means of supplying the army—impressments, and always embarrassed by the scarcity and depreciation of money, within a few weeks after this appointment ... order was introduced every where.... A change which we have the express avowal of General Washington, was attributable altogether to the measure of the new quarter-master-general."[15]

Meanwhile, as Nathanael Greene was getting down to business, in Downingtown, Private Martin was still enjoying the pleasant duty and ample provisions of a forager. "We fared much better than I had ever done in the army before, or ever did afterwards," he tells us. "We had very good provisions all winter and generally enough of them. Some of us were constantly in the country with the wagons; we went out by turns and had no one to control us." Downingtown, while only twenty miles west of Valley Forge, was distant enough from Philadelphia to have eluded the coercive foraging depredations of the British, which were hardly as cordial as the American efforts. Somewhat surprisingly, Martin explains, by and large, with the exception of their horses, most civilians were remarkably friendly and cooperative with the American foragers. "When we were in the country we were pretty sure to fare well," he writes, "for the inhabitants were remarkably kind to us. We had no guards to keep; our only duty was to help load the wagons with hay, corn, meal, or whatever they were to take off, and when they were thus loaded, to keep them company till they arrived at the commissary's, at Milltown; from thence the articles, whatever they were, were carried to camp [Valley Forge] in other vehicles under guards.

"I do not remember that during the time I was employed in this business," Martin continues, "which was from Christmas to the latter part of April, even to have met with the least resistance from the inhabitants, take what we would from their barns, mills, corncribs, or stalls, but when we came to their stables, then look out for the women." Horses were for the farmers the very lifeblood of their industry, whether for plowing, hauling, pulling a carriage, or just riding to church, and their loss could not easily be made good. Since it was well known that the American foragers had no interest in harming anyone, their threats proved worthless, and whatever horses were confiscated were often stolen directly back by the ladies who owned them, initiating a never-ending game of cat and mouse.

Today it is difficult to fathom what the United States was like during the Revolutionary period, when often farm families and even city dwellers knew very little of the world beyond their own doorsteps. Hence towns fifty miles away were unknown, while the customs, habits, and people living in distant sections of the country may well have seemed as odd and threatening as creatures from another planet. By and large Martin found the people of Pennsylvania to be "worthy characters," but he thought that "Southern women" (that is, the women of Pennsylvania) had some odd notions about people from other parts of the country, most notably the inhabitants of New England, commonly referred to as Yankees.

Indeed, Joseph tells an amusing story of just such an encounter he had while out foraging, and it is a tale worth recounting: "I happened once to be with some wagons, one of which was detached from the party," he explains.

I went with this team as its guard. We stopped at a house, the mistress of which and the wagoner were acquainted. (These foraging teams all belonged in the neighborhood of our quarters.) She had a pretty female child about four years old. The teamster was praising the child, extolling its gentleness and quietness, when the mother observed that it had been quite cross and crying all day. "I have been threatening," she said, "to give her to the Yankees." "Take care," said the wagoner, "how you speak of the Yankees,

I have one of them here with me." "La!" said the woman. "Is he a Yankee? I thought he was a Pennsylvanian. I don't see any difference between him and other people."[16]

It would take quite some time before the people of the United States would come to truly understand one another, if, in fact, that mutual appreciation has ever actually come to pass, just as it would take far more than days or even weeks for Baron von Steuben and Nathanael Greene to succeed at the new jobs they had been charged with. But just as a journey of a thousand miles begins with but a single step, so too does the provisioning, training, and reconfiguration of an entire army. With Steuben and Greene in place, however, General Washington had now at least a realistic hope that the conditions at Valley Forge might soon begin to improve.

SEVEN

Steuben

You say to your soldier, "Do this," and he does it;
but I am obliged to say, "This is the reason why
you ought to do that," and then he does it

In mid–March the weather changed briefly, offering a momentary taste of spring for men weary of snow, ice, and the cold that invariably produced them, not to mention the dark, dingy conditions that always waited inside their cramped quarters. On March 17, for instance, the weather warmed, and it was reported that "Frogs croak in the swamps." The following day it was more of the same as "Frogs still croak in the swamps," and on the 19th the weather remained clear and unseasonably warm.[1] Perhaps this was a good omen, for it was on the morning of the 19th that Baron von Steuben finally mounted his horse and rode for the first time to the Grande Parade intending to begin training the Continental Army in the drill and methods employed by the king's army of Prussia. In that sense, for both Steuben and the United States of America, it was a moment charged with great potential.

As the sun rose, as the day warmed, and as the frogs commenced their croaking, those areas surrounding the Grande Parade—which was situated in the center of the encampment—began to reek of offal, horse carcasses, and improperly disposed of food and waste, all previously neglected, scattered across the ice-covered grounds. All this undisposed of putrefaction began then to thaw in the warming rays of the sun, adding an unwelcome and intensifying stench to the Baron's first lesson. Orders had already been issued to deal with the problem, but they had yet to have an effect: "Sanitation now has become a Camp problem. The carcasses of dead Horses have to be buried. The filth and nastiness about the Hutts must be removed, else it will putrefy and occasion sickness. All offal and damaged Provision is to be burned. The Camp is to be cleaned. The Vaults [latrines] are to be filled with earth and fresh ones dug each week. Fresh earth is to cover each day's accumulations and the animal dropping are to be buried."[2]

The Baron had for some time been hard at work devising a method by which he could impart the basics of close order drill, along with the highly choreographed movements of large and small unit maneuver to a ragtag army of individualists, used to performing all of these actions— indeed, if they could perform them at all—by means of a dozen or more methodologies. Fortunately, he had struck upon a sound idea, and the General Orders of March 17 reflected as much: "Orders today for one hundred men to be annexed to the Guard of the Commander in Chief as a cadre to be instructed in the Manoeuvres necessary to be introduced into the Army. This is the model Corps to serve to execute Genl de Steuben's orders. Troops are to be draughted [drafted] from other States."[3]

The method of instruction selected by the Baron was of the simplest variety imaginable. At the time General Washington maintained a headquarters guard of some fifty specially selected Virginians, among the most intelligent, responsible, and physically imposing in the army. To this select group another one hundred were to be added from other regiments, preferably the most alert and intelligent soldiers from those units, as well. At the changing of the guard on the morning of the 19th, this combined company of one hundred and fifty men was then to assemble on the Grande Parade and begin the new form of training, this under the direct tutelage of the Baron.

Steuben had been working on the problem for days, and what he had now in mind was to drill this model company until they understood, and could perform, every movement and command as well as he understood and could perform them himself. Once so drilled, they would be dispersed throughout the army to perform as surrogate instructors. It was a very sensible idea, and the only practical method by which the entire army might be trained before spring arrived, ushering in with it a new season of campaigning. Moreover, in the interest of efficiency, he had stripped the Prussian system of commands down to the bare bones, hoping that a less ornate structure would work quicker and better for the more practically minded Americans. The question still on everyone's mind, however, was would this method work in an American army of shopkeepers, farmers, carpenters, day laborers, and such, all unused to the strict discipline of Prussian drill? It was a good question, and many at the time were sure the answer was no.

Washington now referred to Steuben as his new Inspector General, but it was a symbolic reference only. While Thomas Conway had been essentially banned from Valley Forge, he still held the actual position of Inspector General, authorized by Congress, so Washington could not technically replace him, no matter how much he would have liked to do so. So, for the time being, then, Baron von Steuben would serve as a sort of volunteer instructor, but a volunteer serving with Washington's full blessing, a fact that for the assembled model company carried enormous weight.

While the new honorary post of "Inspector General" was surely a boon for the Baron's ego, it hardly conferred upon him the undisputed authority he was accustomed to, as when in years past he had addressed new Prussian recruits. The men he would be trying to train today, after all, were not raw, Prussian peasants, but veteran American soldiers, free men, many of whom had already marched and fought and starved for three long years in pursuit of what many observers worldwide considered little more than a quixotic fantasy. These were not troops, Steuben suspected, who would take kindly to the harsh measures of Prussian discipline. How, then, was he to connect with them? Would they even listen to him? While it is true that in many ways he had already developed a deep respect for the American soldier, it was also true that much of America and American customs remained for him a curious Byzantine-like maze. He was an old man in a New World, trying to fathom the mysterious culture of a new political system along with the mechanics of its Continental Army which, from the outside looking in, at least, often appeared confused and irrational. There is little doubt, therefore, that as the Baron rode toward the Grande Parade that morning, he did so with a sense of considerable unease.

The troops were waiting for him, clad in every sort of clothing they had been able to scrape together, from the various state issued uniforms to buckskins and blankets. "The men, hardened veterans of Washington's campaigns, were drawn up in line of battle, two ranks deep, on the frozen, packed earth of the Parade. They craned their necks to catch a glimpse of the portly German as his horse cantered toward them. Many of them had seen him as he made his rounds of the camp, not entirely sure as to who he was or what he wanted from them. Perhaps now they would find out."[4]

The Baron dismounted and strode deliberately across the Parade to where the men were drawn-up in formation. There he stopped, turned, and took a long, hard look at his prospective pupils as, silently and curiously, they returned his gaze. Paul Lockhart paints a vivid picture of the historic moment:

> The immaculately dressed, well-fed, and bejeweled German nobleman looked very much as one would expect of a Prussian soldier: his hat of fine black beaver, a bicorn blocked in the French style, sitting atop queued and powdered hair; dark blue cloak; knee-high riding boots wrapped impossibly tight around his calves. Standing before the company—a little soft, perhaps, in the midriff, but still at attention without being rigid, his *Exerzierstock* [fencing stick] gripped in his right hand—he appeared to be the very embodiment of Old World society, of aristocracy and privilege, the very same values the men were fighting against.[5]

There were so many things wrong with the Continental Army that Steuben realized he had to begin with the most basic and important drills, delegating the rest to future training. Recently, for instance, the General

Orders had lamented the current state of the army, while signifying that change was on the wind:

> No such thing as military discipline has existed in this Army. We have had no regular formations. One regiment, so called, is composed of 3 platoons, another of 5,8,9 and the Canadian Regiment of 21. The formation of Regiments is as varied as their mode of drill, which consists only of the manual of exercises. Each Col seems to have had his own system, one according to the English, and Muhlenberg's according to the Prussian, and some according to the French style. Only one thing in this Army has been uniform, our way of marching, all having adopted the files used by the Indians. This is now being changed.[6]

Since the men knew essentially how to fire their muskets, Steuben bypassed that drill, and focused instead on marching in unison, first in small squads, then later in units of increasing size. First, he had the men stack their muskets. Then he selected a small squad to work with personally, while having the rest gather near and observe. He had three aides with him, Duponceau, Ponthière, and the Frenchman Jean Baptiste Ternaut, recently assigned to the Baron on a temporary basis. Alexander Hamilton and John Laurens were also present, functioning as interpreters. Steuben began with the most basic position of all, that of attention. He explained what he wanted in broken French to the twenty or so men before him, this translated for the troops by Hamilton and Laurens. Then he demonstrated the precise stance himself, showing the men exactly what he wanted them to do: stance erect, shoulders back, head held firmly in place, heels together with feet spread open at a slight angle. Inspecting the line, he walked slowly in front of the troops, stopping here and there to make a correction, praising and scolding, swearing in French and German, making absolutely sure that each and every man had the stance down precisely. Not until this most elementary of all martial positions had been accomplished by every man to his absolute satisfaction did he move on to the next subject.

With the position of *attention* now accomplished, he began on topic number two, the proper method of dressing the ranks: "*To the left—dress!*" Steuben barked, demonstrating again precisely the maneuver he wanted them all to perform, this over, and over again until performed with consistent perfection. And then to the right: "*To the right—dress!*"[7]

These basic drills of forming and dressing did little more than bring the company into proper stance and alignment, but they were the essential preparatory commands before the more involved systems of marching and maneuver could be taught. Once the men could form and dress, the lesson moved on to proper marching, this including regulation step and cadence. These were skills the Continental Army had never learned, yet they were essential for coordinated movement to, on, or from the field of battle. Utterly absorbed in his work, pleased beyond measure that the men were trying hard to follow his instructions, the Baron continued barking orders, laughing, swearing, correcting and praising, as the men stumbled along. Over time the entire company fell into common rhythm: *"To the Right—Face! To the Left—Face! To the Right, about,—Face! To the Front,—March! Halt!"* The *common step* was taught (marching seventy-five steps per minute), then the *quick step* (one hundred and twenty steps per minute), the line of Continentals now moving in perfect unison, faultlessly dressed as they marched.[8] Having been up for much of the previous night charting precisely how he wanted to present the sequence of orders, in just over an hour Steuben had completed the first lesson. The men were praised for their effort and told to reassemble later in the afternoon for the second lesson of the day. It seemed to everyone involved that the morning's work had been a definite success.

That afternoon the Grande Parade began to attract a smattering of onlookers, the numbers of which grew considerably as the day warmed. This, after all, was something new, something very curious to observe, the cream of the army being transformed before their very eyes. The Baron did not disappoint his new audience, barking out orders, swearing in various foreign languages as Hamilton and Laurens translated the profanities into English, much to the howling delight of the soldiers. Steuben did not mind the amusement; he could sense that he was connecting with these tough, hungry, jaded Americans, and that personal rapport meant everything to him.

The Continentals, to their credit, responded with a spirit of their own, perceiving at once that the gruff, profane Steuben cared deeply about the drills he was trying to impart. Never, after all, had an officer of such rank—or virtually *any* rank, for that matter—bothered to work with them literally man-to-man, stopping to correct every little detail as the lesson progressed.

Baron von Steuben at Valley Forge, 1777. Painting by Augustus G. Heaton.

It is often said that actions speak louder than words, and in that sense the fact the Steuben's grasp of English remained primitive at best may actually have helped him to bond on some instinctual level, for the troops—those drilling as well as those observing—could see for themselves just how desperately he wanted them to succeed. As seasoned soldiers, too, they undoubtedly grasped the fact that the specific drills he was training them to perform were precisely what had eluded them for years: how to march, and move, and fight as a cohesive force.

The afternoon drill began—as is typical for any good teacher—with a thorough review of the morning's lessons. The model company was broken down into individual squads, and once again the Baron strode across the Grande Parade, shouting commands, his assistants frantically trailing behind, supporting, translating, or simply trying to conjure just what Steuben had in mind. Once the morning's drills were repeated to Steuben's strict satisfaction, new commands—far more complex—were initiated.

Now that the company could form well-dressed lines and march forward, halting, about-face, then return to the point of origin, the next test would be to wheel as they marched, that is, each line pivoting on a single point (one stationary soldier at the end of each file) either to the left or right, like a door swinging open or closed.[9] This is a difficult drill, particularly for the line to remain perfectly dressed as it swings, and as a result throughout the course of the afternoon there was much stumbling and failure, confusion and cursing. When the lessons broke down, as often they did, Steuben grew

Pen and pencil illustration of Lieutenant Colonel John Laurens. This etching was done by Henry Bryan Hall in 1871, while the original artist remains unknown. The illustration is signed by Laurens. From the Miriam and Ira D. Wallach Division of Art, Prints and Photographs, New York Public Library.

red-faced, angered, and impatient, not with the men, but with himself. "He vented his exasperation in streams of shouted invective and profanity, directed at no one in particular. To a civilian, these outbursts would have appeared inappropriate and maybe frightening, but the men of the model company—like soldiers everywhere—were discriminating connoisseurs of foul language. They approved heartily."[10]

The afternoon lesson lasted no longer than the morning's had. Steuben carefully insured that his drills never became tedious or tiresome, lest the troops shy away from the next day's tutorial. When the last command had been given, and the model company dismissed, the troops headed back to their huts, smiling and laughing, recreating for one another many of the various stances and movements they had learned during the course of the day. For Baron von Steuben, their departing interest and levity, obvious to everyone gathered near the Parade, must surely have been invigorating. That night men throughout the entire encampment discussed the events of the day, what they had seen, heard, and what it all meant. A spark of enthusiasm had been lit within the Continental Army, and it was a spark desperately needed. Just how far and wide that spark would ultimately flare for the time being, however, remained a complete unknown.

The instruction the following morning began as it had the day before, indeed as it would for all the days remaining in March—in serious drill. The lessons were prepared every preceding night by the Baron, writing at his desk into the wee hours of the morning, then rising early, reviewing all he had written and making any necessary corrections. Each drill session always began at the appointed hour, with no exceptions, and the model company was always punctual and prepared. The company, as before, was broken down into individual squads, and all prior lessons reviewed, starting with the most basic. Then the new drills were introduced and practiced until each, and every squad could perform them with absolute precision.

The audience ringing the Grande Parade grew daily, privates and officers alike marveling at the transformation that was taking place. Observing the almost miraculous results, officers, in particular, began to reevaluate the distant relationship they had always maintained with their troops in light of the Baron's hands-on, dramatic, and compulsive approach to training, not to mention his loud, profane, and almost hysterical insistence upon perfection. An entirely new model of an officer's responsibilities was being demonstrated for them as they watched. Steuben's approach would very soon create a reformation in the entire American officer corps, and a reformation that would survive for centuries.

In a remarkably short period of time the Baron had the model company performing feats of military drill and maneuver very few before had thought possible. No longer as individual squads, but as an entire unit of 150 men, the company was able to come to attention, face left and right, march with speed and exactness both forward, then reversing, to the rear. They had become capable of marching at either the common, quick, or oblique step, never losing the proper dress of their ranks as they did, and, particularly important, learning how to reload their muskets while in motion. Lastly, the company learned how to wheel to either the left or right—that is, to change direction as an entire unit—with stunning precision.

General Washington was watching closely, and he liked what he saw. If the model company was not yet equal to the best of Prussian infantry units, they were rapidly closing the gap, and there was absolutely no question that they were performing like no other Continental unit had ever performed before. Moreover, the men and Steuben appeared to have bonded in some not quite definable way. The men, as Americans, had no desire to become true Prussian soldiers, of course, but they had demonstrated a willingness to perform as true *professional* soldiers, just so long as the drills made sense to them. And Steuben, very much to his credit, came soon to understand that American soldiers, as free-thinking individuals, would perform superbly, but only when they thought what he was teaching them made sense. Writing to an old friend, for instance, he tried to put into words this new understanding of the American citizen-soldier: "The genius of this nation," he'd discovered, was far different than that of European nations. When a military commander on the Continent shouted an order, the men responded at once. But it was not so in America. "I am obliged to say," the Baron continued, "This is the reason why you ought to do that, and *then* he does it."[11] There seems little doubt that, as the men were learning to march and drill as Prussian infantrymen, Valley Forge's resident Prussian drillmaster had come to appreciate something deeply illuminating regarding the individual American psyche.

By late March the company drill, which had begun only a week or so earlier, expanded into the Baron's next phase of training. The individual members of the model company would now be dispatched to other units throughout the army to initiate the same training, all done with an identical insistence upon precision and detail. On March 24, for instance, the general orders reflected this level of success: "At nine this morning the new commands and manoeuvres were explained to each Regiment on parade. Parades followed most of the morning. In the afternoon the parading was by Brigades, beginning at 4 o'clock and finishing at five. Progress is being made in the military arts."[12]

Success quickly followed success. With Washington and his staff observing at the Grande Parade, the model company put on quite a show. "The Baron de Steuben's Company of Guards is where he wishes them to be. They are all well advanced in the manouevres, well-dressed, their arms are clean and in good order. They paraded in the presence of all Officers and exhibited the results of their training. They formed in columns, deployed, attacked with bayonet, charged front, &c. This was an agreeable sight for our Officers. The Baron, having gained his point, dispersed his apostles, the Inspectors, and his new doctrine is now widely embraced. His system is to be applied to Battalions, then to Brigades."[13]

Everything was coming together. The men of the model company were pleased; Washington was enthused, and so was the Baron. Now the individual members of the company would go forth like Steuben's martial disciples, spreading his gospel brigade-to-brigade, while the Baron and his newly increased staff hovered over the whole—watching, correcting, cursing, and praising—like a flock of mother hens. As historian John B. Trussell Jr. writes: "Valley Forge is correctly regarded as a monument to endurance and dedication. But Valley Forge is equally a symbol of the translation of a group of sincere but minimally trained, loosely organized, and highly individualistic men into a hard-hitting, dependable and efficient army."[14]

The astonishing transformation, which began in misery as the Continental Army marched through the cold and snow to encamp upon the snowy hills of Valley Forge, had now taken a tangible leap forward. But Steuben's accomplishments of March 1778, impressive as they were, remained painfully basic, thus far from complete. An enormous amount remained to be done before the Continental Army could break camp come spring, and march off to confront the British, fully trained to Baron von Steuben's exacting standards. Nevertheless, a large step toward that goal had now been achieved with remarkable focus, energy, and skill, and a sense of hope, essential for any army's survival, was now in the air.

EIGHT

Lee

Washington is not fit to command a Sergeant's Guard

In mid–April the plot thickened at Valley Forge, though not because of any aggressive adventures on the part of the British. On the 21st General Charles Lee, mentioned in Chapter Three as one of the suspects, along with Horatio Gates, with whom General Washington believed the Conway Cabal had been itching to replace him, returned from a lengthy captivity with the Redcoats, initiating an undercurrent of hostility that would fester for months. Much to his surprise, General Lee discovered the army's fighting capabilities considerably improved over the one he had departed in the fall of 1776 and, despite nagging difficulties, conditions at camp that were steadily progressing as the weather warmed:

> Cattle, as many as 500 are slowly coming from the North East, expected to cross the Schuykill at Pottsgrove.
> Our Commissary Department is getting into better regulation. Our difficulties and distresses have not arisen so much from a scarcity of provisions as from improper persons, or rather none at all, being employed.
> Droves of cattle are crossing the Delaware at Easton.
> Winds SSE and very warm and sultry. Willows in leaf.
> Troops of every description are coming into Camp each day: draughts, reenlisted deserters returning, absentees, &c.
> Recruits are being inoculated for small pox. Training provisions for new recruits are established, and they are being supplied.
> Our medicine chests, long empty, are now being filled again.
> Troops from Virginia arrived in Camp, four hundred strong, with fifes colors and wagons coming in under Col Smith.
> We now have prospect of more cattle than we need. The surplus are to be fattened for future use.[1]

In April the army's manpower returns took an enormous leap, from 5,642 men fit for duty in March, all the way up to 10,826.[2] Almost like an undiscovered formula in physics, as the weather cooled the army shrank, but conversely as the days warmed the army expanded, and the weather was warming noticeably now. Not only that, in one month only, General Greene's effect on the Commissary Department had proved remarkable, as supplies from all across the North and Middle Atlantic States began arriving in prodigious quantities. Some of this, of course, was simply due to the thawing roads, but Greene's systematic approach to every detail of the process was clearly paying dividends.

With his wife Caty now in camp to accompany him, Greene must surely have felt invigorated. Her presence, however, had hardly gone unnoticed. "Genl Greene's Quarters are frequented by the foreign Officers as his lady is a handsome, elegant and accomplished woman. She speaks French and is well-versed in French literature." As noted previously, these gatherings percolated at a very low key, only coffee, tea, and conversation being considered appropriate. "No dancing or amusement of any kind," we are assured, took place, "except singing. Every gentleman or lady is called on in turn for a song."[3]

It was amidst this light revelry—along with the army's growing numbers and increasingly bountiful system of supply—that General Lee made his grand entrance, having been paroled on April 5, and exchanged for British general Richard Prescott shortly thereafter.[4] While Washington responded by means of an elaborate reception, he could not have been pleased to see this scheming nemesis return to camp.

Washington had known Lee since the French and Indian War, but their current tiff went back to the very beginning of the Revolution when Lee had been utterly convinced that, due to his previous military experience as an officer in both the British and Polish armies, Congress, as a matter of course, was sure to appoint him commander-in-chief. But Washington got the job instead, and years later the outraged Lee made his feelings well known in a discussion with the commissary general of prisoners, Elias Boudinot: "Washington," he blurted, "is not fit to command a sergeant's guard," a declaration that was as impudent as it was imprudent.[5] If that gaffe had been Lee's only verbal transgression, it probably would have been long forgotten but, unfortunately for the abrasive Lee, it was not.

Charles Lee, like Horatio Gates, was English born and educated. Born in 1731 in Darnhall, Cheshire, into the aristocratic Lee family—his father was a colonel in the British Army, his mother the daughter of Sir Henry Bunbury—he received a proper elementary education and was later sent to a finishing school in Switzerland where he was educated across a wide range of subjects, becoming expert in both French and Latin along the way. After Charles completed his schooling in 1747, his father purchased an ensign's commission for him in the 55th Foot (infantry), the unit his father commanded. This purchase was emblematic of the British officer corps of the day, a system designed not necessarily to produce excellent military officers, but certainly to produce an officer corps of aristocratic lineage. Historian

John Buchanan explains: "An officer purchased his initial commission and all subsequent ranks through full colonel. Prices were steep and increased as he went upward. Seniority and ability were not factors. It was a system that effectively kept out men without means and reserved the corps, especially its upper ranks, for the tiny class that ruled Britain. On the face of it the system was iniquitous and has been held up to ridicule, especially when connected with blunders by men whose ignorance was exceeded only by their arrogance."[6]

Enter Charles Lee. At the age of sixteen Lee reported for duty in Ireland and was later sent to North America as a lieutenant at the outbreak of the Seven Years' War, called the French and Indian War in the colonies. He served alongside George Washington during Braddock's Defeat, and later married a Mohawk princess who bore him twins. For his acerbic tongue and violent temper, the Indians named him *Ounewaterika,* Mohawk for "Boiling Water"[7]; this was a telling description.

Short, slovenly, frightfully skinny, with a large head and nose, Charles Lee was a physically unimposing specimen, but whatever gravitas he may have lacked in the flesh, he attempted to make up for ten-fold with an imperious air, obnoxious tongue, and bloated ego, all of which many people found quite disturbing. While Lee was unquestionably well-traveled and versed in all forms of literature including Enlightenment thought, his personal downside often far overshadowed his positive attributes. Almost pathologically opinionated, prone to violent outbursts, he was the type of person capable of offending at virtually every turn. Wounded, for instance, during the British assault on Fort Ticonderoga in 1757, he was treated then transported to New York to recover. There an army doctor—whom Lee had earlier attempted to throttle for some unknown reason while seething with rage—recognized him and returned the favor, giving him an instant pummeling that continued until the doctor was dragged off the frantic Lee by onlookers.[8] Arguments, oaths, threats, even duels unfortunately were to follow General Lee throughout his entire life.

Lee was recalled to England after the Seven Years' War, and later served in Portugal where, as a lieutenant colonel, he fought with skill at the Battle of Vila Velha. When his unit was disbanded, Lee moved on to Poland as an aide-de-camp to the king, and it was while in Poland that he was promoted to the rank of major general. This service was primarily ceremonial or as an observer, however, and it is important to keep in mind that General Lee's service during this period did not involve handling troops in combat, most certainly the command of large-scale operations. He later moved to America in 1773, siding with the colonists in their rising conflict with the crown, and purchased a tract of land in Virginia, not far from present day Shepherdstown, West Virginia. In 1774 he spent the better part of a week visiting with Washington at Mount Vernon where the two men discussed the current political climate.[9]

As war between the colonies and Great Britain loomed ever larger on the horizon, Lee resigned his standing commission in the British army, naturally feeling his credentials merited command of the American forces then gathered at Boston. Congress thought otherwise, however, and unanimously picked Washington instead. Lee did have extensive military experience, however, particularly as an engineer of fortifications, a topic the fledgling Continental officer corps was desperately in need of. While he had purchased many of his commissions (like most officers in the British Service at the time), he had nevertheless been able to intimidate, convince, or simply con many members at Congress into thinking him a military genius of sorts, in all probability a product of his imperious air and prior Polish generalship. Washington, realizing he needed all the help he could get, also reasoned that Lee's knowhow could be of considerable use, and therefore had no objections to his being commissioned a major general in the Continental Army.

During Washington's New York campaign, Lee was sent hastily South by Congress to oversee the American forces at Charleston, then preparing to repel a British invasion by sea. Upon arrival, General Lee found the defenses under the command of General William Moultrie, who was in the process of constructing forts on the islands surrounding Charleston Harbor which, upon inspection, fell short of Lee's ideas of appropriate defensive engineering. Lee fancied that Moultrie's battlements—constructed of native palmetto trees, layered with sand and marsh clay—would crumble almost immediately once subjected to the withering bombardment of British man-of-wars, and ordered Fort Moultrie on Sullivan's Island evacuated. But the South Carolinians ignored him, and the British seaborne assault, ill-planned and sloppily executed, turned chaotic in the shallows surrounding the islands, and devolved quickly into a fiasco.

The American gunners at Fort Moultrie returned fire with stunning effectiveness as the British war ships bobbed about in the narrows, offering themselves as tantalizing targets. Meanwhile, the British bombardment, while fierce and unrelenting, proved utterly ineffective. The palmetto logs, a particularly soft wood, simply absorbed the British shells with almost no adverse effect. Fort Moultrie held, while the British warships suffered horribly. A land invasion launched with even less foresight by the Redcoats floundered in chest high water, and had to be recalled. By day's end the firing died out altogether; the Americans had scored an unprecedented victory.

"Firing slackened with the setting sun. All firing ceased at 9:30 P.M. At 11:30 P.M., silently, without the usual piping of bos'uns' whistles, the ships slipped their cables, and on the tail end of the ebb tide withdrew to Five Fathom Hole. In the morning *Actaeon* was set afire by her crew and abandoned. It was all over."[10] Charles Lee—technically the commanding officer, like Horatio Gates at Saratoga—received the bulk of credit for the defense of Charleston but had contributed almost nothing of substance to earn that applause. The defense of Charleston had been accomplished by Moultrie and his gunners; nevertheless Lee returned North to a hero's welcome, which, in all likelihood, served only to swell his already inflated delusions of grandeur.

Charles Lee reported to the Continental Army in New York in October of 1776, his newly gilded reputation preceding him. He was to handle a full division, but for all intents and purposes, Lee had become Washington's second in command. At the time, no one in New York, Washington included, understood that Lee's heralded feats at Charleston truly belonged to Moultrie and his stout band of South Carolinians, so Lee arrived with his reputation considerably enhanced. He was present for the unfortunate defeats at White Plains and Fort Washington, and it was after Fort Washington that Lee's true, simmering ambitions began to surface.

At the time Washington was unsure of British intentions, but fearful of having his army cut off on the eastern side of the Hudson River should the British cross over into New Jersey. Hence on November 10 he gave specific instructions to Lee to cross his troops over the Hudson if the Redcoats did the same. "If the Enemy should remove the whole or greater part of their force to the West side of Hudson's River, I have no doubt of your following, with all possible dispatch, leaving the militia & Invalids to cover the frontiers of Connecticut in case of need."[11] At the same time Washington ordered General Heath to move to the New York Highlands for defensive purposes with his division of 2,000 men. Then on November 19, the British crossed the Hudson in force, scaling the palisades on the western bank, and pouring into Fort Lee almost unopposed. It was yet another incompetent, dismal Continental defeat, and all Washington could do was gather what few troops he still had left and begin a stumbling retreat across New Jersey. Washington had just over 2,000 Continentals at the time, while Lee's Division numbered 3,400, but despite the British crossing, for some unknown reason Lee's Division remained on the other side of the river. So, Washington wrote again on the 21st from Hackensack, New Jersey, insisting that Lee put his division in motion at once. "I am of the Opinion & the Gentlemen about me concur in it, that the publik Interest requires your coming over to this Side of the Hudson with the Continental Troops."[12] Despite this second specific order, for some reason Lee's Division still failed to budge. Why?

General Washington became befuddled by Lee's inaction and could not sensibly grasp his intentions at the time. With the benefit of hindsight, however, it becomes much easier for us today to take a stab at what Lee really had in mind. It appears he had no desire to remain second in

An engraving of Charles Lee circa 1775, done by C. Corbutt. Lee would rise to the rank of major general in the Continental Army before his failure on the field at Monmouth Courthouse. National Archives.

command, especially as Washington then had at his disposal a smaller force than Lee himself commanded and was retreating after a string of disastrous defeats across Jersey. Soon, Lee surely expected, Washington's force would be routed by the pursuing British, or simply wither away to nothing as it plodded across the Jersey marshlands. Then Congress, as a matter of simple logic, would have to turn to him, the savior of Charleston, and he would at last command center stage, precisely where he believed he belonged. To achieve this objective, then, Lee's tactical calculation became one of simple delay; to let Washington twist in the wind, so to speak, while Lee consolidated his strength at a distance. And that is precisely what he did—for weeks! While Lee's inaction might appear as sensibly tentative, potentially no more than mildly insubordinate, the truth is it was profoundly insubordinate, clearly undermining Washington's authority and capacity to fight.

Washington continued to write to Lee, ordering him to move at once, but Lee continued to dawdle, often not replying at all. Then Lee attempted to appropriate Heath's entire corps, all 2,000 Continentals, by intimidating Heath into compliance. But Heath can be greatly credited for his resistance, noting that his orders came directly from Washington, and that Lee, though superior to him in rank, did not have discretion over his troops. After much fulminating, Lee eventually backed away, but once more his efforts appear entirely self-serving. Had Heath complied, Lee would have almost doubled his strength, while subsuming another independent command entirely within his own. By observing his actions alone, it becomes apparent that General Lee did not care about orders, the chain of command, or even the propriety of defending the New York Highlands. He appears to have been scheming to augment the strength of his division at Washington's expense, hence augmenting his own power and prestige.

While Lee remained east of the Hudson, Washington began a retrograde movement across New Jersey, his goal Pennsylvania. These were dismal times for Washington's Continentals, but the commander-in-chief had little choice. Yet amidst a thousand and one problems and complaints, he maintained an impassive attitude, moving the army along, one day at a time. Indeed, the contrast of these two commanding figures at this critical moment in history—the stoic Washington compared to the scheming Lee—serves as one of the most striking during the entire Revolutionary period.

So important was the safe withdrawal of the American Army across the Jersey lowlands, that Washington detailed others to take the lead while he commanded the rearguard himself, often within musket, or even shouting range of the pursuing British. Trees had to be felled across roads as obstacles, bridges burned, artillery properly placed, and George Washington dared not leave the supervision of these vital activities to officers of lesser skill. It was during this period of retreat when an eighteen-year-old lieutenant from Virginia first encountered his commander-in-chief, and the image of the composed Washington directing the rearguard while almost in sight of the enemy made a lasting impression on him. To him Washington seemed to possess "A deportment so firm, so dignified, but yet so modest and composed, I have never seen in any other person."[13] That young officer was James Monroe, who like Washington would one day rise to the presidency of the United States, and in his later years Monroe readily admitted that the image of Washington he encountered that day remained imprinted upon his consciousness forever.

As the Americans marched south, Washington continued sending orders for Lee to join him, which Lee conveniently found reason to ignore. The Continental Army finally gained the Delaware River at Trenton during the first days of December, but Washington still had no idea where Lee and his absent division was located. By then Phillip Schuyler had ordered fresh troops from the Northern Department to march to Washington's support, but when Lee got wind of their location in Jersey, the approaching column seems to have provided General Lee with handy fodder for yet another perfidious scheme. Despite the fact these troops were bound for Washington's command (and since Lee's previous attempt at commandeering Heath's entire division had failed entirely) he now fancied he would commandeer this fresh detachment, usurping them to his own design. So, on December 4 Lee wrote to the commander-in-chief, carefully polishing his intentions, of course, but providing an explanation that was simply breathtaking in its audacity. As for the troops marching to Washington's relief he wrote:

> I shall put myself at their head tomorrow. We shall upon the whole compose an Army of five thousand good Troops in spirits. I should imagin, Dr General, that it may be of service to communicate this to the Corps immediately under your command. It may

encourage them and startle the Enemy. In fact this confidence must be risen to prodigious heighth, if They pursue you, with so formidable a Body hanging on their flank, or rear.[14]

Here Lee's attempt at usurpation, although veiled, remains painfully obvious: It would be General Charles Lee who would now be calling the shots, designing the grand strategies that would "startle" the enemy. While his suggestion of hanging on the enemy's rear bore some strategic plausibility, these were the sort of operations he was free to suggest, but not to pursue without approval. But it was obvious by now that orders meant nothing to him. The chain of command meant nothing. Congress's wishes meant nothing. General Lee intended quite literally to hijack Washington's troops and operate under his own, separate jurisdiction, immune from Washington's directives, all under the ruse of sensible cooperation. Not only that, but he openly suggested that George Washington, along with the rest of the army, might at once cheer and celebrate his scheming. Amazing.

Well, Washington had had enough. He decided to send an officer, Major Robert Hoops, off on a mission to locate the missing Lee. Riding for days, Hoops inquired everywhere about the Jersey hills until on December 8 he finally located Lee's Division, which had not moved terribly far from Morristown. Hoops promptly galloped into Lee's headquarters with a dispatch from Washington. The major made it clear just how depleted Washington's "corps" was, and that a passage on the Delaware had been prepared for Lee's division with boats at the ready.

To this order Lee responded at once, but still demurred as to compliance, arguing that his own idea of harrying the enemy's rear and flank was preferable. "I am extremely shock'd to hear that your force is so inadequate to the necessity of your situation," he wrote, "as I had been taught to think you had been considerably reenforc'd.... I have put myself in a position the most convenient to cooperate with you by attacking their rear—I cannot perswade myself that Philadelphia is their object at present as it is almost certain that their Whole Troops lately embark'd have directed their course to the Eastern Provinces.... It will be difficult I am afraid to join you but cannot I do you more service by attacking their rear? I shall look about me tomorrow and inform you further."[15]

Hoops must have made a resounding impression on Lee, however—not an easy thing for a junior officer to have on the imperious general—because on the 12th Lee ordered his division to begin a movement toward the Delaware under General Sullivan. Whether he really intended to follow orders this time around, or this initial movement was but another delaying tactic will never be known, however, for on December 13 Providence intervened. As his division prepared to move off to the south, Lee decided to spend a night in a tavern in Basking Ridge, possibly in the arms of a professional lady, though the rumor is unproven. Early the next morning, however, the tavern was surrounded by a British raiding party under the command of Lieutenant Colonel William Harcourt, immediately killing several of Lee's bodyguards, and wounding others. Threatening to burn the tavern to the ground, Lee finally gave up and surrendered. Whisked off in his night clothes, the general was ridden off to prison in New Brunswick and, for the time being at least, out of George Washington's hair. Many in the Continental Army, still in awe of Lee's supposed martial credentials, lamented the loss but, to his credit, Washington was somehow able to contain his remorse.

Lee remained in captivity until May 1778, treated well by his captors, cooperating with them it is said, as to how best to defeat the Americans. Paul Lockhart writes, "Later events would cast Lee in a most unflattering light; no American officer, save Benedict Arnold, has been so vilified as he. To some of his detractors, he was little more than a traitor; even his defenders acknowledged that while in British captivity he had given Clinton advice on how best to fight the American rebels."[16]

This, then, was the Charles Lee who appeared at the Valley Forge encampment on the 23rd day of April 1778, unbothered by his capture, unfazed by his suspect past. Much of what we know now of him Washington only suspected at the time; hence he ordered the type of flamboyant martial greeting he knew the general would expect:

> Gen Lee arrived in Camp. All the principal Officers of the Army were drawn up in two lines, advanced of the Camp two miles towards the Enemy. Then the Troops with the inferior Officers formed a line quite to headquarters. All the musick in the Army attended. The Genl with a great number of principal Officers and their suites, rode about four miles on the road towards Philada, and waited 'till Genl Lee appeared. Genl Washington dismounted and received Genl Lee as if he had been his brother. He passed through the lines of Officers and the Army, who all paid him the hightest military honours, to headquarters, where Mrs Washington was, and here he was entertained with an elegant dinner, and the musick of Mrs Washington's sitting room, and all of his baggage was stowed in it. Genl Washington gave him Command of the right wing of the Army, but before he took charge of it, he requested to have leave to go to Congress at York Town, which was readily granted.[17]

Typically, without a moment's hesitation or nod to propriety's sake, General Lee was off to Congress, in part to comply with the terms of his parole, but no doubt to feather his own cap. But he will most certainly be heard from again as our narrative continues, and not for the better.

NINE

Washington

His Excellency dined with Genl Knox and played at
wicket [cricket] with the gentlemen of the Artillery

The budding spring and moderating April temperatures brought relief
from the frigid days of January and February, that is true. Food became
more abundant, clothes and medicines in better supply, and men—new
enlistments, returned deserters, and furloughed officers by the score—
seemed to be pouring into the encampment daily, the division rolls blos-
soming as a result. Due to Baron von Steuben's efforts on the parade
ground, the army had a new step and swagger, and plans for the upcom-
ing campaign were already being discussed. All things seemed suddenly to
have taken on a positive blush, but that blush belied a terrible truth. For it
was precisely during the months of early spring—March, April, and May—
when the greatest number of deaths occurred, these a result of the rampant
diseases—pneumonia, smallpox, frostbite, and typhus, to name but a few—
that swept through the huts and hospitals during the cold winter months.[1]
For months men had lingered at the edge of death at the army's network of
far-flung hospitals, but now that lingering ceased.

The total number of deaths at Valley Forge remains a mystery to this
day, an unknowable figure due to the administrative chaos that plagued
the army throughout most of the encampment. Even after years of searching with modern archeological tools and methods, very few soldiers' graves
have been located at or near the encampment grounds. As a result, the number of deaths remains an estimate only, ranging between 2,000 and 3,000
men.[2] It can be presumed (because of the lack of local grave sites) that most
of these poor souls died either at or en route to the far-flung hospital system previously mentioned in chapter three, all of these facilities located
in small villages such as Ephrata, Lititz, Easton, and Reading. If the ailing
soldier was fortunate enough to survive the bumpy wagon transfer from
Valley Forge during the dead of winter, on frozen, rutted roads, with
almost no blankets to speak of, he would have been removed to "hospitals

most likely established in churches or other facilities that were often over-whelmed far beyond their capacity." These small village hospitals had almost no means of dealing with the influx of patients being unloaded at their door-step, although in fairness they always tried their best. The medical sojourn of Private Elijah Fisher, a volunteer in the Massachusetts Line, lasted from December 19 through January 28, for instance, and provides a compelling example of the fragile, haphazard conditions the sick were often subject to:

> Thare come orders for all the sick to be sent the Hospital and I with the others of the sick belonging to the Reg't was sent to the hospital at Reddin [Reading] but when we come thare the sick belonging to the other Right [Regiment] had taken it up so we was sent to Dunkertown [Ephrata] to the hospital there.
>
> I with one more had leave to go and Quarter at some house where we Could find a Place and after we had taken a good Deel of Pains in seeking for a Place we Come at length to Mr. Miller's, which Place we staid a considerable time where we was used very well and Clever folks they were.
>
> At length I having got a recent Cold by which means the feaver set in I was carried to hospital and a sevear fit of sickness I had for a fortunate [fortnight] after that. I gits better but a Number Dyed. There was between fifty and sixty Dyed in about a month.
>
> I gos back again to Mr. Miller's and stays there till I got well an off to Return to the Regiment again. I with a number of others that belonged to the briggade Left Dunker-stown on the way to the army.[3]

Private Fisher was fortunate enough to recover and return to regu-lar duty. Then late in January he was thrilled when accepted into Washing-ton's "Life Guard," a promotion of some significance. Said he: "I jined the Life guard and liked being there much better than being in the Ridgment."

While the medical journey ended well for Fisher, for many others—as he himself noted—the finale proved far less joyful. For those still alive and well at the Valley Forge encampment, this grim exodus took place well out of sight, hence typically out of mind, but there is little doubt that many of the sick from Valley Forge passed from this earth in distant places, with lit-tle notice. For them—many of them no more than teenage boys—it was a sad and lonely death, in villages they did not know, cared for by people who did not know them. Of the 11,000 or so men who marched into Valley Forge in December 1777, somewhere between 18 percent and 27 percent would fail to march out. These numbers would represent reasonably grim combat totals had they occurred in battle, but the men at Valley Forge did not die fighting the British. They died in camp, fighting an entirely different sort of war. This sad, fatal exodus was that spring's terrible truth—although for the bulk of the army it probably passed as obscure, or even unbeknownst, as winter faded into spring—and today it serves as a somber reminder of just how grim the conditions at Valley Forge truly were.

As the ill withered away in distant locations, the army, much like a phoenix, began to rise from the frozen ashes of the Valley Forge winter.

Supplies of all variety were streaming into camp, as were troops, bringing the regiments up to muster strength once again. As the weather warmed, all eyes began to gaze south toward Philadelphia, curious as to what the British might be up to once the roads sufficiently dried for campaigning. Spies in the American capital were placed on high alert, in search of clues that might belie any potential intent.

In late April outlying detachments were recalled to the main body, this including Private Joseph Plumb Martin and his merry band of foragers who, it can be recalled, had been wintering rather comfortably in the village of Downingtown. Martin received the news with understandable displeasure. "But the time at length came when we were obliged to go to camp for good and all," he tells us, "whether we chose it or not. An order from headquarters required all stationed parties and guards to be relieved, that all who had not had the smallpox [inoculation] might have an opportunity to have it before the warm weather came on. Accordingly, about the last of April we were relieved by a party of southern troops.... We accordingly marched off and arrived at camp the next day, much to the *seeming* satisfaction of our old messmates, and as much to the real dissatisfaction of ourselves. At least, it was so with me."[4]

Having eaten well, been housed comfortably, even having obtained a few articles of clothing that fit tolerably well, the abrupt return to camp life proved unsettling for Martin: "Thus far, since the year commenced, 'Dame Fortune had been kind,' but now 'Miss-Fortune' was coming in for *her* set in the reel," he complained. Not only did he have to forfeit the easy days and comparative freedom of an unsupervised forager, but he returned directly into the highly organized and grinding drill routine established by Baron von Steuben, something that was entirely new for him, and which arrived as a definitive shock. "After I had joined my regiment I was kept constantly, when off other duty, engaged in learning the Baron de Steuben's New Prussian exercises. It was a continual drill."[5]

In late April, then, as Martin took his turn on the Grande Parade, George Washington received two pieces of news—one good, the other stunning—that would alter the face of the war. First, Thomas Conway had resigned his position as Inspector General, allowing Washington to move forward and promote Steuben to Conway's vacated post, something the Baron had both earned and deserved. Secondly, and infinitely more important: "This evening [April 30] we had the agreeable news that the Courts of France and Spain had declared these United States free and Independent.—The *La Sensible*, a Frigate of 36 guns, belonging to his Most Christian Majesty, has just arrived at Falmouth, Casco Bay, in 35 days from France, which she left on the 8th of March, with dispatches from our Envoy at the Court of Versailles, informing us that the Court of France has recognized us."[6]

This foreign recognition arrived like manna from heaven, a much-needed shot in the arm for the cause of American independence. While French recognition had been hoped for and expected ever since the American victory at Saratoga the preceding fall, now it could be genuinely presumed that vast quantities of supplies, army and naval support, even foreign currency, would soon be on their way to the hobbling Continental Army. This changed *everything*, and Washington's mood soared as a result. Although rarely admitted to previously, the prospect of the Americans defeating the British entirely on their own had always seemed a dubious proposition. Now suddenly, with the backing of France and its vast resources, that prospect shifted from dubious to entirely doable. The smiles at Washington's headquarters could hardly be contained.

Washington, known for always keeping his emotions under complete control, responded with uncharacteristic enthusiasm. "I believe no event was ever received with a more heartfelt joy,"[7] he advised Congress, and this sense of newfound elation hardly ended there. Buoyed by the news, he decided to hold a pageant to celebrate the new treaty and show off the strides his army had taken under von Steuben's tutelage. The event was promptly scheduled for the morning of May 6. It was to be an all-day affair, starting with a grand review and ending with rum for the hard-marching troops and a splendid dinner for the officers, their wives, and visitors.

Washington suggested the celebration to Steuben, and the Baron responded with a burst of activity. He pulled out his pad and paper and went straight to work, toiling day and night until he had everything choreographed precisely to his liking. "In just a few days, he worked out all of the intricate details, writing instructions for each brigade and regiment, even drawing diagrams. Everything had to be laid out well in advance so that there would be no room for embarrassing errors."[8] This gala event was to be the Baron's showcase, and he was going to leave nothing to chance.

As these details were being worked out, the army apparently caught wind of Washington's sense of jubilation, for on May 1 the general orders tell us: "The day was spent in mirth and jollity. The soldiers paraded, marching with fife and drum, and huzzaing as they passed the poles [May poles], their hats adorned with white blossoms."[9] These had become heady days for Washington, his officers, and most certainly the men in the ranks.

What a contrast to that dreadful day back in December when the entire army had slipped and stumbled onto the snowy plain at Valley Forge, only then to spend the night hungry and freezing, huddled before open fires. Now there was hilarity in the air, and even George Washington got caught up in the excitement. Late on the 4th, for instance, Washington had dinner with Henry Knox, the army's chief of artillery, and afterward discarded his coat and joined in with Knox's boys for a game of cricket. For

Washington, who was both naturally and necessarily reserved at times to the point of stony aloofness, to have tossed his coat aside and taken up the bat with a bunch of youthful artillerymen, provides a brief and revealing snapshot of a man suddenly as joyous and momentarily carefree as a youngster on a schoolyard playground. At long last his men had food and medicine; they were learning how to march and maneuver as professional soldiers; spring was in the air, and now even the French were on their way. Why not toss the coat aside and take a few swings? One can only imagine just how relieved George Washington must have felt at that moment.

Meanwhile, in Philadelphia American spies were sending back interesting reports of what appeared to be the preliminaries of a British movement. On May 1, for instance, it was noted that "many enemy transports have sailed from Philada. They were empty and their destination is unknown." The British appeared to be up to something for sure, but just what remained unclear. Then this dispatch came in: "The enemy is changing the disposition of his forces. He has lately sent nearly two hundred sail of light transports from Philada."[10] All eyes turned curiously toward America's capital city. Daniel Morgan's expert Virginia Riflemen, now legendary within the Continental Army, were known to be posted well south of Valley Forge, and Morgan had details out scouting near the city's outskirts.[11] If the British began to move, it was hoped Morgan's scouts would spot that movement at once.

The Revolutionary period was a time when the hand of God was oft discerned directing the daily affairs of both man and nature, and for those so inclined, it must surely have seemed that Providence was smiling as dawn appeared on May 6. The morning came on, cool but clear, a cloudless sky painted shimmering blue, a light southerly breeze tossing the leaves in the trees that surrounded the Grande Parade.[12] The day of the grand review was at hand and after a long, bitter winter excitement stirred in the ranks.

> At half after ten o'clock a cannon was fired, a signal for the Troops to be under arms. We began to march the Parade Ground in good order in the following manner: Each Major Genl conducted the first Brigade in his Company to the Ground and the other Brigades were led by their Commanders in separate columns. Words cannot convey an adequate idea of the movements of the Troops to their several Posts of the good order, discipline and brilliancy of their arms, and the remarkable animation with which they performed the necessary salutes and manoeuvres.
>
> His Excellency made a circuit of the lines of review, and the air of the soldiers, the decorum they presented, was in stark contrast to the naked, starving friendless rabble of the winter.[13]

The troops turned in a stunning display, something even the most hopeful had not expected. "The Review went off without a hitch on that crisp, May morning…. The entire army marched by files onto the Grande Parade, and though their uniforms were disheveled, they moved like soldiers, silent and perfectly in cadence, to the music of the fifes and drums."[14] The marching units moved smartly from column to line, forming two long ranks across the expansive Parade. This was in turn followed by three rounds fired by thirteen cannons, each volley perfectly executed. Then the assembled infantry offered a *feu de joie,* an elaborate, synchronized display of musketry, very popular at the time. It began as the two men at the end of each line raised their muskets and fired simultaneously, the firing in turn proceeding down the line from right to left, two men at a time, like a vast string of fireworks going off in perfect order. This was done three times without a single misfire, and the effect on the gathered onlookers was almost overwhelming.

Elijah Fisher was marching with Washington's Life Guard that morning, and he later captured the entire scene in his journal. The Guard had taken a position in the center of the Grande Parade, such that the event unfolded around them; and it all proved an experience Fisher would never forget:

> We had a Rejoicing on the account of the French declaring for us Independent and the howle [whole] of the Continental army was ordered to three larm [alarm] posts in the senter and the army was all around us at there several stations (and there was a grand harber [arbor] bilt and all the Commisioners were Envited to dine with His Excellency) our guard gave the firs fire then thirteen Cannon then the fire began at the rite of the army and went through the howl line and fired three rouns apeace the Artillery Discharged forty-four Cannon and it was followed with three Chears for the King of France and three for the Friendly Powers of Europe and three Chears for the Thirteen United States of Amarica and His Excellency gave orders that every Prisoner should have his Freedom that belonged to the Continental army that they might taste the Pleasur of the Day.[15]

The troops then retired from the Grande Parade with as much precision as they had appeared, marching off to their huts where a gill of rum awaited each man as a reward for his efforts. As the troops headed off, the officers, their wives, and the invited guests all headed for a cold collation of food and drink. "The tables in the center were shaded by elegant marquees raised high and agreeable arranged. An excellent band played. And feast was made still more animated by the magnanimous bearing of his Excellency and by the discourse and behavior of the Officers. Mrs Washington, the Countess Stirling and Lady Kitty, her daughter, Mrs Greene and other ladies, favoured the feast with their presence. Wines and liquors circulated most genially. To the King of France! To the Friendly European Powers! To the American States! To Mr Franklin! To Mr Deane! And other suitable toasts."[16]

During the height of the festivities General Washington took the time to announce Conway's resignation, and for the first time the promotion of Baron von Steuben to the full rank of major general, the army's new Inspector General. The assembled crowd thundered its applause, and Steuben, taken by complete surprise, swelled with pride. It was, after all, precisely what he had traveled from Europe all those months before to attain, and now, because of a job extremely well done, it was his.

The feast finally broke up around 6 o'clock, and everyone returned to their duties and quarters. It had been a wonderful and impressive affair, from beginning to end. Despite the precision of the review, however, a small cloud still hung over the day, an irksome question that no amount of marching or stylized drill could answer, no matter how well performed. Because while the army had surely demonstrated its ability to parade with great skill and coordination, when push came to shove, could they be counted on to fight as well as they had paraded? That issue remained a bothersome unknown and, despite all the levity and applause, it was a question George Washington knew would have to be answered soon.

TEN

Lafayette

It was a very Luckey affair on our side

The opportunity to determine whether the drill routine instituted by Baron von Steuben had turned the Continental Army into a capable fighting force, and not just impressive parade ground performers, came far sooner than anyone had expected.

After the dazzling success of the May 6 review, Washington and his staff turned their thoughts toward the approaching spring campaign. On May 8, for instance, just two days after the event on the Grande Parade, a council of war was convened to discuss various options. Washington, Knox, Gates, Greene, Stirling, Mifflin, Lafayette, and Dekalb were all present, and the debate got down quickly to offensive potentials. In the long run, however, still unsure of British intentions, it was decided "to remain on the defensive and wait events, and not attempt any offensive operations against the Enemy, until circumstances afforded a fairer opportunity of striking a decisive blow."[1]

General Washington was by nature an aggressive leader, more than once in the past anxious, it seemed, to end the war with a single climactic stroke. Waiting and watching, bobbing and weaving, biding his time fit neither his personality nor temperament. Joseph Ellis tells us, for instance, that during the siege of Boston—Washington's first true taste of large-scale operations—he routinely conjured up bold suggestions, but suggestions that were just as quickly and boldly rejected by his staff. "Washington proposed frontal assaults against the British defenses, arguing that 'a Stroke, well aim'd at this critical juncture, might put a final end to the War.' (In one of the plans he envisioned a night attack across the ice with advanced units wearing ice skates.) His staff rejected each proposal on the grounds that the Continental army lacked both the size and discipline to conduct such an operation with sufficient prospects of success."[2]

But that had been early in the war, years before, in fact, when the commander-in-chief commanded little more than a large mass of untrained and undisciplined militias. Now things had changed, and radically, it appeared, for the better. Washington had a new army now, an army trained in the Prussian mold, and he was anxious to kick its wheels, so to speak, and see for himself just how well it might perform. Before he could do that, however, a sober analysis of the military situation had to be carefully taken into account, and on May 9 the Board of War met with Washington and his generals to do just that. Notes from Washington's presentation were compiled, and even today these are fascinating to review, given that they represent the situation precisely as Washington, his staff, and the Board of War grasped them at the time. They read as follows:

> The enemy's whole force within these States is distributed into three Divisions, one at Philada, one at New York, and one at Rhode Island, amounting to between sixteen and seventeen thousand rank and file fit for the field. Their whole force in Philada is about 10,000—the flower of their Army. New York has 4,000 rank and file, mostly Germans and levies. Rhode Island has about 2,000, mostly Germans. The Genl informed the Council that he was not sufficiently acquainted with the European situation to be able precisely to judge what reinforcements the Enemy might expect.
>
> The Continental force consists of about fifteen thousand rank and file. The main body is at Valley Forge, amounting to 11,800 fit for service. The detachment at Wilmington is about 1400. The force on the North river [Hudson River] is about 1400. There is expectation of no more than 20,000 rank and file. The Militia are not to be depended upon. Our ordnance, small arms and military stores are insufficient for a protracted campaign. Provisions are still problematic, and Prospects are somewhat better."[3]

Rhode Island was too distant to consider as realistic for offensive operations. New York, although closer and less well defended than Philadelphia, would still require a long trek across New Jersey, this with a sizeable British force left behind in Philadelphia, capable of striking from the rear and pining the Continental Army between the New York and Philadelphia British contingents, a recipe for potential disaster. No, any realistic action would have to be directed at General Howe's force in Philadelphia, but what Howe intended to do come spring remained unknown. Then suddenly, in a series of intelligence coups, all of that changed. On May 16 word was received from loyal spies that a movement in Philadelphia was afoot. "Our intelligence suggests that the Enemy is preparing to evacuate Philada. We do not know whether he plans to quit our Continent or to concentrate his forces in New York. If the latter, we shall be obliged to give chase and intercept him. So it is necessary to have forage already gathered on the North Road for us." News was also afoot that General Howe was soon to be replaced by General Clinton, and, if true, Clinton by reputation was expected to act far more aggressively than the sluggish Howe ever had.

It is easy to imagine Washington contemplating all this with furrowed brow, his heartbeat beginning to rise ever-so-slightly, as the intelligence began to accumulate. Surely, then, he began to ponder anew his offensive options. He dared not strike the enemy in their Philadelphia defenses, that was a given, but if the British were going to evacuate Philadelphia over-land for New York, then they would have to proceed in a long, slow, snak-ing column. Surely that long column would be vulnerable somewhere as they marched across the Jersey lowlands, and if that were the case, it was at that vulnerable point Washington decided he would strike them—now *that* made perfect sense. But at the time Washington did not believe the enemy would open themselves to such a strike. Then, even more interesting intelli-gence arrived: "We have certain intelligence that the Enemy mean to evac-uate the City and are preparing to embark. The heavy cannon and baggage are already aboard and the transports are taking on food and water."[4]

What Washington didn't know at the time, however, was that, due to the recent treaty between France and the United States, the British force in North America was going to be reduced substantially, a good 5,000 troops being fer-ried to the Caribbean to fight in that theater against the French. Thus hobbled, plans had been made to shift the main body from Philadelphia to New York, a position thought to be more defensible and expeditiously supplied by sea.

To this news Washington responded at once, on May 17 ordering stores to be distributed along the army's potential march route through New Jer-sey. "Magazines are being prepared, forage placed, at Coryell's Ferry, Mor-ris Town, Trenton, Bound Brook and Westfield."[5] But were the British going to evacuate their troops by land or sea? That was still the big question, and it was a question that required an immediate answer. Washington had to have more specific information, and a reconnaissance in force seemed the best way to acquire that intelligence in the most expeditious manner possible. So, the commander-in-chief ordered up a strong detachment of troops capable of defending themselves from any reasonable enemy threat, and General Lafay-ette leaped at the opportunity, volunteering to lead them toward Philadelphia.

To this Washington agreed, but not before providing Lafayette with detailed instructions in writing as to what his objectives were to be, along with safeguards he wanted maintained. "You will remember," Washington instructed, "that your detachment is a very valuable one, and that any accident happening to it would be a very severe blow to this army. You will therefore use every possible precaution for its security, and to guard against surprise.... In general, I would observe, that a stationary post is unadvisable, as it gives the enemy an opportunity of knowing your situation, and concerting plans suc-cessfully against you."[6] The very next morning, May 18, the column departed Valley Forge, almost 3,000 strong, Lafayette riding at their head.

This detachment contained a curious mix. There were approximately 600 members of the Pennsylvania militia, 2,000 Continentals, some 50 Oneida warriors along with a smattering of Canadians—these having recently arrived with Lafayette from Albany—accompanied by a battery of light artillery. We know that both Joseph Plumb Martin and Elijah Fisher marched with the column that day, Fisher with the Life Guard, Martin with the Continentals. Martin sets the scene: "About this time I was sent off from camp in a detachment consisting of about three thousand men, with four field-pieces, under the command of the young General Lafayette.[7] Marching briefly north, the column sloshed across the Schuylkill at Swede's Ford, and then turned east. Setting a leisurely pace, Lafayette led his troops down the Swede's Ford Road, then turning onto the Ridge Road which ran along the ridge that bordered the river, covering some 12 miles before arriving at the tiny village of Barren Hill (modern Lafayette Hill). The small town overlooked Matson's Ford very near where, it might be recalled, our narrative began the preceding December."

Having experienced no difficulty or opposition thus far, it was atop Barren Hill that Lafayette decided to camp for the night, and here he explains the defensive arrangements he employed: "On a good elevation, his right resting upon some rocks and the river, on his left some excellent stone houses and a small wood, his front sustained by five pieces of cannon, with roads in his rear, such was the position of M. de Lafayette. An hundred dragoons whom he was expecting did not arrive in sufficient time; but he stationed six hundred militia on his left at Whitemarsh, and their general, Porter, made himself answerable for those roads."[8] Private Martin recalled, "We marched to Barren Hill, about twelve miles from Philadelphia. There are crossroads upon this hill, a branch of which leads to the city. We halted here, placed our guards, sent off our scouting parties, and waited for—I know not what."[9]

At this point, a description of the local terrain and road network would prove helpful in order to better envision the impending action (see map). Barren Hill sits atop the ridge that borders the northern bank of Schuylkill River, which continues eastward toward Philadelphia. At the time, the crest of the hill itself had been entirely deforested, and the area surrounding it consisted of open farmland and wood lots. Running directly atop the ridge was an east/west pike imaginatively named the Ridge Road. Paralleling the Ridge Road a mile or so to the north was Swede's Ford Road, also running west from Philadelphia, but then turning south toward the Schuylkill and ultimately descending all the way to Swede's Ford. As the Swede's Ford Road ran abreast of Barren Hill, however, another smaller road forked off which ran south, directly into Barren Hill. Thus there was a crossroads at Barren Hill—just as Martin had noticed—this formed as the fork crossed over Ridge Road, from there descending south to Matson's Ford on the river. An abandoned church with stone wall and graveyard sat at the south/east corner of this intersection. Another ford across the Schuylkill named Levering's was also located several miles east of Barren Hill. All these roads and locations will come into play, as the action commences. Now that the scene has been set, we will return to our narrative.

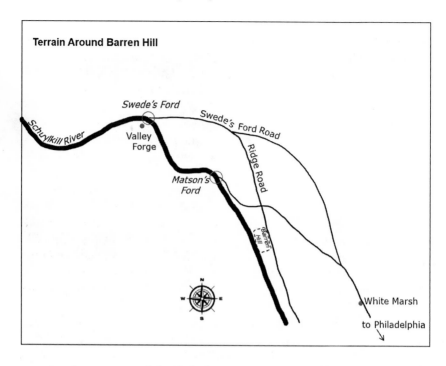

Terrain Around Barren Hill

On the evening of the 18th the column bedded down at Barren Hill for the night. As Lafayette described, he had sent his entire militia detachment out to Whitemarsh, a small town north of Barren Hill located on the Swede's Ford Road, to picket that area, and report back regarding any enemy approach. He also sent his Oneida warriors along with a group of Morgan's riflemen east toward Philadelphia along the Ridge Road to serve as another picket post. These two moves should have successfully blocked the two known major routes by which the British could have advanced upon Barren Hill. As the Americans bedded down for the night, therefore, all seemed in order, but this was far from the case.

The British, with an elaborate system of spies all their own, already knew of Lafayette's departure, and had concocted an elaborate scheme to bag the young Frenchman, along with his entire detachment. Indeed, so confident were they of success that General William Howe's brother, Admiral Richard Howe, had ordered a British frigate readied to serve as fitting quarters for Lafayette once he had been placed in their custody as a prisoner of war. The Americans remained atop Barren Hill the following day, awaiting the return of their scouting parties which had fanned out toward Philadelphia the preceding afternoon. As Lafayette's troops sat tranquilly in position atop Barren Hill, Martin, rather typically, used the time for a little amusement of his own with some of the Oneida warriors.

"There was upon the hill, and just where we were lying," he tells us, "an old church built of stone, entirely divested of all its entrails. The Indians were amusing themselves and the soldiers by shooting with their bows, in and about the church. I observed something in a corner of the roof which did not appear to belong to the building, and desired an Indian who was standing next to me to shoot an arrow at it. He did so and it proved to be a cluster of bats.... The house was immediately alive with them, and it was likewise instantly full of Indians and soldiers. The poor bats fared hard.... They killed I know not how many.... I never saw so many bats before nor since, nor indeed in my whole life put all together."

As Martin was frolicking with his newfound Indian friends, however, the British were planning a little sport of their own, and on the night of the 19th, they put their plans into action. Late that evening, and during the early hours of the 20th, the Redcoats—ten thousand strong accompanied by fourteen field pieces—marched out of Philadelphia, headed for a rendezvous with General Lafayette. Under the command of both William Howe and Clinton, one full division marched west on the Ridge Road directly toward Lafayette's position on Barren Hill, while two other divisions started out the Swede's Ford Road. The attack on the Swede's Ford Road was under the command of General Charles Grant, and as this column came abreast of the country lane that forked south toward Barren Hill, these two divisions split, one continuing up the Swede's Ford Road, the other taking the fork that led directly toward the sleeping Americans. If everything went as planned, the Americans would be entirely cut off, British divisions pinning them front, side, and rear against the banks of the Schuylkill, which was then thought to be running much too high to ford, thanks to the spring thaw. For Lafayette and his men, the British imagined, there could be no escape.

On May 19, as the British were readying their plan, Martin pulled guard duty and had yet another curious experience, worth retelling. "The next day I was one of a guard to protect the horses belonging to the detachment," says he. "They were in a meadow of six or eight acres, entirely surrounded by trees. It was cloudy and a low fog hung all night upon the meadow, and for several hours during the night there was a jack-o'-lantern cruising in the eddying air. The poor thing seemed to wish to get out of the meadow, but could not, the air circulating within the enclosure of trees would not permit it. Several of the guard endeavored to catch it but did not succeed."[1]

---

1. Martin refers here, I believe, to the historic understanding of the term jack-o'-lantern, that is, a will-o'-wisp, ghost light, or ignis fatuus, and not the modern meaning, which is a carved, illuminated pumpkin. These lights are often seen in misty or swampy areas, and are today considered a product of swamp gases, but historically were often thought to be paranormal in nature.

As dawn approached on the morning of May 20, Martin, Lafayette, and the rest of the American force suddenly found themselves the unsuspecting objective of three rapidly closing enemy columns, and Martin quickly forgot, it can be presumed, the hovering phantom of the night before. In fact, Private Martin, still guarding the horses, was one of the first alerted to the danger. "Just at dawn of day the officers' waiters [servants] came, almost breathless, after the horses. Upon inquiring for the cause of the unusual hurry, we were told that the British were advancing upon us in our rear."[10] Word of the impending disaster began to spread through the ranks. Elijah Fisher, for instance, on watch with the Life Guard near Lafayette's headquarters, later noticed the confused commotion, and got wind of the predicament the detachment was in. "This Morning [May 20] at Nine of the Clock there Come Express [message] to the General Quarters and brought Entelegence that the howl [whole] of Gen. How's Army was Advansing upon us in three Colloms."[11]

General Lafayette, thinking his position still well defended, had no idea what was happening. Early that morning he was discussing with a young, local girl the possibility of her going into Philadelphia for a look around on the Americans' behalf under guise of visiting her relatives, when he was suddenly and rudely interrupted. "A miller who lived near the Swede's Ford Road rushed to Lafayette's camp to report the proximity of Grant's column. Around the same time, American pickets to the south along the Ridge Road encountered a body of British light dragoons, the lead elements of the Howe-Clinton column."[12] The distinctive crack of musketry was already audible, just down the Ridge Road. Lafayette had no idea what was going on around him. "On the morning," he writes, "of the 20th, M. de Lafayette was conversing with a young lady ... when he was informed that the red dragoons were at Whitemarsh," that is, moving toward his position directly up the Swede's Ford Road. What to do? "For greater security, he [Lafayette] examined carefully into the truth of the report; and, ascertaining that a column was marching on the left, changed his front, and covered it with the houses, the wood, and a small churchyard. Scarcely was that movement ended, when he found himself cut off by Grant on the Swedes's Ford Road."[13]

This is what Lafayette now understood: Grant, with one British division, had already traveled the Swede's Ford Road to where it turned south; hence that enemy division was now behind him, effectively cutting off any withdrawal toward Valley Forge. Another column of Redcoats, this under General Grey, was on the country lane that forked off the Swede's Ford Road, and was closing rapidly on Barren Hill, threatening his left flank. Still another column—under Howe, Clinton, or both—was attacking directly up the Ridge Road, already just minutes from Barren Hill. Lafayette now faced disaster, envelopment on three fronts! The impending calamity was hardly lost on the troops themselves. Says Martin, "How they got there [the British columns] was to us a mystery, but they *were* there. We helped the waiters to catch their horses and immediately returned to the main body of the detachment. We found the troops all under arms and in motion, preparing for an onset."

The American position had changed abruptly from one of sleepy tranquility to frantic preparations for imminent battle. How had this happened? The answer, although simple enough, is astonishing. The Pennsylvania militia under General Porter had simply vacated their post along the Swede's Ford Road, marching off to points unknown without even bothering to inform Lafayette of their departure. This represented an astounding breakdown in basic protocols that has never been fully explained, but surely provides firm evidence as to why Washington insisted throughout the Revolution that only a thoroughly professional army could ever win the war. Regardless, Porter's disappearance had placed the American detachment in jeopardy of being enveloped—in fact, an envelopment that was already dangerously near completion.

Meanwhile, back down the Ridge Road, the main British column had stumbled headfirst into the Oneida warriors and Morgan's riflemen, a group who had fortunately taken their assignment seriously. Muskets cracked and warriors whooped, startling the unsuspecting dragoons who rode out in front of the British vanguard. "Capt McLean and the Indians had been posted at Mile Post 9 along the Ridge Road. When the red-coated British neared the Indians war-whooped and the British as well as the Indians departed the field, the latter discharging their pieces at the Light Horse. Terrified, the British Horse scampered off and the Indians collected some cloaks which the Enemy had dropped in his flight."[14] Morgan's riflemen, utterly outnumbered, then began a fighting withdrawal accompanied by the warriors back up the Ridge Road toward Barren Hill, for the moment at least, delaying the British advance from that direction.

Expecting an immediate attack by overwhelming numbers, Lafayette's first instinct was to change fronts, anchoring his new line on the old church, while throwing a line of infantry across the country lane on his left, down which an attack was expected at any moment. Martin: "Those of the troops belonging to our brigade were put into the church-yard, which was enclosed by a wall of stone and lime about breast high, a good defense against musketry but poor against artillery. I began to think I should soon have some better sport than killing bats. But our commander found that the enemy was too strong to be engaged in the position we then occupied."

Digesting dispiriting reports from various quarters, Lafayette very quickly concluded that he was facing a force perhaps three or four times the size of his own. Realizing that a defense against those sorts of odds, closing rapidly from three sides, would be suicidal, he decided to vacate

Barren Hill immediately, and make a dash for the river. Unfortunately, Matson's Ford was known to be running very high at the time; nevertheless that crossing represented the only real option the Americans had left. With his back against the wall, and fleeting time decidedly against him, Lafayette had but one choice: withdraw with all haste toward the river!

The British had been careful to cut off access to Swede's and Levering's Fords—the latter east of Barren Hill—but they appeared unfamiliar with Matson's Ford, which lay almost directly below the American position. Moreover, they seemed to have been unaware of the small country lane that snaked its way down the ridge from Barren Hill, all the way to the Schuylkill River. This seems a distinct failure in reconnaissance for an army that had an abundance of dragoons, and that for months had enjoyed the free, open run of the area. It appears they had set a large and sophisticated trap for a mouse, while neglecting to plug all the mouse holes.

Atop Barren Hill the Continentals were in rapid, but disciplined, motion. Shouted orders to switch from line to column rang-out across the treeless hilltop and, in the blink of an eye—as men raced, accouterments clanked, and officers leaped to their horses—the maneuver was completed with admirable haste; something, that just months before, would have been inconceivable. The Baron's constant drill had just reaped stunning dividends. Once formed, the column started off toward the river at the quick step, dust trailing their movement in the slanting rays of the warming sun. It would be a race for their lives.

Lafayette placed the lead in the hands of another officer, while keeping to the rear himself. "He [Lafayette] placed himself as the rear guard, and marched on with rapidity, but without precipitation. Grant had possession of the heights, and M. de Lafayette's road lay immediately beneath him."[15] The desperate escape had just begun, and the Americans still had miles to travel. "It was about three miles to the river," Martin tells us. "The weather was exceeding warm, and I was in the rear platoon of the detachment except two platoons of General Washington's Guards. The quick motion in front kept the rear on a constant trot. Two pieces of artillery were in front and two in the rear. The enemy nearly surrounded us by the time our retreat commenced, but the road we were in was very favorable for us, it being for the most part and especially the first part of it through small woods and copes [small stands of trees]. When I was about halfway to the river, I saw the right wing of the enemy through a lawn about half a mile distant, but they were too late." Elijah Fisher, marching with Washington's Guard, was only yards from Martin as the column dashed for the river. "We took a road that lead to Schoolkill river (for we were obliged to retreat Enstently [instantly]) and the Enemy was so Nigh on our right flank that we Could see them Plain."[16]

If the British had moved quickly, they still might have sprung their trap, but instead they hesitated, confused by what they were observing. From high atop the Ridge Road they had spotted glimpses of an American column where no column was supposed to be. What was happening? Were the Americans retreating or attacking? General Lafayette explains: "His [Lafayette's] apparent composure deceived his adversary; and perceiving that he was reconnoitering him, from among the trees and behind curtains."[17] Whether it was Lafayette's remarkable composure, as he claims, or simply the infamous "fog of war"—a term coined by the Prussian officer Carl von Clausewitz decades later—for whatever reason, the British halted in order to try and determine just who or what they were observing in motion below. That momentary hesitation provided the escaping Americans the few precious minutes required to gain the river. "They saw our rear guard with two fieldpieces in its front," Martin suggests, "and thinking it the front of the detachment, they closed in to secure their prey, but when they had sprung their net they found that they had not a single bird under it."

Lafayette now took the point, riding headfirst into the cold water, leading the column across the rushing river. But it was no easy passage for the infantrymen, struggling all the way against the swift, tumbling current. Fisher, still with the rearguard, recalls the passage. "Our howl [whole] Party Crossed the river and the warter was up to our middle and run very swift so that we were obliged to hold to each other to keep the Corrent from sweeping us away and all in a fluster expecting the Enemy to fire in upon us for we could see them Plain but the reason was they Could not git thare Cannon to bare on us but we got all Safe across without the loss of any save fore or five of our party that the Enemy's Lite horse Cut to pieces."[18]

The Americans emerged on the south bank of the river, then scampered to higher ground where they formed at once, awaiting attack. Booming guns had been heard in the distance as the column first entered the river, but the rumble had not been occasioned by British artillery, but rather cannons at Valley Forge, miles away, sounding the alarm. Seems the disparate Red-coated columns had been spotted by Washington's scouts, and the garrison at Valley Forge, fearing attack, immediately scrambled to the battlements.

Meanwhile, Lafayette and his men stood to their arms along the riverbank. "We crossed the Schuylkill in good order," Martin explains, "very near the spot where I had crossed it four times in the month of October the preceding autumn. As fast as the troops crossed they formed and prepared for action, and waited for them to attack us; but we saw no more of them that time, for before we had reached the river the alarm guns were fired in our camp and the whole army was immediately in motion."[19] According to Lafayette, upon spotting the American escape, the British "generals quarreled, and although the commander in chief [Howe] had invited some ladies to sup with him [Lafayette, that is], although the admiral (Howe's brother) knowing him to be surrounded, had prepared a frigate for him, the whole army, (of which half had made a march of forty miles) returned, much fatigued, without having taken a single man."[20]

The British, hearing the report of the distant guns themselves, suddenly worried that they might soon be under assault from Washington's entire army, and broke off their offensive initiative; thus ended the so called Battle of Barren Hill. Lafayette's column slowly marched back to Swede's Ford then returned to Valley Forge on the 21st. Truthfully, Barren Hill had been an engagement that even in Revolutionary terms hardly rated the designation of skirmish. Wary of a larger engagement, the British determined not to pursue, still unsure of just who they were chasing, but certainly aware by now that the entire American detachment had somehow managed to slip through their fingers. It had been a clumsy affair for both sides.

As far as the Americans were concerned, Colonel Henry Dearborn, known as a straight shooter himself, minced no words while summing up the operation in his diary. "It was a very Luckey affair on our side," he wrote, "that we Did not Loose our whole Detachment."[21] Lafayette later polished the incident in his *Memoirs*, but it was impossible to polish away the fact that he had come very near capture himself, his troops facing the uncomfortable prospect of annihilation or capitulation. He had failed to keep a keen lookout and had taken up a stationary post against instructions, hence allowing the British to target his detachment, and had escaped by the skin of his teeth, everything Washington had warned him to avoid at all cost. His was a poor performance, and everyone knew it.

Nevertheless, the incident at Barren Hill did serve to highlight two important facts. The first was the Continental Army's continued lack of capable leadership at the division level. Lafayette's safe return had been a product of good fortune, and nothing more. Sadly, the officers Washington trusted the most were generally inexperienced, while the experienced officers—Gates and Lee come to mind—he dared not trust. But there was one emphatic plus that could be gleaned from the incident as a whole and that was just how well the troops had marched and reacted under pressure. Barren Hill demonstrated that Washington now had something very close to a professional army to work with. Pity the same could not be said of his senior lieutenants.

ELEVEN

Washington

We pass a most tiresome time of inactivity and suspense in Camp

The officers and men of the Continental Army publicly applauded General Lafayette's return from near entrapment on Barren Hill, but privately they were far more circumspect. If Dearborn was aware of all the details, after all, it can be assumed most everyone else was, as well, and his analysis, quoted in the preceding chapter, was probably common. No doubt Washington exhaled a huge sigh of relief—especially once the details became known—but he could not afford to admonish the Marquis too severely, especially given the fact that he had given Lafayette operational command in the first place. It was becoming clear, however, that training at the royal court of France as a Musketeer and handling a division in the field against the British were two very different things. The commander-in-chief was not one to cast aspersions, however, especially on those he relied upon, but in a private letter to Landon Carter, a fellow Virginia landowner, on May 30, Washington offered a hint as to his true opinion. "The Marquis by depending on the militia to patroll the roads on his left, had very near been caught in a snare—in fact he was in it—but by his *own dexterity* or the enemy's *want of it,* he disengaged himself in a very soldierlike manner."[1] In the long run Washington could only hope Lafayette had learned a valuable lesson, and that during his next mission he would adhere far more closely to instructions.

The next few weeks at Valley Forge proved a period of great uncertainty. While it was widely accepted by both officers and rank and file alike that the British were soon to vacate Philadelphia, precisely when and how that movement was to be made, and just where the enemy were bound remained subjects of much conjecture. Increasingly, however, information was coming in favoring the idea that the heavy guns and baggage would be shipped by sea; hence there was at least a chance their infantry might make the trip by land across New Jersey. On May 27, for instance, the General Orders speculated as follows: "The most recent intelligence from

Philadelphia is, that the Troops [British] drew yesterday three days provisions and had their canteens filled with rum, that the women and children had embarked, some of the sick had been removed from Hospitals and bettering house.... The number of Transports amounts to 180 vessels, averaging 250 tons each. This does not appear to be adequate to the number of Troops, and makes us think that the Enemy will retreat through the Jerseys, after embarking their heavy cannon and baggage."[2]

(It might be noted that 18th century correspondence often refers to New Jersey as "the Jerseys." This is because from 1664 to 1702 there were actually two Jerseys, one West Jersey, the other East Jersey, each with its own governor and capital. The area of New Jersey was first claimed by the Dutch and originally named New Netherlands, but later claimed by the British in victory as a result of war. The British later renamed the area New Jersey after the British isle in the English Channel, and in 1702 the two Jerseys were united into one political unit. The habit, however, of referring to New Jersey as "the Jerseys" remained a rhetorical constant for years after the unification.)

Two days after this intelligence had been posted, General Washington—now believing the British intended to withdraw their infantry across New Jersey—wrote to Gouverneur Morris in Congress, providing his most current strategic analysis. "The enemy seem to be upon the point of evacuating Philadelphia—and I am persuaded are going to New York—whether as a place of rendezvous of their whole force, for a general imbarkation, or to operate up the North River [Hudson River], or to act from circumstances is not quite so clear."

The recent treaty between the United States and France had thrown a wrench into British strategic thinking, and it was impossible for Washington to judge at the time how they might react. He continues to Governor Morris: "Equally uncertain is it, whether the Enemy will move from Philadelphia by Land or Water. I am inclined to think the former, and lament that the number of our sick (under inoculation, &c.), the situation of our stores, and other matters, will not allow me to make a large detachment from this army till the enemy have actually crossed the Delaware and began their march for South Amboy,—then it will be too late; so that we must give up the idea of harassing them *much* in their march through the Jerseys, or attempt it at the hazard of this Camp."[3]

Here Washington's thinking seems clear. If he moved prematurely against any British march across New Jersey, he would leave the Valley Forge camp open to potential attack. But if he waited until the British crossed over the Delaware, they would have stolen the march, and he would not have sufficient time to pursue the fleeing column. This analysis, however, remained firmly embedded in the notion that the British would move the vast bulk of their equipment, baggage, etc., by water, and that any march across New Jersey would therefore consist only of unencumbered infantry, this moving swiftly enough to avoid harassment. Still, Washington saw potential in all of this, and the day after writing Morris, he issued orders, preparing the army to march on short notice—just in case. "The Commanding Officers are to hold themselves in readiness to march. Wagons are to be drawn from the Quarter Master. Baggage is to be ready. Camp utensils and necessaries are to be ready for the field. Hard bread and salt meat is to be readied for issue. Guards are to be on alert."[4]

Washington still may have thought his chances of intercepting the British slim, but he was readying everything should that slim chance emerge somehow into firm reality. One can almost sense his mind at work, as day after day he issued a series of pragmatic orders, preparing for the fight he hoped to find somewhere on the long route through New Jersey between Philadelphia and New York. On May 29 New Jersey state troops were dispatched across the Delaware under General Maxwell to harass the British, for instance, should the enemy eventually emerge from Philadelphia.

Meanwhile, Baron von Steuben continued his incessant drilling, taking his instructions to ever more complex levels of maneuver. These now involved large scale exercises, what today might be called war games or mock combat. Whole brigades or even divisions were involved, each drill designed to inculcate the sort of precise movements required for real battlefield synchronization. Moving, wheeling, moving from column into line of battle, then reforming quickly on the battlefield was the hallmark of Prussian infantry, and Steuben wanted his American units to perform up to the same standard. This was difficult, technical work, but in combat such training could easily be the difference between victory and defeat. "Now each division would be formed up in a deep, narrow column, its width equal to the battle-line width of one platoon, twenty to twenty-five men across, with the platoons following closely upon one another in succession. Such a column could move forward much more rapidly, and was much more maneuverable, than a division in line of battle."[5]

From this new line the column could halt, then wheel clockwise to face a foe, or from there counterclockwise back to its original position, offering a range of tactical possibilities, all achieved with remarkable speed. Then firing drills were added to the mix, allowing the divisions to move forward or backward, individual platoons firing and reloading in sequence for a steady succession of musket fire as the division either attacked or withdrew. Practiced repeatedly, this would allow for command of the battlefield far beyond anything the Continental Army had ever before achieved. By late May Steuben had a reasonably clear understanding that Washington intended to go after the British if and when that opportunity ever presented itself, and he was determined to provide the commander-in-chief an army functioning at the highest level possible, given the timeframe available.

It was during Lafayette's Barren Hill escapade that General Charles Lee returned to camp, up from his meetings with Congress in York. What he discovered as he toured the Valley Forge encampment this time around did not please him. It had long been Lee's emphatic belief that the Continental Army—formed essentially of untrained, unprofessional militias—could never stand up to the British in pitched battle, no matter how much training they received. Training, from Lee's perspective, then, amounted to little more than wasted time and effort. Lee despised Washington's authority, a man he adjudged his military and social inferior, so by extension he naturally denigrated the army's newfound training routine, which served only to support Washington's desire for a conventional fighting force, a view Lee considered preposterous. What he witnessed now was an army capable of battlefield maneuver equal to, or perhaps even superior to, some elements of the British Army (the loyalist foot, for instance), but that obvious development failed to make the slightest dent on his long-held beliefs. Moreover, he returned to Valley Forge to the unhappy realization that there were now many new generals in Washington's inner circle whose views the commander-in-chief seemed to value, perhaps more than his own. None of this sat well with the self-important and overbearing Lee, and he began a subtle form of agitation against the progress he was seeing.

In particular, Lee began to focus his ire on Baron von Steuben, whose good work he tried to undermine through a campaign of whispers and innuendo. Historian Paul Lockhart tells us, "Steuben had superseded Lee as the army's resident expert on military affairs, and had displaced Lee's ally Conway as inspector general. He was a newcomer, too, and close to Washington. Steuben encouraged Washington's irrational belief that American soldiers could be made the equal of their British foes. And as if to rub salt into a raw wound, Steuben made no attempt to conceal his low opinion of the British military."[6]

Unfortunately, Lee still carried such an aura of martial intellect about him that over time his efforts began to pay off, inspiring several brigadiers to complain to Washington of Steuben's ever-growing authority. Washington resolved the complaint by providing all Continental commanders henceforth the authority to drill their own troops, but only in the presence of either Steuben or one of his inspectors. All commands regarding drill routine and schedules would now come from Washington's headquarters. Thus, Steuben no longer had the authority he previously held, but that authority now ran through Washington's office, so from that point forward Steuben's commands derived authority by means of Washington himself, and no one was about to quarrel with the commander-in-chief. Problem solved.

But that resolution did not stop Lee from continuing as a thorn in Washington's side. Despite being given command of one of the army's five divisions, he continued to champion his already disproven insistence that American soldiers could not be trained to fight conventionally against the British, a foe he still considered the best fighting force in the world. Worse still, he persisted in his veiled campaign against the Baron, an intrigue that over time would so infuriate the Prussian that Steuben ultimately demanded satisfaction, challenging Lee to a duel. Fortunately, Lee apologized, and the duel never took place, but Lee's rampant narcissism, disdain for Washington, and unrealistic conviction in the superiority of British arms would very soon create a crisis in the ranks of the Continental Army.

Meanwhile, as Continental divisions wheeled and fired their flintlocks in mock display on the Grande Parade, preparing for the fight many now considered imminent, tensions at headquarters continued to increase. Arrangements were put in place for surgeons to remain behind once the army marched, and 1,900 stands of new arms were received, finally bringing the army up to full firepower. News from Philadelphia continued pointing toward a British withdrawal, but the precise details remained sketchy at best. Representative of just how climactic the current moment in time seemed for Washington and his staff, on May 20 the General Orders read: "We are verging fast on one of the most important periods that America ever saw."[7]

Despite the mounting tension at headquarters, and acknowledgment of the climactic times that were fast approaching, since many of the soldiers at Valley Forge were little more than boys, those boys continued to be boys. On May 30 Elijah Fisher of the Life Guard, for instance, tumbled headfirst into the Schuylkill while simply trying to help a friend, an episode in which he came close to forfeiting his life, and which provides our narrative with an interesting look at the daily activities of camp. "I unhapely falls in to Schoolkill River and had Enliked to have been drowned one of my messmates having gon over the River after some Milk and comes and Calls for some one to Come with the Canew and fetch him acrost but none would go after him." Fisher, responding to his friend's conundrum when no one else would lift a finger, pushed off in the canoe, but he was unused to boats, and very soon found the current—which was still swimming high and brisk—more than he could handle. "I shifted the setting Pole on the other side to keep the head of the bote up" he tells us, "[but] it happened to Catch on a side of a rock and as I shoved the Pole slipped off and pitches me out of the other side and being surprised and current strong with all, made for the shore but the current was so swift it Carried me Down Stream." Fighting against the current with all his might, Fisher very soon became exhausted, and "after struglen for some minnets," almost went under. Fortunately, his friends dove into the river and dragged him from the water, and Fisher's calamity ended well. "Blake the young man that I was going after Come as fast as he could swim after me and come to me and soon a number was there and they helped me home to the barrack and the Doctor blooded but I was very unwell for several days."[8] Bloody, banged up, and exhausted, Elijah would nevertheless recover in time to march with the army in the coming campaign.

Day after day American reports trickled in reaffirming the same thing—the British seemed prepared to move immediately, but for some unknown reason had not, and this delay—inexplicable as it was—continued to weigh heavily on Washington and his staff. What was going on? "We pass a most tiresome time of inactivity and suspense in camp."[9] Then the cause for delay became suddenly manifest. Colonel Daniel Morgan, at his headquarters near Gulph Mills, received an envoy representing the British crown, up from Philadelphia. "Dr. Adam Ferguson was a noted professor of moral philosophy at the University of Edinburgh. Ferguson appeared as secretary of the so-called Carlisle Commission, which recently landed in Philadelphia with an offer of reconciliation from George III to the Continental Congress. Morgan had no authority to grant Ferguson a pass to enter the American lines, but he agreed to give Washington a copy of the commissioners' instructions, including the peace offer. The document carried the seal of a loving mother caressing her children."[10]

The British, now faced potentially with a far more expanded war with France, became suddenly willing to offer an olive branch to their unruly colonies. "The reason for Genl Clinton's delay in quitting Philada now is clear. Today the British commissioners for Peace arrived in Delaware Bay. The enemy now seems more disposed to negotiate a peace than to fight. He has sent letters suggesting reconciliation to his Excellency, who in turn has sent them to Congress."[11] Then on June 5 Clinton sent Major Loring along under a flag of truce to deliver a message directly to Washington that he intended to evacuate Philadelphia, and that, as a result, an exchange of prisoners ought to be arranged as soon as possible. Washington responded at once with a flurry of activity.

Realizing that the hunt for the evacuating British column would soon be on, on June 5—immediately following the reception of Clinton's message—Washington had Martha pack her bags and depart for Mount Vernon. Then he wrote to Philemon Dickinson, a general in the New Jersey militia, offering a range of suggestions as to how best to slow the enemy's march once they crossed over the Delaware River, chiefly, thought Washington, by round the clock bushwhacking with the smallest units possible:

I take the liberty of giving it to you as my opinion, also, that the way to annoy, distress, and really injure the enemy on their march (after obstructing the roads as much as possible) with militia, is to suffer them to act in very light bodies. Were it not for the horse [cavalry], I should think parties could not be too small, as every man in this case acts as it were for himself, and would, I conceive, make sure of his man between Cooper's Ferry and South Amboy, as the enemy's guards in front, flank, and rear, must be exposed, and may be greatly injured by the concealed and well directed fire of men in ambush. This kind of annoyance ought to be incessant day and night, and would I think be very effectual."[12]

Lastly, on the same day, he sent orders to Elias Boudinot to hasten to Philadelphia to begin negotiations for the exchange of prisoners. It is clear that by the evening of June 5, 1778, General Washington had his gaze set firmly on New Jersey, and he was doing everything he could think of to prepare for the hunt.

At 8 o'clock in the morning on June 10 the army said goodbye to its original Valley Forge encampment, crossing the Schuylkill River and moving about a mile onto open fields that bordered the river.[13] Here the ghastly odors of dead animals, foul latrines, rotting food, and the unhealthy, wretched huts were replaced by fresh air and the enticing fragrance of spring flowers. Tents were pitched, and the men of the Continental Army relaxed under the glow of a warming June sun. This move also represented a preparatory expedient, the army shedding much of its unneeded winter gear, trimming down for the march that was now looming, surely only days away.

The British commissioners, unsuccessful in their attempt to negotiate either a truce or peace, on June 18 departed Philadelphia, sailing off down the Delaware, bound for the open Atlantic. The British Army followed very soon thereafter, evacuating the city and crossing the Delaware River at several locations. Morgan's scouts, who had been watching closely, spotted the evacuation almost immediately. "Morgan, whose advanced parties discerned this movement, sent scouts into the Quaker City even as the last British rear units were retiring. On his command, bellmen went through the streets that night crying that the populace should stay inside until morning when the patriot leaders would officially take control of the city."[14] Before the following dawn smiled on the city, however, Morgan had his men already on the march, bound for Coryell's Ferry, a passage on the Delaware about twelve miles north of Trenton, New Jersey.

Headquarters became a sudden beehive of activity. Immediately upon receiving news of the British evacuation, Washington put several units of the Continental Army into motion. Then he wrote Congress, explaining both the situation and his intentions. "I have the pleasure to inform Congress, that I was this minute advised by Mr. Roberts that the enemy evacuated the city early this morning. He was down at the Middle Ferry on this side, where he received the intelligence from a number of the citizens, who were on the opposite shore.... I have put six brigades in motion; and the rest of the army are preparing to follow with all dispatch. We shall proceed toward Jersey, and govern ourselves according to circumstances."[15]

General Washington had charted a course for his troops, from Valley Forge across Pennsylvania to Coryell's Ferry, and very quickly the entire army was in motion. Chomping at the bit to get after the British, Washington had written Lee's orders—who was to lead the van out of Valley Forge—weeks before, waiting impatiently only for the opportunity to have them made operational. Specific in detail, the orders may have reflected the commander-in-chief's desire to avoid the problems he had encountered with the wayward Lee during the fall of 1776. They read: "Poor's, Varnum's and Huntington's brigades are to march in one division under your command. The quartermaster-general will give you the route, encampment, and halting-days, to which you will conform as strictly as possible, to prevent interfering with other troops, and that I may know precisely your situation on every day.... Begin your march at four o'clock in the morning at latest, that it may be over before the heat of the day, and that the soldiers may have time to cook, refresh, and prepare for the ensuing day."[16]

The vanguard marched off promptly on the 18th, the remainder breaking camp the following day, marching east on muddy roads through a heavy rainstorm. Regardless of the conditions, early the next morning they were all up and moving again. Drums tapped and fifes pealed as the long columns departed Valley Forge. Few men looked back. Elijah Fisher recorded the momentous departure in his journal: "June 20th. We left Schoolkill and Marched and Come into Bucks County after Marching fifteen miles and Pitched our tents."[17]

Already, however, the June sun seemed to be longing for summer. Temperatures began to spike higher and higher, and along the narrow, dirt roads men began to sweat profusely as they marched ever eastward toward the Delaware. If the army moved quickly, they just might catch the Redcoats in mid-march, somewhere along that long stretch of road that ran between Philadelphia and New York. For George Washington and his dusty, sweating Continentals, this was everything they could ever have wished for. The Redcoats were finally out of their defenses, and the Americans were hot on their trail. On the 20th the vanguard, led by Lee and "Mad Anthony" Wayne, crossed over the Delaware into Jersey, and took up defensive positions on the first good ground they could locate. The days of cold, famine, illness, and lingering death were over. The Continental Army had somehow managed to survive the grueling winter. Shedding their Valley Forge defenses, as of June 20, 1778, they had gone over to the offensive. Now the hunt was on.

TWELVE

Clinton

I have the Honor to inform your Lordship that pursuant to His Majesty's Instructions I have evacuated Philadelphia

On June 18, George Washington and his Continentals assumed the role of the hare, leaving by default the role of tortoise to Sir Henry Clinton and his royal troops, although it appears playing the turtle was at the time a part Sir Henry relished. Commanding a movement of "some 20,800 people, forty-six artillery pieces and ammunition stores, perhaps 5,000 horses, and 1,500 horse-drawn wagons packed with provisions for six weeks,"[1] for the sake of convenience, the British soon divided the expedition into two columns as they crossed into southern Jersey. The Redcoats started their journey north at a snail's pace due to the heat and heavy thunderstorms that were likewise impeding the Continentals, who were by then crossing the Delaware some thirty miles to the north.[2]

Clinton's columns contained not only his soldiers and their personal belongings, but numerous Tory families fleeing Philadelphia along with all the possessions they could pack aboard the overburdened wagons. Clinton had wisely detailed an engineer to make a thorough study of the road network in southern New Jersey prior to evacuating the city, removing the possibility of delay or misdirection once his troops had been disembarked on Jersey soil. Taking advantage of the road system, the dual columns—one under Clinton, the other under General Knyphausen—crawled slowly north on two different roads, headed for the village of Mount Holly where the two roads finally merged. The British movement contained some of the finest fighting units in their entire army—Queen's Rangers, Jaegers (Hessian sharpshooters), Grenadiers, Black Watch (Royal Highlanders), and British Light Dragoons—and they were well drilled in screening the vanguard, rearguard, and flanks of any column. Clinton's column contained approximately 10,000 effective troops, Knyphausen's about 8,000. Hence Clinton was not concerned with skirmishes with the Continentals, nor was he worried about local militia interference, which he expected to simply brush aside as the columns lumbered northward. So, Clinton had decided to take his time while traversing New Jersey, and if Washington happened to stray too near, then he would be happy to offer battle, should the situation favor confrontation.[3]

Interestingly, the British appeared to be leaving Philadelphia with fewer troops than they had arrived with so many months before, as many had apparently discovered America to be a far more welcoming and prosperous land than the countries they had left behind in Europe.

> He [Howe] had landed certainly 15,000 (it is confidently believed 18,000) men at the head of Elk River, and been since largely reinforced from New York. About a thousand had fallen in battle or been made prisoners, and their loss by sickness could not have been very great; for comfortable quarters had kept their army comparatively healthy. But great numbers had deserted. Their intercourse with the women of that place, with whom many intermarried, and with the European settlers, particularly the Germans, induced many to wish to remain in the country. Among the Hessians, the spirit of desertion was universal. Their countrymen who had been captured at Trenton, were comfortably disposed of in a part of Pennsylvania inhabited by Germans, and possessing every thing that could tempt men to escape, or to carry off with them some of their companions in arms. On their retreat through the Jerseys, it is thought that not less than one thousand more effected their escape."[4]

It seems that not even the severest British punishments could induce many to remain under arms, when the prospect of freedom and a far better life was there for the taking, right below their noses.

The British evacuation had so far been a masterpiece of martial engineering, initiated in stages, involving hundreds of moving parts, all expertly choreographed. It began late in May with the systematic loading of heavy artillery onto British transport ships, this followed in turn by mountains of supplies and provisions. Those supplies that could not find a place onboard were tossed into the Delaware River, or burned along the docks, the Redcoats not wishing to leave anything behind that might prove useful to the enemy. Once it became clear that the Royal Navy did not have transports enough to evacuate the entire army, Sir Henry—now commander-in-chief of all British forces—began planning an evacuation across the Delaware River of his infantry and their loyalist friends, knowing that he would have to move overland to New York. That movement began in mid–June, when the first troops were rowed across the river at Cooper's Ferry, from there fanning out once ashore to establish a beachhead. More troops followed, ferried across the river in an almost constant flow over a four-day period, again at Cooper's Ferry, slightly north of Philadelphia, then finally at Gloucester, just south. Once firmly astride the Jersey side of the Delaware, several units marched to Haddonfield, some six miles southeast of Philadelphia, and established a defensive perimeter. Sir Henry had every reason to be proud so far of his effort, later reporting to Lord Germain in London: "I have the honor to inform your lordship that pursuant to His Majesty's Instructions I evacuated Philadelphia on the 18th of June at three o'Clock in the Morning, and proceeded to Gloucester Point without being followed by the Enemy."[5] Mount Holly lay northeast of Haddonfield some fifteen miles as the crow flies, more distant over the bumpy, roundabout roads of the day, and it was toward the Mount that the twin columns first set their course.

Clinton was of course expecting disruptions from American militia units upon reaching New Jersey, and in this regard American militias did not disappoint. Trees were felled across roads, bridges burnt or dismembered. Shots routinely rang out from hilltops, barns, farmhouses, and tree lines all along the line of march, but the musketry did little damage, and each British marching column contained a company of pioneers practiced in the art of clearing roads and repairing bridges. Virtually every bridge that spanned the creeks and small ravines along the line of march was found burnt or dismembered, but the pioneers worked their magic while the infantry covered the approaches, and in that manner delays were kept to a minimum. Each column was slowed somewhat by these incessant disruptions, but Mother Nature, far more than militia actions, began to take her toll on the speed of the march. The temperatures soared daily into the ninety-degree range, only then to be followed in turn by booming thunderstorms featuring whipping winds and torrential downpours. Dirt roads were soon reduced to rivers of mud, and Clinton's 1,500 horse-drawn wagons quickly turned the mud into impassable quagmires. The columns—once joined—were immense, stretching out along the roads some 12 to 14 miles, a lengthy distance painfully difficult to defend, while at the same time offering tantalizing opportunities for lightning like raids of the hit-and-run variety.[6]

The British columns crawled along at a snail's pace, tortured by the heat, mud, mosquitoes, and nagging militia disruptions. In Paul Lockhart's words, "There was something more behind the sluggishness of Clinton's retreat than the vicissitudes of a harsh summer. Clinton's cumbersome baggage train—some fifteen thousand wagons carrying the personal belongings of the officers, spare camp equipage, and all the comforts of home taken from Philadelphia—slowed the army, as did the unusually large number of noncombatants that followed in the army's wake. Alongside British columns walked some one thousand civilians, including more than seven hundred women and children."[7] It was almost as if the British had put half of Philadelphia on wheels, and were now attempting to drag the lot of it across New Jersey while simultaneously fending off the enemy and Mother

Nature in the process. Of course, the sluggish pace had not been designed for Washington's benefit, but in hindsight, it certainly played into his hands.

On June 19 Clinton led his column out of Haddonfield, bound for Mount Holly. It was a brutal passage, heat, storms, and incessant rebel sniping taking their toll on everyone's nerves. Ahead, around, and behind the Redcoats, Maxwell's Brigade, in concert with Dickinson's New Jersey Militia, were swarming like bees, making life as miserable for the British as possible. Clinton marched into Mount Holly on the 20th after a nasty fight with bushwhacking rebels at a bridge just outside of town.[8] There Sir Henry decided to settle down for a brief rest while awaiting Knyphausen's column, which was still working its way north. Knyphausen appeared the following day, having experienced no opposition to speak of, and the twin columns then departed Mount Holly early on the 22nd, Clinton sending General Alexander Leslie off on a more westward sweep with a contingent of troops to serve as a screen for the main column. Despite the rains and nagging musketry, so far the withdrawal had gone smoothly if slowly, and Sir Henry must surely have been satisfied with his progress.

Clinton, like Cornwallis, Charles Lee, Horatio Gates, and the Howe brothers, was a product of English aristocracy, but of a considerably more refined pedigree. Clinton's precise date of birth remains unclear but is thought to have been between 1730 and 1738. His father was Admiral George Clinton, his mother the daughter of a general, his grandfather the Sixth Earl of Lincoln. In 1741 his father was named the Royal Governor of New York, and in 1743 young Henry accompanied the rest of his family to the New World. Little is known of Henry's upbringing or education in New York, but it can be presumed the young Clinton was well tutored. In 1746 his father purchased a

Sir Henry Clinton.
From an English Print.

Sir Henry Clinton, here portrayed in a pen and pencil illustration. Clinton arrived as second in command of British forces in 1775, and rose to full command in 1778. From *The Pictorial Field-Book of the Revolution*, Vol. 2, by Benson J. Lossing.

commission for him, and he was briefly stationed at Fort Louisbourg in Nova Scotia on garrison duty. Returning to England in 1751, he was commissioned a Captain in the Coldstream Guards, an elite unit which surely represented a feather in his cap. Seven years later he was commissioned a Lieutenant Colonel, and he later fought in Germany during the Seven Years' War. Clinton served with distinction during that war, was wounded, and was later promoted to the rank of Colonel. His star appeared to be in ascendance.

Twelve years later Clinton was promoted to Major General and elected to the British Parliament. He was by then married and the father of five children, but his wife, Harriet, died just days after the birth of their sixth child, a loss that sent Clinton spiraling into a deepening despair. He finally left England for a lengthy trip to try and recuperate, and returned to Great Britain in 1774, apparently recovered from his bout with depression. In 1776 he was dispatched to North America in order to deal with the rebellion, and over the course of the war he consistently displayed a keen sense of tactical and strategic ingenuity. Now, as he departed Mount Holly in the early hours of June 22, Sir Henry would have to marshal all his tactical knowhow in order to deliver this slow, hulking column to New York unharmed.[9]

The American forces, while not yet consolidated, were beginning to close on the British advance. Washington, relying heavily upon Daniel Morgan and his Virginia riflemen—a group that had played prominently in the American victory at Saratoga—ordered Morgan to be reinforced for reconnaissance efforts, and hopefully engage the British when and where advantageous. "Each Brigade is to furnish an active, spirited Officer and twenty five of it's best marksmen immediately; These parties to join Colo. Morgan's Corps and continue under his command 'till the Enemy pas thro' the Jerseys after which they are to rejoin their Regiments without further orders."[10] Heavily reinforced, Morgan's Virginia riflemen were the best scouting and combat unit Washington had in the field and, despite the delayed start, Colonel Morgan's men were some of the first to pass the ferry into New Jersey.

But the going remained slow, both sides straining to make headway on mud laden roads, the passage made far more difficult by the insufferable heat. On the 21st Elijah Fisher noted that "We Left Buck's County [Pennsylvania] at ten of the Clock in the four noon and after ten miles March we arrived at Carrell's ferrey and the Life guard Crossed at four in the afternoon and Marched to Mr. Haises in Hunberton's County where his Excellency had his Quarters and Pitched our tents."[11]

Meanwhile Clinton proceeded north, brushing aside any minor annoyance the American militias managed to toss in his path, reaching the vicinity of the Black Horse Tavern late on the 22nd. On the same day that Clinton reached Black Horse Tavern, Washington wrote to Henry Laurens at Congress, advising that he had established his headquarters in New Jersey, and was preparing to locate and assault the British, if possible.

> I have the honor to inform you that I am now in Jersey, and that the troops passing the river at Coryell's, and are mostly over. The latest intelligence I have had respecting the enemy was yesterday from General Dickinson. He says they were in the morning at Morestown and Mount Holly; but that he had not been able to learn what route they would pursue from thence; nor was it easy to determine, as, from their situation, they might either proceed to South Amboy, or by way of Brunswic. We have been a good deal impeded in our march by rainy weather. As soon as we have cleaned the arms, and can get matters in train, we propose moving towards Princeton, in order to avail ourselves of any favorable occasions, that may present themselves, of attacking the enemy.[12]

On June 23 Clinton's column approached Crosswicks and found Maxwell's entire brigade deployed on high ground above the bridge that spanned Crosswicks Creek, apparently stewing for a fight. The long column halted as Clinton considered his options. First the dragoons, who had been leading the advance, made a dash at the Americans, but they were promptly repulsed by a torrent of long-range musketry. Clinton then decided upon flanking operations to dislodge the rebels, leading one assault himself. The British moved to within musket range where they became heavily engaged with Maxwell's troops. Muskets cracked back and forth for some time as Clinton worked to get his flanking assaults into position. While all this was going on, the British opened on the Americans with artillery, spitting antipersonnel shells at the rebels from reasonably close range. Lacking artillery to respond, and now out gunned, the Americans finally backed away, but not before having given Clinton a healthy taste of what he could expect waiting for him at virtually every bridge, stream crossing, or defile on the path ahead.[13]

Next morning the British were up and marching again, slowly rumbling northward toward Allentown, a road junction where Clinton realized he would have to make a decision, either heading directly north toward New York City, or east where he might rendezvous with the British Navy near Sandy Hook on the Atlantic. As he later advised Lord Germain: "Thus far ... my March pointed equally towards the Hudson's River and Staten Island by the Rariton [Raritan River]. I was now at the Juncture when it was necessary to decide ultimately what course to pursue."[14] Sir Henry had a decision to make; the American were beginning to close on him, events were naturally accelerating, hence some sort of brush with the enemy appeared more and more imminent.

The British were disposed to cross New Jersey on a northeast path, a total distance of roughly 90 miles from Philadelphia to New York. Washington, on the other hand, by crossing farther north at Coryell's Ferry, was from there proceeding almost at a right angle to the British march. If a line were to be drawn roughly straight from Coryell's Ferry across New Jersey to overlap with the British line of march, those two lines would intersect very near a sleepy hamlet containing about forty houses and a district court building, then known as Monmouth Courthouse (present day Monmouth, New Jersey). Unknown to either Clinton or Washington at the time, of course, that is precisely where the converging columns would collide.

Thirteen

Washington

We are intirely at a loss where the army is

General Washington established his headquarters at Hopewell, New Jersey—some ten miles east of Coryell's Ferry—and then commenced the trying task of digesting all the diverse intelligence reports he was receiving from his vanguard units. Typical for an army on the move, the situation remained murky. He had received intelligence from Dickinson that the enemy appeared bound for Allentown, a hamlet where the road was known to split. So, once the British passed Allentown, geography and the road system alone would force them to reveal their true destination, either moving north toward the Raritan River, or east toward Sandy Hook. If they marched toward Sandy Hook, it was assumed the column would meet the British Fleet along the Atlantic coast and be ferried the short distance from there to New York City. Once at Allentown the British would have completed almost half their trek, and whether they moved north or east, it was apparent that opportunities to damage them would begin to diminish considerably, once they began moving directly away from Continental forces. What to do? Washington responded by calling a council of war.

On the 24th General Washington met with eleven of his top officers. He reviewed the strategic situation, as it was understood at the time, then asked for opinions. The result, for the aggressive Washington at least, was dispiriting. General Lee was firmly, and typically, of the opinion that no contest with the retreating British column ought to be sought, and that the Redcoats should be allowed to retreat unmolested. Characteristically, Lee still fancied the British Army the very apex of military forces then on the world stage and was happy to make his opinion known. According to Lafayette, who along with Steuben was among the eleven officers in attendance, "Lee very eloquently endeavoured to prove so that it was necessary to erect a bridge of gold for the enemy," and further, "the English army had never been so excellent and so well disciplined." This was, of course, little more than boilerplate Charles Lee, his respect for British arms animating his every opinion, and Lee's reputation ultimately carried the day, the majority of officers finally agreeing that a confrontation was at present unwarranted.

Lafayette insists, however, that he was of a different opinion, and objected to Lee's passive suggestion. "M. de Lafayette spoke late, and asserted that it would be disgraceful for the chiefs, and humiliating for the troops, to allow the enemy to traverse the Jerseys tranquilly; that without running any improper risk, the rear guard might be attacked."[1] While Lafayette's suggestion seemed based upon a sense of martial élan more than any strategic considerations, he nevertheless had a point. What was the purpose, after all, of marching men for days on end through mud, heat, and thunderstorms if nothing of substance was to be gained by the effort? After months of starvation and drill at Valley Forge, and now days hard on the march, was "tranquility" the best the army could hope to accomplish?

No clear agreement was achieved by the council, but that was hardly surprising.[2] The notion that eleven men of different experience, skill, and temperament were going to come to a firm agreement on any particular course of action had been remote to begin with. Washington, apparently disappointed by the council's outcome, simply retired to his office. Of course, he was in no way bound by the council's vote so, despite the tepid response of his officers, Washington decided to send forward a detachment under General Charles Scott of 1,500 men to harry the enemy.[3] It was a small-scale effort, but surely Washington thought it superior to nothing at all.

Scott departed on the afternoon of the 24th, marching through Princeton, his objective Allentown, the small village about ten miles south and east of the college town where the British were expected soon to arrive. Marching with that column was Private Joseph Plumb Martin, and as usual his recollection of events is worth revisiting. "Here I was again detached with a party of one thousand men, as light troops," he explains, "to get into the enemy's route and follow him close, to favor desertion and pick up stragglers." The distance between Hopewell and Princeton was about nine miles, and by dinner time Martin's column had reached the town's outskirts. "Our detachment marched in the afternoon and towards night we passed through Princeton," he recalls. "Some of the patriotic inhabitants of the town had brought out to the end of the street we passed through some casks of ready-made toddy. It was dealt out to the men as they passed by, which caused the detachment to move slowly at this place." Martin apparently enjoyed an ample ration of toddy then marched on, taking in the scenery as he did. "The young ladies of the town, and perhaps of the vicinity," he observed happily, "had collected and were sitting in the stoops and at the windows to see the noble exhibition of a thousand half-starved and three-quarters naked soldiers pass in review before them." The gathering of young women made quite an impression on the teenage soldier. After months in the wilds of Pennsylvania, and now with a good taste of whiskey under his belt, Martin literally glowed in admiration as his platoon continued through town. "I chanced to be on the wing of a platoon next to the houses, as they were chiefly on one side of the street, and had a good chance to notice the ladies, and I declare that I never before nor since saw more beauty, considering the numbers, than I saw at this time. They were *all* beautiful." Whether Martin's observations were fact or simply the whiskey talking, we shall never know, for the detachment continued out of town and eventually "encamped on the open fields for the night, the canopy of heaven for our tent."[4]

As Martin's detachment was bedding down outside of Princeton, Washington was joined again in his office by Lafayette, Greene, and Hamilton, the latter having attended the council of war as Washington's aide. As candlelight flickered off the walls, all three, according to Lafayette, conferred with the commander-in-chief then urged him to consider a more forceful course of action. Since this advice—probably much welcomed by Washington—dovetailed with the commander-in-chief's far more aggressive inclinations to begin with, Washington agreed, and immediately decided to augment his forward divisions still further with yet another detachment.[5] In that General Wayne had joined the conversation, and concurred entirely with the other officer's views, Washington decided to send Wayne's troops ahead, this adding another 1,000 men to the vanguard.

This decision was greeted with delight all around, but it simultaneously highlighted an obvious problem. With the addition of Wayne to the forward mix, there would now be five significant American units—Morgan, Maxwell, Wayne, Scott, and Dickinson—all maneuvering independently of one another as they approached the British column. These units could mistakenly bump into one another (especially at night) causing a friendly fire incident (thus alerting the British to their location), or at a minimum fail to appropriately cooperate during a time of necessity. Moreover, such a large body of troops operating near the enemy might inadvertently bring on a major engagement, should the British interpret their presence as a serious threat, and respond accordingly. Washington also realized that he would now have to shift the main army to within supporting distance of the forward units in order to avoid a potential disaster, and then hold the army on ready alert to march on a moment's notice.

The situation screamed for a controlling hand, an officer capable of riding forward, taking charge of the situation, and imposing coherence over disorder, but the pickings for such an officer were unfortunately slim, as the bumbling affair at Barren Hill had aptly demonstrated. The movement of the main army could be easily achieved, but the selection of an officer capable of handling the forward units represented, for the commander-in-chief, a serious dilemma. Washington had essentially two choices at hand, Lee or Lafayette, and both came with their own positive and negative attributes.

Washington first offered the command to Lee, and this selection was warranted. To begin with, Lee, being a senior officer, deserved the position, while he also had the presumed experience required to handle the situation. Lee's downside, on the other hand, was that he had just passionately argued against the very maneuver he was now being asked to oversee, and Washington had good reason to mistrust him, even with written orders, given Lee's actions outside of New York earlier in the war. Lee demurred, however, arguing that the nominal size of the operation was unworthy of an officer of his stature. There was, of course, some truth to this assertion, but Lee's refusal also points directly to the fact that his essential motivation— his raison d'être—seemed grounded entirely in personal vanity. Washington was in a sticky situation, he needed help; he graciously sought that help from Lee and got little more than snubbed for his effort.

So, Washington had but one option left, and he turned to the Marquis for help, to which Lafayette jubilantly responded. While Washington knew Lafayette was loyal and enthusiastic, he also realized—post Barren Hill— that a command of such magnitude may well have been beyond the Marquis' depth. So, he crafted Lafayette's orders with great care:

> You are immediately to proceed with the detachment commanded by Genl. Poor, and form a junction as expeditiously as possible with that under the command of Genl. Scott. You are to use the most effectual means for gaining the enemy's left flank and rear, and giving them every degree of annoyance. All Continental parties, that are already on the lines, will be under your command, and you will take such measures, in concert with Genl. Dickinson, as will cause the enemy the greatest impediment and loss in their march. For these purposes you will attack them as occasion may require by detachment, and, if a proper opening shd. be given, by operating against them with the whole force of your command. You will naturally take such precautions, as will secure you against surprise, and maintain your communication with this army.[6]

Importantly, while von Steuben had earlier agreed with Lee's analysis and conclusion as to allowing the British to pass through Jersey unmolested, after conferring with Lafayette, he had reversed his opinion, and agreed that some form of action should be taken before the British got too far away for practical operations. Given the Baron's experience in intelligence gathering with the Prussian Army, Washington immediately dispatched him on an important mission. Washington had to know which way the British turned when they marched out of Allentown—north toward the Raritan River or east toward Sandy Hook—in order to craft an offensive strike, and Steuben enthusiastically accepted the assignment. Of equal importance, Washington wanted to attack the rear of the British column once it had separated from the lead division, so he had to know when that separation took place in order to time his attack. "Sometime in the evening of the twenty-fourth, before Lafayette had departed, Steuben—accompanied by Duponceau, Ben Walker, and a small cavalry escort—slipped out of camp at Hopewell to find the British army."[7]

The following day, the 25th of June, the Continentals were in motion. Washington marched with the main body, moving from Hopewell through Rocky Hill to present day Monmouth Junction in order to better support his forward operations, while Steuben and his small group rode toward Allentown, tracking the British across the New Jersey countryside. Elijah Fisher noted the day's activities: "We left Kittorn at Nine of the clock A.M. and Marched and Come to Rockey hill and Pitched our tents there awhile."[8] Meanwhile, south of Rocky Hill, Private Martin was marching with Scott's detachment as it closed on Allentown.

> Early the next morning [June 25] we marched again and came up with the rear of the British army.... We had ample opportunity to see the devastation they made in their rout; cattle killed and lying about the fields and pastures, some just in the position they were in when shot down, others with a small pot of skin taken off their hind quarters and a mess of steak taken out; household furniture hacked and broke to pieces; wells filled up and mechanics' and farmers' tools destroyed. It was in the height of the season of cherries; the innocent industrious creatures could not climb the trees for the fruit, but universally cut them down. Such conduct did not give the Americans any more agreeable feelings toward them than they entertained before.[9]

Lafayette, greatly enthused, rode forward that day to take over his new command. Toward evening he met with Alexander Hamilton, who had ridden to Cranbury Town earlier to establish a new headquarters while also trying to discern the current situation in the field. The two met that night, Hamilton sharing a dispatch he had recently forwarded to Washington:

> The enemy have all filed off from Allen Town on the Monmouth road. Their rear is said to be a mile Westward of Lawrence Taylor's Tavern, six miles from Allen Town. General Maxwell is at Hyde's Town, abt. three miles from this place. General Dickinson is said to be on the enemy's right flank, but where cannot be told. We can hear nothing certain of General Scott but from circumstances he is probably at Allen Town. We shall agreeable to your request consider and appoint some proper place of rendezvous, for the union of our force, which we shall communicate to General Maxwell & Scot and to yourself.... I am told Col Morgan is on the enemy's right flank. He had a slight skirmish with their rear this forenoon at Robert Montgomery's, on the Monmouth road leading from Allen Town.[10]

Hamilton's note made it clear that very little was known at the time about the whereabouts of the American advanced units. At this point, all was guesswork and hearsay, precisely the situation Washington hoped the appointment of Lafayette would soon resolve. But Lafayette had his eyes on the British who, according to Hamilton's intelligence, had turned east and were marching toward Monmouth Courthouse, fast disappearing through the heat and dust. The detachments Lafayette had joined had already out marched their supply train and were now severely short of rations. Despite this, early the next morning the Marquis had the troops up and on the road again, departing at 5:00 a.m. in the hopes of catching up to the British. Colonel Dearborn, of the New Hampshire Continentals, recalls the day: "26th we march'd Early this Morning after the Enimy. The weather is Extreemly Hot, we are Obliged to march very Modirate. The Enimy Desert very fast, we are Join'd to Day by the Marquis De Lefiette with a Detachment of 1000 men. We advanced within three miles of the Enimy, & Incamp'd.

This painting by John Turnbull features Alexander Hamilton later in life, long after his work as a valued member of General Washington's staff at the Battle of Monmouth Courthouse. National Archives.

The Enimy are about Monmouth Court House, on good Ground."[11]

Lafayette was now at Robin's Tavern, some eight miles north of Allentown on the road to Monmouth, but by noon his troops were already breaking down from intense heat, exertion, and the lack of food. Hamilton was also there, and he alone seemed to have a firm grasp of the tactical situation as it was then understood, circumstances that were far from comforting. He jotted down an urgent message to Washington, explaining the state of affairs: "Our reason for halting is the extreme distress of the troops for want of provisions. General Wayne's detachment is almost starving and seem both unwilling and unable to march further 'till they are supplied. If we do not receive an immediate supply, the whole purpose of our detachment must be frustrated. This morning we missed doing anything from a deficiency of intelligence." Lafayette had raced ahead, not only beyond his capacity for supply, but also beyond the ability of the army to support his detachment, a dire prospect that Hamilton grasped at once. "We are intirely at a loss where the army is, which is no inconsiderable check to our enterprise; if the army is wholly out of supporting distance, we risk the total loss of the detachment in making an attack."[12]

This was hardly the news George Washington wanted to hear. He had sent Lafayette forward to consolidate the advanced units under a single commander, who would then hopefully coordinate a sensible plan of attack against the enemy's rearguard, not to charge off half-cocked, placing his entire detachment in harm's way, which was precisely what Lafayette had managed to accomplish. Neither Lafayette nor Hamilton had at the time any idea where many of the scattered American units were operating, nor, it appears, had Lafayette been able to make contact with many of them. And this, more than anything, had been his primary task.

Once again, the lack of competent leadership at the senior level had bedeviled Washington's plans, and there was nothing the commander-in-chief could do now but take charge of the situation himself.

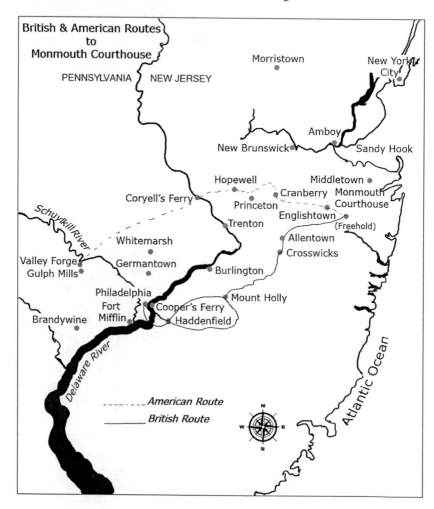

"Light Horse" Harry Lee offered this insight into the Marquis' initial appointment: "The marquis was young, generous, and brave, like most of his brother generals, yet little versed in the art of war."[13] In fairness to Lafayette, however, it must be noted that it was Washington who had orchestrated the befuddled tactical arrangement in the first place, augmenting the vanguard piecemeal, and only after the troops moved ahead had the confused nature of the operation he had initiated become apparent to him. The disjointed organization now in the field was Washington's fault, and now Lafayette had done virtually nothing to straighten it out.

Washington checked his map and noticed the small village of Englishtown, about five miles northwest of Monmouth Court House, the village where the British column was then known to be encamped. So late that day he sent instructions to Lafayette to forgo any offensive operations, and consolidate all forward detachments upon Englishtown, where they could be better supplied and supported by the main army. This was a sound move, correcting a mistake that had yet to be corrected.

This was accomplished the next day, June 27, another day of sweltering heat under an unforgiving sun. Dearborn: "We march. Early this morning within one mile of the Enimy & were ordered by an Express from Genrl Washington to Counter March to where we Incamp'd Last night, & from thence to file off to English Town."[14] Like Dearborn, Martin and his mates suffered through the same heat and confusion, marching and countermarching. "We were marching on as usual, when, about ten or eleven o'clock, we were ordered to halt and then to face to the rightabout. As this order was given by the officers in rather a different way than usual, we began to think something was out of joint somewhere, but what or where our united wisdom could not explain.... We, however, retraced our steps till we came to our last night's encamping ground, when we left the route of the enemy and went off a few miles to a place called Englishtown. It was uncommonly hot weather and we put up booths to protect us from the heat of the sun, which was almost insupportable."[15] So insupportable, in fact, that many men had already collapsed during the long day's march and countermarch. Ultimately, the heat would take almost as many lives—for Continental and British alike—as would musket balls during the Monmouth Campaign.

As at Barren Hill, good fortune had again spared Lafayette from being discovered and attacked, but at headquarters, General Lee's pride was now boiling like steam hissing from a teapot, gumming up Washington's plans beyond what fate and foolishness had already accomplished. Upon grasping the full scope of the command Washington had ultimately extended to Lafayette, General Lee suddenly changed his mind, deciding that command of such a combined detachment should naturally fall to him as a consequence of his senior status. He demanded in writing on the 25th that Washington restore him to the position, despite the fact Lafayette had already marched from camp, accompanying Wayne's troops. After outlining again his argument against fielding the vanguard detachment in the first place, Lee then continued, insisting that "if this detachment with Maxwells Corps Scotts, Morgans and Jacksons are to be considered as a separate chosen active Corps and put under the Marquis's Command until the Enemy leave the Jerseys—both Myself and Lord Steuben will be disgrac'd."[16]

Not disappointed, mind you, or even distressed, but disgraced. Even stipulating the elaborate martial etiquette of the day, Lee's demand—considering the current tactical situation then confronting the commander-in-chief—can be viewed only as an extraordinarily self-serving piece of business. Note that Lee included the Baron in his claim of potential humiliation (Steuben, who had voiced no such complaint, and who was at the time off happily on a reconnaissance mission of his own) simply, it would appear, to bolster his own assertion. One can only speculate as to what Washington's reaction to this declaration might have been, but the term flabbergasted does come to mind.

Now having to deal with not only a military situation that remained confused and potentially dangerous, but also a command decision fraught with powerful tactical and emotional implications, Washington nevertheless settled upon a middle ground, and presented it to Lee in writing on the 26th: "Your uneasiness, on account of the command of yesterday's detachment, fills me with concern, as it is not in my power, fully, to remove it without wounding the feelings of the Marquiss de la Fayette—I have thought of an expedient, which though not quite equal to either of your views, may in some measure answer both; and that is to make another detachment from this Army for the purpose of aiding and supporting several detachments now under the command of the Marquiss & giving you the command of the whole, under certain restrictions." Those restrictions were that Lee would move forward with two additional brigades, advising Lafayette of his approach, and upon reaching the front Lee would then take command of the entire vanguard, unless Lafayette was already in some manner engaged, or involved in "some enterperize," at which time Lee would lend his full support to Lafayette's efforts.[17] To this proposal both Lee and Lafayette fortunately agreed.

It was the best Washington could possibly have proposed under the circumstances, and with its acceptance, Lee's public disgrace was thankfully averted. And while this solution may have served to soothe ruffled feathers, as a command element, it was far from perfect. If, for instance, Lee's approach were to take place just as Lafayette was responding to a threat, or actively fighting off a sudden attack, the actual chain of command could easily have devolved into a state of confusion, given Lee's sense of operational vanity, and Lafayette's desire for glory. That this did not occur was a matter of good fortune far more than good design, and the additional fact that the British were at the moment more interested in escape to New York than battle in New Jersey. But, as we shall see, Lee's last-minute demand, and Washington's awkward acceptance of it, would prove the very source of almost all the problems that would disrupt the Continentals' morning affair at Monmouth, and drive historians to distraction for years afterward.

Thus, as June 27 drew to a close, General Washington had much to be thankful for, whether he knew it or not. His vanguard was reunited at Englishtown, while the main army had marched to within supporting distance, all of this accomplished without the loss of a single brigade. Meanwhile, the British had managed a full day of rest and recuperation at Monmouth Courthouse, but were expected to resume their march the following morning.

One critical thing had changed, however. Washington had just replaced an enthusiastic commander—who had unfortunately proven himself too young and inexperienced to handle such an involved assignment—with another who he knew had a penchant for disobeying orders, disagreeing with Washington's own offensive impulse, and consistently voicing his disapproval of the very plan he was now being asked to implement, worse still, while detached at some distance from the main army. In a perfect world, given his experience, it would be hoped that Lee would provide a firm and guiding hand, utilizing the Marquis' exuberance to best effect, while Lafayette would be placed in a position where he might gain the glory he desired through the execution of a sensible offensive scheme. Unfortunately, the world was then, just as it is today, far from perfect.

As the sun set on that miserably hot June 27, 1778, all the marching and countermarching had blessedly come to a halt. The weary troops were bedding down for the night, hopeful of an evening breeze that might offer at least a modicum of relief. By day's end a new arrangement of combatants had been established as a result of the day's considerable efforts, errors, and confusions, however, and that new arrangement is worth noting.

The British, we know—as reported by Colonel Dearborn—had encamped at and around Monmouth Courthouse, some ten miles northeast of Robin's Tavern, an encampment on good defensive ground, well established and properly picketed. The American vanguard (minus Morgan's small detachment, which still hung on the right flank of the British column, Lafayette having failed to make contact) was now concentrated at Englishtown, five miles northwest of the courthouse. Washington had by sunset of the 27th moved the main body forward from Cranbury to Manalapan Bridge, roughly four miles from Englishtown; nine miles total from Monmouth Courthouse (or Freehold), now in reasonable supporting distance of the vanguard. By day's end, the lead elements of both armies were separated by no more than a few miles.

On the afternoon of the 27th General Washington rode into English-town to confer with General Lee. There they met in a local tavern and discussed the nature of the attack Washington wanted launched come first light the following morning, Sunday, June 28. Washington's blood was up, and some sort of attack seemed surely in the air.

FOURTEEN

Lee

This, I understood from General Washington, was in pursuance of his intention to have the enemy attacked, and conformable to the spirit of previous orders he had given General Lee for that purpose

The early morning hours of June 28, 1778, would inaugurate one of the most confused, bewildering, and perplexing events in American military history, that being the initial phase of the Battle of Monmouth Court House. Historians have combed over the details—numerous as they are—for generations, trying to fathom *precisely* what took place that morning, but for quite some time that precision eluded discovery. Fortunately, we have much to work with, from fact to speculation, facts that are a bit confused, and speculation that ultimately ranges from Lee as traitor outright, to having led a competent, soldierly withdrawal. What we do know for certain is that the initial attack launched by General Lee ended in a fumbled mess, a bewildering withdrawal of Continental troops, many of whom had not yet begun to fight, and most of whom considered their retreat a profound blunder. Foremost among that group was His Excellency George Washington, who stumbled upon the fleeing remnants of his vanguard as he approached the field of battle late that morning. Fortunately, over the years a baseline of facts has been cobbled together, and it is to that compilation to which we will now turn our attention.

We know, for instance, that the general orders issued by Washington on the 27th were short and ominous, clearly preparing his army for battle. "As we are now nigh the Enemy and of Consequence Vigilance and Precaution more essentially necessary, the Commander in Chief desires and enjoins it upon all Officers to keep their Posts and their soldiers compact so as to be ready to form and march at a moments warning as circumstances may require."[1] From this it is easy to determine that Washington expected a fight sometime in the very near future, but just when and under what circumstances remained uncertain.

We also know—as mentioned in the preceding chapter—that on the afternoon of the 27th Washington rode to Englishtown in order to confer with General Lee. We know that they met in a local tavern, and that in addition to Lee and Washington, Wayne, Lafayette, and Scott also attended, these being the officers of the vanguard units expected to deliver the assault the following morning. Regrettably, since no notes or record of that meeting exist, little is known of the actual discussion beyond the after battle statements of the officers involved, and these, generally speaking, were recorded at the court-martial hearing of General Lee, initiated on July 4, several days after the close of action. By then Washington had ordered Lee's arrest and, while we can assume all of the officers present were men of honor, their testimony may well have been tainted, if ever so slightly, by loyalty to their commander-in-chief. Fortunately, however, not all the statements available for scrutiny are post-battle. Some were made before the action, others before the outcome of events then unfolding were known. Those statements, therefore, made innocently and seemingly without malice, would seem to carry considerable weight when it comes to discerning the truth.

The principal question regarding the meeting between Washington and Lee has always been: what specific orders did Washington issue to General Lee for the morning's attack? Were those orders restricted or flexible (the latter termed discretionary in military terms)? The evidence clearly indicates that Washington's orders were discretionary and, frankly, it would have been foolish for him to have done otherwise. Washington had not personally inspected the ground or the British positions near the courthouse; he had no idea when the British might move or even if they intended to move at all (or perhaps even to remain and fight) come morning; and he would be nine miles away at Manalapan Bridge when dawn broke the following morning. In short, Washington understood that Lee would face a potentially fluid and unpredictable situation come morning, and that his second in command would have to respond accordingly. Of course, Lee had always presented himself as a man of prodigious military experience and expertise (indeed, Washington's superior in that regard). He had demanded as a matter of his seniority and standing the command he now held, and Washington had every right to expect Lee to discharge his orders with the know-how and due diligence his bluster and resume suggested.

It would be entirely sensible, therefore, to propose that Washington had ordered an attack, but an attack that was to proceed and develop according to the circumstances Lee discovered on the ground. And that is precisely what the pre-battle correspondence indicates. The clearest evidence of this comes from Washington himself in a dispatch to Congress written on the morning of June 28 at approximately 11:30 a.m. while moving with the main body through Englishtown, still some six miles from the front. "We have a select and strong detachment more Forward under general Command of Major Genl. Lee," he wrote, "with orders to attack their rear, if possible. Whether the detachment will be able to come up with it, is a matter of question, especially before they get into strong ground."[2] This dispatch, more than any other testimony or arguments, appears to clarify the situation. Washington expected Lee to attack the British rearguard in the morning, his only worry being that the British might move off to the heights east of Freehold (Monmouth Courthouse) near Middletown before Lee could get at them. There seems to be no question, according to Washington's own words, that his orders to Lee were discretionary ("if possible"), while at the same time he obviously expected Lee to attack the British rearguard, unless confronted by some major and unforeseen impediment.

The problem with discretionary orders has always been that they can be confused or misinterpreted. Perhaps the second most glaring instance of this in American military history was Robert E. Lee's now famous order delivered to Confederate General Richard Ewell, late on the first day at Gettysburg. Lee wanted Ewell, then in command of a full Confederate corps, to push the retreating Yankees off of Culp's and Cemetery Hills just outside of Gettysburg, two heights that dominated the landscape and would obviously prove severe impediments if left in the hands of the enemy. Lee subsequently ordered Ewell to take those heights, "if practicable," a term Ewell could not immediately comprehend, and history turned that day on the meaning of those two words. Ewell could not make sense of the order and ultimately failed to move against the hills, while the Yankees dug-in on those same heights, positions from which they would never be moved. When commander and lieutenant are of a like mind, discretionary orders can work wonders, but when they are not, the same order can lead to fiasco, and very few officers in American military history were less like-minded than George Washington and Charles Lee.

So, we know that General Washington had given Lee orders to attack in the morning, but in all probability left the details of that attack for Lee himself to work out. This would hardly have been unexpected for an officer of Lee's experience, in that an advance against the enemy's rearguard (as expressed by Washington to Congress that morning) should not have been difficult for him to arrange. Late on the afternoon of the 27th, Lee had met with his sub-commanders—Wayne, Maxwell, and Lafayette—at Washington's insistence, but Lee offered no plan of attack for the following morning at that meeting.

Why had Lee provided his subordinates with no tentative plan of attack, when attack is precisely what he had been ordered to do? This seems a fair question. At this point, then, the inquiry turns from one regarding the nature of Lee's orders—which we can stipulate as being discretionary—to one involving those normal arrangements he should have taken in preparation for a morning attack, now just hours away. Put differently, what actions did General Lee take to sensibly prepare his command for the morning attack he had been ordered to perform? The answer to that question appears rather simple—virtually nothing!

Instead of preparing for an attack, at 7 o'clock that night Lee wrote to Washington, complaining that he knew nothing of the ground ahead, the British positions or intentions; that the local inhabitants were decidedly unhelpful; and that a plan of attack would have to await a more substantive analysis.[3] In other words, he had done absolutely nothing to organize the attack he had been *ordered* to deliver, and he appeared to have no intention of doing anything significant before dawn—at the earliest. This response of Lee's had the same, tired ring of the Lee of old, the officer who could never quite comply with Washington's orders, and who always seemed to have superior ideas to those of the commander-in-chief. Recall this response for instance, from Chapter Eight: "I cannot perswade myself that Philadelphia is their object at present as it is almost certain that their Whole Troops lately embark'd have directed their course to the Eastern Provinces.... It will be difficult I am afraid to join you but cannot I do you more service by attacking their rear? I shall look about me tomorrow and inform you further." The new list of tribulations offered up by General Lee had the distinct sound of an officer trying to establish a case for doing as little as possible, when it was well known that the British might begin moving out as early as 3 o'clock the following morning. While we cannot know what General Lee had in mind late on the afternoon of the 27th, it is nevertheless apparent from his glaring lack of activity that he assumed command of the forward corps without anything resembling a firm grip or sense of urgency.

Small wonder, then, that Washington suddenly felt the need to send another dispatch to Lee, apparently fearful the British would steal the march on his subordinate and disappear over the horizon, before his second in command had even bothered to get out of bed. "Washington directed Lee to send a party of 600–800 men forward to close with the British. If Clinton did march, this force was to skirmish and slow him enough for Lee to bring up his full command. Hamilton then had a light horseman carry this dispatch to Lee in the middle of the night, arriving sometime before 2:00 A.M."[4] Both American and British forces had been commencing their marches deliberately in the very early hours to avoid the awful summer heat, and there was absolutely no reason to believe the British would fail to follow this same pattern come morning. So, if Lee were to move at all, he would have to initiate offensive operations at a very early hour.

The peculiar thing about Washington's dispatch is that Charles Lee had been practically raised in the British Army, knew virtually all its senior officers, and certainly understood its marching procedures. Washington knew all of this as well as anyone, so why suddenly the need to remind Lee that the British might depart early? Or was it that Lee's 7 o'clock dispatch had given the commander-in-chief the sudden, nagging suspicion that Lee really had no intentions of fighting at all, and needed specific instructions—delivered at 2 o'clock in the morning—in order to force him into action? We will never know for sure, but Washington's late-night dispatch surely hints of a profound uneasiness simmering at Washington's headquarters that night. When questioned about the nature of this late order during the court-martial of General Lee, Alexander Hamilton, for instance, stated under oath, "This, I understood from General Washington, was in pursuance of his intention to have the enemy attacked, and conformable to the spirit of previous orders he had given General Lee for that purpose."[5] In other words, Washington had repeatedly made it clear that he wanted the British attacked "if possible," and this late night dispatch was simply another amplification of this theme.

What is known, however, is that when Hamilton's dragoon galloped into Englishtown that night with Washington's late-night directive, he did not find Lee's headquarters a beehive of activity, as might be expected, given the situation. This might have been fine, had arrangements for an early morning assault—marching orders delivered, units shifted into place, etc.—already been accomplished, but in fact, nothing had been accomplished at all. In fact, Lee was asleep when Hamilton's dragoon appeared, and was awakened only by the commotion of his arrival. Then one of Lee's staff members signed for the dispatch, and in turn sent fresh orders out to various vanguard commanders with instructions conforming to Washington's newest set of instructions.

One of these directives was particularly botched, however, ordering Morgan to attack the enemy "tomorrow morning," when in fact tomorrow had already arrived. Thus, Morgan was given to think the attack had been scheduled for the following day, Monday, June 29.[6] Morgan's biographer, Don Higginbotham, explains: "Morgan got such a message sometime after three o'clock on the morning of the 28th. It also contained word of Lee's intention to attack after sunrise and of his desire for Morgan to assist by pushing against the British right. But Lee did not call Morgan back toward the main advance force, nor did he tell Morgan when or where he was to co-operate with Lee's troops. Morgan apparently expected further information from Lee before the battle; he failed to get it."[7] Poor staff work, then a complete lack of communications from Lee would keep the Continental Army's most elite fighting unit entirely out of Sunday's engagement.

Meanwhile, back at Monmouth Courthouse, Sir Henry Clinton had no intention of waiting around for the Continentals to strike. He had decided to march to Sandy Hook on the Atlantic coast, and to send his baggage train ahead under the protection of one division, while holding the other division momentarily behind. "The Approach of the Enemy's Army being indicated by the frequent Appearance of their Light Troops on our Rear," explains Sir Henry, "I requested His Excellency Lieutenant General Knyphausen to take the Baggage of the whole Army under the Charge of his Division.... I desired Lieutenant General Knyphausen to move at Day-break on the 28th, and that I might not press upon him in the first Part of the March in which we had but one Route, I did not follow with the other Division till near 8 o'clock."[8]

Just here it is worthwhile remembering that Baron von Steuben had been dispatched by Washington on a mission to track and report British positions and movements, and at this the Baron had been hard at work. After three days in the saddle, riding through heat, swarms of mosquitoes and thunderstorms, von Steuben had finally caught up to Clinton just outside of Monmouth Courthouse. Moving in to closely observe the British encampment—a very dangerous piece of business, in the dark, early morning hours, something that had apparently not occurred earlier to General Lee—Steuben's hard work and diligence finally paid off. "At around three o'clock on Sunday, the men of Knyphausen's division emerged from their improvised brush shelters—like Washington's men, they were travelling without tents—extinguished their fires, and formed up for the last leg of the march to Middletown. Within an hour they were on the road north, with their baggage train following immediately behind. Clinton's army was in motion; the moment Washington was waiting for had finally arrived."[9] Steuben then found General Dickinson, whose militia troops were maneuvering very near the British, and alerted him as to Knyphausen's departure.

Dickinson promptly sent dispatches to both Lee and Washington, and around 5 o'clock that morning Lee had it in hand. Written at 4:15 a.m., the message from Dickinson read: "A Major who was on Duty on the Lines last Night, this moment informs me, that the Enemy are in Motion—marching off."[10] Dickinson was then operating just north of the courthouse, so his message should have reached Lee no later than 5 o'clock. By then Lee had complied with the first aspect of Washington's new orders, which was to order a party of 600–800 men against the British rearguards as early as possible. Lee had selected Grayson's detachment for this chore, ordering Grayson to march to within three miles of the British, then wait and report further as to the enemy's activities.[11] Just what Grayson was supposed to observe or accomplish at night from a distance of three miles remains a mystery, but those were his orders.

At any event, Grayson did not march from Englishtown until 6 o'clock that morning, a sluggish response given that Washington's orders had been received via dragoon some four hours earlier. Local guides, knowledge of the ground, intelligence of the enemy, the preparation and positioning of fighting units, all of this and more had been ignored by General Lee even though he had been expressly ordered to attack in the morning. Only once rousted from bed by Hamilton's horseman would the general and his staff begin to initiate Washington's new directives, and by then, at least for some important aspects of the operation, it was already too late. As we shall see, Lee's indifference to Washington's clearly stated desires, and his lethargic adherence to standard military protocols on Saturday, June 27, would cause the early stages of the Battle of Monmouth Courthouse to begin, not with a bang, but a sputter.

That said, could Washington really have expected anything more of Lee, given the circumstances? He had agreed to virtually shoehorn Lee into this divisional command at the very last moment, and he should have been aware of the obvious limitations that movement entailed. In that respect, then, the true blame for the bumbling early hours at Monmouth belongs to both Lee *and* Washington, for both had a hand in creating a command situation that was so lacking in basic military understanding and protocols that it bordered on dysfunction from the moment it was conceived. To begin with, it was Washington, not Lee, who had sent out five separate forces marching toward the British under no comprehensive command structure, only to realize—well after the fact—just what he had done. Not only that, but these units were filled with "select men," that is, the best hand-picked troops in the army. While the idea was to increase the fighting capacity of these forward units, the move also served to break down unit cohesion by placing men in regiments with which they were entirely unfamiliar. Then Lee, of course, added his vain flourish by demanding a position he had already declined, this while the advanced units were already in the field, perhaps only hours away from combat. But Washington *agreed* to this, authorizing the strange command instructions referenced in the preceding chapter, knowing all the while that Lee had argued repeatedly *against* the very action he was now being ordered to perform, not to mention his long, established record of disobeying orders.

Thus, in the early morning hours of Sunday, June 28, General Lee had been ordered to deliver some sort of discretionary attack, although he did not know the ground upon which he was to maneuver and fight (and the terrain around Monmouth Courthouse would prove some of the most peculiar and difficult for staging combat operations during the course of the entire war), did not have a firm grip of the positioning of his own troops, the road network, the British positions or their strengths. Moreover, he had a hopelessly inadequate staff with which to coordinate the movements of his dispersed units, had no experience working with most of his Continental subordinates, had no scouts or guides to assist him, and had made no efforts to remedy any of these problems or shortcomings during the course of the 27th. The fact is, General Lee had demanded that he be inserted into an almost impossible command situation, but Washington had granted his wish and shares, at least to some degree, responsibility for the ensuing folly the morning hours at Monmouth produced. Taking all of this into consideration, it appears that the initial phase of the Battle of Monmouth Courthouse was simply an accident waiting to happen. Indeed, given the utter lack of preparation with which Lee approached the morning's offensive operations, it is a wonder the Continental Army did not stumble into disaster.

FIFTEEN

Lee

I know My Business

Whatever evidence of apathy Charles Lee had displayed on the 27th of June, as daylight greeted the 28th he appeared a changed man, if not reanimated, at least awake and preparing his detachment to march. At around 4 o'clock that morning, for instance, Lafayette discovered the general weary, but up and busy, and was told that the forward units had already been put into motion. The Marquis, thinking himself an unassigned volunteer at the time, asked how he might contribute, and was told to attach himself to the select men, a position Lafayette thankfully assumed.[1] It can be recalled that, in an attempt to comply with Washington's early morning order, Lee and his staff had instructed Colonel Grayson to move forward with a company of about 700 men to within three miles of the enemy, and once there carefully take post and observe the enemy's progress. Grayson, however, due to a lack of guides and knowledge of the ground ahead, did not depart until almost 6 o'clock in the morning, a significant delay, and a direct result of Lee's general lack of preparation.

Knyphausen's Division of the British Army—which included the long baggage train—had risen early and moved off toward Sandy Hook around 4 o'clock in the morning, but Clinton had remained behind with the other division, intending to follow Knyphausen out around 8:00 a.m. This was precisely the tactical situation Washington had been waiting for, hoping to strike the enemy's rearguard while they remained behind, separated from the van as it marched off toward Sandy Hook. As a result, as Knyphausen continued his march, his ability to support Clinton was decreasing steadily with every step, thus increasing the Continentals' odds of success as they approached Monmouth Courthouse.

Some minor skirmishing broke out north and west of the courthouse in the early hours as Steuben continued his reconnaissance efforts, trying to get a clear look at the British defenses. "As he continued to reconnoiter the British positions, he and John Laurens rode so close to the British lines that Steuben was immediately spotted, recognized ... and pursued. The British generals were aware of his presence, and Knyphausen had issued orders that every effort should be made to capture the distinguished Baron unharmed. Two dragoons broke from the British lines and charged straight for him. He paused only long enough to draw both of his enormous horse pistols from the holsters lashed to his saddle and fire each of them at his pursuers; then he turned his horse about and galloped to safety, so fast that his cocked hat flew off his head during his retreat."[2]

Meanwhile, back at Englishtown, the vanguard troops were struggling to march from the small hamlet due to the previous night's lack of proper positioning by either Lee or his aides. They finally managed to get things straightened out by around 7 o'clock, at which time they headed down the road toward Grayson, Wayne and Scott leading the column, followed in turn by Maxwell and Jackson. The morning was clear, the day already hot and sultry. Private Martin recalls the early hours:

> We were early in the morning mustered out and ordered to leave all our baggage under the care of a guard (our baggage was trifling), taking only our blankets and provisions (our provisions were less), and prepare for immediate march and action.
>
> After all things were put in order, we marched, but halted a few minutes in the village, where we were joined by a few other troops, and then proceeded on. We now heard a few reports of cannon ahead. We went in a road running through a deep narrow valley, which was for a considerable way covered with thick wood; we were some time in passing this defile. While in the wood we heard a volley or two of musketry, and upon inquiry we found it to be a party of our troops who had fired upon a party of British horse, but there was no fear of horse in the place in which we then were.[3]

As Martin was proceeding on his march, General Lee rode forward to confer with General Dickinson, who now bore ominous intelligence. Dickinson, contradicting all the earlier reports, insisted that the British were still at Monmouth Courthouse in full force, in fact arrayed for battle. This brought Lee and his entire column to an abrupt halt, as well it should have. Here Lee thought he was marching out to strike the enemy's rearguard, only to be told that the enemy was prepared to meet him in force, and might even strike first, driving in Grayson's small group now posted just ahead. As the American column waited in the warming sun, the situation ahead was argued over by the officers in attendance. Finally, Benjamin Walker, a member of Steuben's staff, joined the discussion around 8:30 a.m. Walker insisted that the original reports were correct; that Knyphausen's Division had marched earlier that morning, as reported, and that only remnants of Clinton's other division remained behind.[4] Lee finally accepted Walker's report but, sensing now that the situation ahead might be far more dangerous than previously anticipated, called back for General Wayne to come forward and take the lead, replacing Grayson. Lee knew Wayne to be a capable, veteran commander. It was a sound move, but more valuable time would be wasted making the change.

The switch in commanders accomplished, Lee and Wayne then rode ahead in order to survey the situation nearer the courthouse. As they closed on the small village, Wayne rode even further ahead, sat his horse, and pulled out a small field glass for a closer look at the British, now clearly arrayed in the fields just ahead. This is what he saw: "I had a fair prospect from my glass of the enemy. Their horse seemed so much advanced from the foot, that I could hardly perceive the movement of the foot, which induced me to send for Colonel Butler's detachment, and Colonel Jackson's detachment, in order to drive their horse back." Butler's detachment then came up and went after the British cavalry, driving them into the village, after which the British moved off and began to form again at a distance. General Wayne was watching all the while through his glass, and at the time estimated the British strength as follows: "Their number then about five or six hundred foot, and about three hundred horse."[5]

This was a small detachment which appeared to Wayne as nothing more than a modest rearguard left behind to screen Clinton's withdrawal. In that the American vanguard now consisted of some 5,000 troops and component artillery (once fully deployed), the party that Wayne observed should have been easy work for the Continentals to brush aside or drive back down the road toward Middletown. Lee then returned to Wayne's side, and the two had another good, long look at the British, now forming again in the distance. Lee agreed with Wayne's assessment of the enemy's strength, and it was at this point—perhaps around 10:00 a.m.—that Lee struck upon a clever scheme.

Rather than simply drive the British away from Freehold, he decided instead to have Wayne's troops demonstrate across the enemy's front, while simultaneously sending a substantial column of select troops around to the left (the British right) in order to march behind them unseen, then sweep them up between the two American commands like a school of fish snared in an angler's net. No question it was an elaborate plan for dealing with such a small contingent of the enemy's force, but if successful it would surely bag the British rearguard, and probably without much of a fight, once the Redcoats realized just how badly they'd been trapped. Moreover, it was the sort of clever gambit that might be recounted by knowing observers approvingly for years to come, hence a rather gaudy feather in the general's cap. Lt. Col. Brooks, of Lee's staff, later confirmed the nature of Lee's plan during testimony at the court-martial, but also added this ominous detail. "It was impossible, on the ground that you [Lee] were on when you reconnoitered the enemy, to see the rear of the enemy left or the road that led to their rear, so that a precise plan could not be formed."[6]

In other words, an accurate plan would require knowledge of the enemy's position and possible strength beyond what both Wayne and Lee had so far observed. So, Lee sent Captain Edwards off on a scouting mission along with two light horsemen to scout along the enemy's right and see if he could confirm their strength. Edwards took a road that ran behind cover and soon discovered the British right flank. There he stopped, and estimated their strength at "five or six hundred filing off from the court house, perceptibly retreating."[7] But had anyone bothered to reconnoiter the British left, as Brooks noted later at trial, or the road leading back toward Middletown, those areas Lee could not see clearly from his initial vantage point? The answer is no. Thus, when Edwards returned from the British right, his estimate was essentially the same as had earlier been

GENERAL WAYNE.[1]

General "Mad Anthony" Wayne, as drawn by illustrator Benson J. Lossing and published in his *Pictorial Field-Book of the Revolution*.

adjudged by both Wayne and Lee, this serving to embolden the American commander. Lee promptly ordered Edwards to lead Col. Durgee's Brigade along with two guns to the British right, this as Lee moved to take command of the remaining column and move behind Edwards and Durgee up the same narrow road with the intention of completing his envelopment.

It should be recalled that General Wayne, upon reconnoitering the British, called for Butler's and Jackson's detachments to move up and push the British horse from their current position. This was initially accomplished by Butler's Brigade, the British riders moving off without much in the way of a fight. Later, however, the British dragoons returned as Butler was marching toward the British right flank under orders from Wayne. The British horsemen, chasing a scattered element of American militia cavalry, came dashing at the Continentals at full tilt. Nimbly, both Butler and Jackson changed front and gave the charging British a full volley at short range, unhorsing many, and sending the remainder off at the gallop. This, in fact, was the sound of musketry that Private Martin had heard along his march, and it essentially inaugurated the Battle of Monmouth Courthouse.

Immediately after their clash with the British horse, Butler and Jackson resumed their movement toward the British right, Jackson trailing the lead brigade by about one hundred yards. Both units were under Wayne's command, and it is here where the confusion of the morning's action begins. We are told that Wayne was supposed to demonstrate in front of the British, thus pinning them in place, and not move off on his own. Either Wayne misunderstood his orders, or the orders given him were not clear, because at this point in the action, his troops were already moving off.

Interestingly, as both Butler and Jackson marched on, their movement toward the British right either changed their angle of observation or brought into view something previously unseen. For Jackson now saw a far more threatening force than had previously been spotted by Wayne and Lee. "At this time," said Jackson, "I could see a very heavy body of the enemy as far as I could see from their left to their right." Asked later to estimate the number of British soldiers he saw at this time "from their left to their right," Jackson responded. "I should have supposed the apparent number to be at least three thousand men, but I saw no end to them, I had reason to suppose there were more."[8] Both American brigades then came under an intense cannonade from the British, so intense, in fact, that they had to seek cover in the woods to their left.

What was happening? Lee was now racing off, fully confident of bagging a rearguard he had guessed at no more than 1,500 to 2,000 men, but Jackson—only moments later, in fact—had spotted an enemy force substantially larger, worse still, perhaps growing. Was the British force the Americans were observing departing or arriving? Was it a rearguard, as assumed, or a vanguard on the move toward them, entirely unanticipated? These were very serious questions, but General Lee had already put his offensive into motion and would not be in position to second guess his decision until it was too late.

Now, there was nothing technically wrong with Lee's plan, and nothing wrong with the steps he had taken thus far to bring it to fruition—that is, if the enemy's force was a mere rearguard as he had estimated, of no more than 2,000 men. Not only was he following Washington's orders, but he was going to comply with a display of martial flair—an envelopment.

As a result, at that moment Lee seemed a man supremely confident, not only of his strategy, but of his assessment of the entire situation. Edwards had already scouted the area (to the American left) at his behest and returned, confirming the fact that that the roads would indeed lead to the enemy's right and support the transport of artillery, to boot, all this further bolstering Lee's self-assurance. If all went as planned, the operation would be like taking candy from a baby. So confident was General Lee, in fact, that he boasted openly to Lafayette, "My dear Marquis, I think those people are ours,"[9] confidently assuring success, almost before a single boot had struck the ground. And when General Forman approached him with an offer to lead a detachment to the left in order to strike the enemy's right flank, Lee declined the superfluous suggestion, informing Forman, "I know my business."[10]

But did he? Did General Lee really know his business? That seems a fair question. Soldiering is a brutally unpredictable occupation, after all, as combat often embarrasses even the best laid plans, while turning ill-conceived operations into ruin, quite often in the blink of an eye. That is why it is imperative to follow certain long-standing norms and protocols, no matter how fruitless those protocols may momentarily appear. As suggested, there was nothing wrong with what General Lee had so far conceived or accomplished, but it would be the small, simple things he failed to conceive and accomplish that morning that would ultimately prove his undoing, and we will begin by examining the most glaring examples.

To begin with, General Lee appears to have conflated his initial assessment of the battlefield with reality, a danger in any line of work, but often fatal in warfare. He had made a snap decision, and one that would not suffer alteration until too late. What he viewed that morning with General Wayne was a momentary snapshot only, the smallest sliver of enemy potential. He was sure he had spotted a modest rearguard. But had he? Was it possible, for instance, that a substantial enemy force remained hidden from view, perhaps behind those trees over there, or behind that hill just yonder, or around the next bend on the road to Middletown? No doubt General Lee understood what he saw directly in front of him, but he appeared uninterested in other potential scenarios. Recall that only moments after Lee's initial assessment, Jackson had spotted a British detachment, from left to right, as far as they eye could see, quite possibly growing in strength far beyond Lee's initial evaluation.

In warfare a constant flow and reappraisal of intelligence is critical to any operation. For General Lee that morning, however, his grasp of reality seemed already to have been set in stone, a critical error from which many other errors would soon flow. Lee was confident his trap would work because he *knew* that most of the British strength had already vacated Monmouth Courthouse and was now long on the march. As a result, the area directly behind the observed rearguard had to be free and open to American maneuver. Indeed, that was precisely what he had told Lt. Col. Brooks. But was it?

Recall that the general's goal was to march a substantial force beyond the enemy's right flank, then have them swing behind the British rearguard, capturing them all between his two deployed detachments, front and rear; an envelopment. It was an intelligent, aggressive plan but, like all military strategies, a plan that naturally entailed certain risks. The American column would be marching into uncharted territory, for instance, paralleling somewhat the direction in which the British were then known to be withdrawing in force, potentially exposing first their right flank, then later their rear and left flank, to attack if the British happened to be watching and waiting. Were they watching? Were they waiting? General Lee assumed they were not, because he emphatically believed most of the British force had already marched off some distance toward Sandy Hook.

But that was a *dangerous* assumption, hardly a given. To turn that assumption into fact, a reconnaissance was required, a job given, perhaps, to a few mounted officers who knew their business. Riding cross country, they might parallel the Middletown Road for a few miles, locating the departing Redcoats in the process (this as the American assault force was being brought into line), along with confirming that no force was near at hand on the British left. Sensible operations always require hard facts: How far down the road to Middletown had the British moved? Were they out of supporting distance? Was there danger on the British left? These questions could, and should, have been answered before the flanking column ever stepped off.

Unfortunately, General Lee never thought to ask these questions because, events clearly suggest, he believed he already knew the answers: the British were long gone and there was nothing to fear. In fact, Lee gave Lafayette exactly that impression prior to the march, that time was wasting and there were no problems to fear beyond the few British already observed. "My idea of the matter," Lafayette later explained at trial, while speaking directly to Lee, "was that you wanted to cut off a small part of the enemy's rear, and that nothing was to be feared but to lose time or ground."[11] In other words, Lee's only concern at the moment was that he might not move quickly enough to ensnare the departing British.

Lee's second failure (or command oversight), equally as important as his first, was that as the American units deployed, it was vital for the general to immediately locate—or task a qualified engineer or officer to locate—a suitable fallback position, should the vanguard somehow stumble into misfortune. It did not matter how utterly convinced of success he was at that moment. Selecting a fallback position was standard practice, utterly essential, and consisted of nothing more than locating good defensive ground where the vanguard's retreating elements might form and rally around a chosen unit or two, deployed at the select location to serve that purpose alone. Did General Lee see to this task? No, he did not, and it would cost him dearly. Lee's other command failures—and they are numerous—will become obvious as our narrative continues.

Meanwhile, across the field, on the American left General Lee was hurrying the turning force off on their mission, Varnum's Brigade in the lead, Lafayette following, now in command of Wayne's old detachment.[12]

But dark clouds were already forming on the horizon. As Lee moved off, Wayne sent word to him that "the enemy seemed to be forming on the hill by the fork in the roads," and that Wayne was expecting an attack, but Lee discounted this intelligence.[13]

General Lee continued his march, Private Martin in tow, and we will allow Martin to describe the movement from the foot soldier's perspective. "It was ten or eleven o'clock before we got through these woods and came into the open fields. The first cleared land we came to was an Indian cornfield surrounded on the east, west and north sides by thick tall trees. The sun shining full upon the field, the soil of which was sandy, the mouth of a heated oven seemed to me to be but a trifle hotter than this ploughed field; it was almost impossible to breathe."[14]

Lee, leading the turning column, also now emerged from the trees, and moving out into the blistering heat of the sun-drenched fields had the opportunity to take a fresh glance at the enemy. Unfortunately, this new view proved decidedly unsettling. The British were now arrayed in strength—far greater than he had originally estimated—and a strong column had emerged from their left and was making its way toward the courthouse. If it gained the village, it might cut the American vanguard off from the roads leading back to Englishtown, severing Lee from Washington's main body—a disaster. Moreover, one brutal fact must have shaken even the supremely confident Lee as he beheld the field at that moment, which was this: rearguards do not emerge in strong marching columns of assault. Only attacking forces

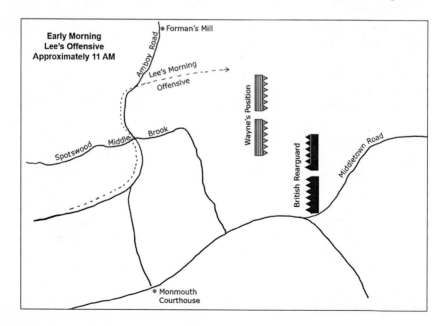

do. Lee was no longer the hunter. He had now become the hunted, all this in the blink of an eye.

What had happened? Paul Lockhart explains: "Lee saw what he thought might be a golden opportunity to cut off and envelop the rearmost elements of Cornwallis's division, which he estimated at no more than 1,500 to 2,000 men. This prospect, however, quickly vanished, for soon a growing body of British infantry began to move south toward him on the Middletown Road. Clinton was not retreating; quite the opposite: he was turning to fight with the bulk of his forces."[15]

To General Lee's credit, he did not panic, but responded quickly and calmly. He attempted to patch a battle line together to halt what he feared would be a British onslaught, sending Lafayette with his force rushing toward the courthouse in the hopes of cutting off the column of Redcoats he had just spotted marching in that direction. Said Lafayette: "An Aide-de-Campe from General Lee told me that the enemy were gaining our right, and that I should prevent them by gaining their left."[16] But Lafayette had scarcely moved before his troops came under heavy cannonade, and the situation on the field began to devolve into chaos.

Lee was desperately trying to arrange a defense, but he had entered the day with a staff utterly inadequate to the task, another small but critical oversight. He had insisted upon being given command of a vanguard numbering nearly 5,000, but with a staff of but a few officers he really had no capacity to enforce battlefield control under normal circumstances, much less under the sudden duress in which he now found himself. This insufficiency he could have taken steps to resolve before marching, but had neglected to do so, and now, along with his men, he would suffer the consequences. Confusion and chaos naturally ensued, as many of the American unit commanders had no idea what to do and received no new orders from Lee. As more British columns appeared (three in total), then advanced toward the Americans, many brigade commanders rightly feared being entirely cut off or encircled, and had no option left but to withdraw, orders or not. Lafayette: "I was surprised, then looking back, to see some of our troops forming towards the village of Freehold, as they were behind me."[17]

Some units scattered and retreated in disorder, pressed by the British advance, while most simply turned and withdrew in disciplined fashion. Unfortunately, no one had any idea where they were to go or reform as, once again, General Lee had failed to find and prepare a fallback position upon taking the field. Hence, even more chaos now ensued. Late in the game— indeed, *very* late in the game—Lee tried desperately to locate good ground upon which to reform, but the ground near and about Freehold was cut by vast ravines called morasses, with woods, fields, hills, and streams adding bewildering dimensions to the lay of the land. Martin: "By the time we had got under the shade of the trees and had taken breath, of which we had been almost deprived, we received orders to retreat, as all the left wing of the army, that part being under the command of General [Charles] Lee, were retreating. Grating as this order was to our feelings, we were obliged to comply."[18]

Adding yet another critical note to the sorry tune now being played out, the area to which the Americans had to withdraw was dominated by only a single bridge across a creek called Spotswood Middle Brook. Thus, all the forward units now in the field would have to cross this one bridge, surely inaugurating a bottleneck bound to leave the fleeing Americans virtually mobbing in the open while trying to cross, hence entirely vulnerable to cannonade, cavalry, and infantry pursuit. The ground beyond the bridge was high and defensible, but Lee had failed to secure either it or the approaches to the bridge, despite having been warned about the problems inherent in the terrain earlier that morning by General Davidson. Had he simply posted a small reserve on the high ground, and a brigade forward to defend the approaches to the bridge, he would have provided for a seamless withdrawal but, of course, he had not.

Colonel Dearborn recalled the morning approach and vanguard collapse in his journal.

> We ware Ordered, together with the Troops Commanded by the Marquis & Genrl Lee (in the whole About 5000) to march towards the Enimy & as we thought to Attact them, at Eleven o Clock A.M. after marching about 6 or 7 miles we ariv'd on the Plains Near Monmouth Court House, Where a Collumn of the Enimy appeared in sight, a brisk Cannonade Commensid on both sides, the Collumn which was advancing towards us Halted & soon Retired, but from some movement of theirs we ware Convince'd they Intended to fight us, shifted our ground, form'd on very good ground & waited to see if they Intended to Come on. We soon Discovered a Large Collumn Turning our Right. & another Coeming up in our Front With Cavelry in front of both Collumns. Genrl Lee was on the Right of our Line who Left the ground & made Tracks Quick Step towards English Town. Genrl Scots Detachment Remained on the ground we form'd on until we found we war very near surrounded—& ware Obliged to Retire which we Did in good order although we ware hard Prest on our Left flank. The Enimy haveing got a mile in Rear of us before we began to Retire & ware bearing Down on our Left as we went off & we Confin'd by a Morass on our Right.[19]

While General Lee had incorrectly deduced the situation at first glance, his opponent, Sir Henry Clinton, working from a different playbook, had responded with strength and clarity of mind. As he moved off with his division, he tells us that

> Intelligence was at this Instant brought me that the Enemy were discovered marching in Force on both Flanks. I was convinced that our Baggage was their Object; but it being at this Juncture engaged in Defiles which continued for some Miles, no Means occurred of Parrying the Blow but attacking the Corps which harassed our Rear, and pressing it so hard as to oblige the Detachments to return from our Flanks to its

assistance. I had good information that General Washington was up with his whole army, estimated at about 20,000; but as I knew there were two Defiles between him and the Corps at which I meant to strike [Lee's vanguard], I judged that he could not have passed them with a greater Force than what Lord Cornwallis's Division was well able to engage; and had I even met his whole Army in the Passage of those Defiles, I had little to apprehend, but his situation would have been critical. The Enemy Cavalry, commanded it is said by Mr. la Fayette, having approached within our Reach they were charged with great Spirit by the Queens Light Dragoons. They did not wait the Shock but fell back in Confusion upon their own Infantry."[20]

Clinton intended to hit Lee with Cornwallis's entire division, and he had caught General Lee in mid-career, utterly unmindful of any British offensive intentions. It has been pointed out by Lender & Stone in their excellent account of the battle that one of the first tasks Sir Henry had seen to as he entered the fray was to establish a sound fallback position, the precise cautionary protocol Charles Lee had completely neglected. "Behind the columns, Clinton posted the brigade of Hessian Grenadiers in reserve.... Following standard procedure, Clinton had ordered them to remain in place in case the attack went badly and the forward troops had to retreat."[21]

On the field the disparate American units were now withdrawing before the sudden British advance in confusion, some in disorder, others in good order. Once again, Steuben's relentless drill at Valley Forge was paying dividends. Lee's orders, such that they were, were surely confused, but far more alarming was the fact that no one knew where to go. Lt. Col. Fitzgerald, for instance, riding into the withdrawal at the direction of General Washington, later stated: "They mostly retreated rather in disorder, which appeared to me to have proceeded as much from being ignorant of the place they were to go, as from the retreat itself."[22] Lt. Col. Harrison, also riding on Washington's behalf discovered the same state of confusion amongst the officers. Coming across Lt. Col. Rhea, for instance, Harrison later stated, "he appeared to be very much agitated, expressed his disapprobation of the retreat, and seemed to be equally concerned (or perhaps more) that he had no place assigned to go where the troops were to halt." Departing Rhea, Harrison then came upon General Maxwell, who was in the same confused funk. "He appeared to be as much at a loss as Lieutenant-Colonel Rhea, or any other officer I had met with," Harrison stated, "and intimated that he had received no orders upon the occasion, and was totally in the dark what line of conduct to pursue."[23]

General Lee had been caught by complete surprise, and no better example of the extent of his bewilderment can be found than what Lee's own staff officer, John Mercer, told Fitzgerald on the field as the collapse continued. Recounted later by Fitzgerald, Mercer exclaimed essentially that "We were all very much deceived, and that instead of finding a covering party as was expected, the enemy's whole force was drawn up to receive them."[24] Mercer's astonishment can be forgiven, however, because it was a direct byproduct of nothing more than his General Lee's sudden, unbounded confidence in his own assessment of the situation, that the British before him were nothing more than a small rearguard, soon to depart; hence no reconnaissance in order ("My dear Marquis, I think those people are ours"), hence Wayne's ominous intelligence that he was facing a large force of an aggressive nature, something only to be dismissed as uninformed. Contrary to Mercer's claim, however, General Lee and his staff had not been "deceived" by the enemy at all; they had deceived themselves.

Self-deception can be a powerful thing, but when it finally collapses under the weight of stubborn reality, the new truth it unleashes can have a sudden and disorienting effect on the self-deluded mind. As the Americans stumbled back toward the rear, essentially bereft of sensible orders or of a strong position to rally upon (or any position at all, for that matter), General Lee's rock-solid understanding of the situation evaporated before his eyes like an early morning mist. The usually cocksure Lee was suddenly stunned, confused, and almost speechless. Lt. Col. Meade, for instance, sent forward by General Washington to determine the situation on the field, located a disoriented and uncommunicative Lee. Asked to clarify the situation, Meade later explained, "His [Lee's] reply was, they were all in confusion. I told him that General Washington would be glad to know the particulars; asked again General Lee replied again, that he had nothing to say, but they were all in confusion."[25] Likewise, when asked to describe General Lee at the apex of the collapse, Lt. Col. Lawrence said, "I thought General Lee seemed to be a good deal embarrassed, and that his orders were indistinct." When pressed for the reasons for his conclusion, Lawrence stated simply, "I imputed it to a want of presence of mind."[26]

Fortunately, a clearer mind and firmer hand were now nearing the scene. General Washington, riding at the head of the main body, was then approaching Monmouth Courthouse, expecting good news because that was all that had been communicated to him during the morning hours by General Lee and his subordinates. Suddenly, however, incongruent signs of disaster began to stab his sense of assurance: first a young, panicked fifer whose story of collapse the commander-in-chief could scarcely credit, then more fugitives in flight. Then, as Washington rode farther forward, he came upon whole units stumbling to the rear, exhausted, disheartened, but somehow unfought and obviously undefeated. *What* was going on? Washington could hardly believe his eyes, and ordered officers to ride ahead—Fitzgerald, Harrison, and Meade—to discern the situation. As he approached the debacle then unfolding on the fields around Freehold, General Washington's temper began to flare, and why not? His vanguard was in ragged retreat while hardly a shot had been fired. What was Lee up to? He rode on, across a small bridge then up a short hill, discovering the extent of the unfolding fiasco as he continued, until just ahead he spotted its architect, his horse cantering gamely toward him. Anger boiled in Washington's chest as Lee approached, and he set his jaw firmly, now about to engage in surely one of the most heated, bitter, controversial, yet historic confrontations in American military history.

SIXTEEN

Washington

A Damned Poltroon

George Washington was furious, and there was no concealing it. Somewhat fortuitously—for our narrative, at least—Private Martin, who had fallen back with the American left wing, was seated nearby just as Washington made his appearance, and the hard-marching Martin provides a first-hand description of the event. "We had not retreated far before we came to a defile, a muddy, sloughy brook. While the artillery were passing this place, we sat down by the roadside. In a few minutes the Commander in Chief and suite [staff] crossed the road just where we were sitting. I heard him ask our officers 'by whose order the troops were retreating,' and being answered, 'by General Lee's,' he said something, but as he was moving forward all the time this was passing, he was too far off for me to hear it distinctly. Those that were nearer to him said that his words were 'd----n him.' Whether he did thus express himself or not I do not know. It was certainly very unlike him, but he seemed at the instant to be in a great passion; his looks if not his words seemed to indicate as much."[1] Lee then approached Washington expecting, it has been suggested, to be congratulated for having saved the vanguard from a British pummeling, but General Washington was apparently in no mood for offering compliments. Moreover, while it's true the advance had not so far been destroyed by the British, the individual unit commanders had made most of the decisions to withdraw based on the changing facts on the field (the approaching British columns that were making their individual positions untenable), not as a consequence of any directive from General Lee. Later suggestions that Lee deserved some praise for having overseen a skillful withdrawal seem, given the facts, overstated.

What transpired between Lee and Washington has been grist for historians for almost 250 years—in that few observers were near enough to overhear—and while their precise exchange remains open to debate, the general flow and nature of the confrontation are reasonably well understood. Washington was furious, and his fury alone appears to have stunned Lee, who was expecting only accolades for his conduct. Washington demanded an explanation, Lee stammered, and Washington repeated his demand. Lee, simultaneously embarrassed and flummoxed, complained that his orders had been disobeyed, that his intelligence had been faulty, and that he did not wish to fight the British, numerous and professional as they were known to be. Some say Washington cursed Lee, others that he was obviously infuriated, but civil, yet there seems little doubt that Lee was stunned virtually speechless that hot afternoon as Washington repeatedly demanded an explanation for the flight of the vanguard before the British.

There are many accounts of the exchange that differ slightly, but I believe the one that may come closest to the truth is offered by historian Henry B. Dawson in his book *Battles of the Unites States; by Sea and Land*, published in 1858. Dawson was reportedly a meticulous historian, took his business quite seriously, and in his description of the Battle of Monmouth he repeats an account of Washington's meeting with Lee supposedly passed on by Lafayette on Sunday, August 15, 1824, to Daniel D. Tompkins, then vice-president of the United States. This description is probably not precisely accurate, but I suspect it captures the essence of their exchange:

> At this instant the guilty author of the mischief, General Lee, rode up, and the commander-in-chief demanded, in the sternest manner, "What is the meaning of this, sir?"
>
> Disconcerted and crushed under the tone and terrible appearance of his chief, General Lee could do nothing more than stammer, "Sir, sir?" When, with more vehemence, and with a still more indignant expression, the question was repeated.
>
> A hurried explanation was attempted—his troops had been misled by contradictory intelligence, his officers had disobeyed his orders, and he had not felt it his duty to oppose the whole force of the enemy with the detachment under his command. Farther remarks were made on both sides, and, closing the interview with calling General Lee "a damned poltroon," [coward] the commander-in-chief hastened back to the high ground between the meetinghouse and the bridge, where he formed the regiments of colonels Shreve, Patton, Grayson, Livingston, Cilley, and Ogden, and the left wing under Lord Stirling.[2]

Those who discount Washington's use of profanity at this moment generally do so on the basis of the commander-in-chief's long-standing sense of decorum, dignity, and self-control. But Washington was known to have a terrible temper that was rarely displayed, but volcanic once unleashed, and everyone who saw him that day testified to his obvious state of extreme agitation. One other minor exchange that seems to have the ring of truth about it was later reported by Lt. Thomas Marshall of Grayson's Regiment who insisted he heard Lee state, "Sir, these troops are not able to meet British Grenadiers." To this Washington reportedly replied rather hotly, "Sir, they are able, and by God, they shall do it!"[3] If true, this would surely have been in keeping with General Lee's unrivaled admiration of British arms, a view he had espoused since the war's inception. It is also in keeping with another statement James McHenry, one of Washington's aides, overheard Lee make later that day, a comment which will be duly reported as our narrative continues.

Regardless of whatever words passed between the two generals that morning, however, the situation on the field was growing ever more dangerous for the Americans with every passing second. The British, in three columns, were now pressing close, and unless immediate steps were taken to slow their advance, much of the American vanguard appeared doomed. Bernardus Swartout, retreating with Scott's detachment at the time, later recalled the critical moment. "We retired in great haste but in good order—the enemy pressed hard on our rear. After retreating two miles was met by Gen. Washington who was amazed to find us retreating—he ordered us to halt, form on a hill immediately in our front and face the enemy, accordingly did so, with alacrity, on a good piece of ground—the enemy had been advancing on us very fast, cutting our rear to pieces."[4]

Leaving the dumbstruck Lee behind, Washington then rode forward, only to discover firsthand the dire state of his retreating vanguard, and the menace that was fast approaching. Lt. Col. Tilghman recalls the scene: "The General seemed entirely at a loss, as he was on a piece of ground entirely strange to him; I told him what Lieutenant-Colonel Rhea had told me of

"George Washington at Monmouth, June 28, 1778." The romanticized engraving done by G. R. Hall in 1858 shows General Washington approaching the battlefield as the Continentals retreat and General Charles Lee approaches the commander-in-chief on horseback. National Archives.

his knowing the ground; he desired me to go bring him as quick as possible to him; to desire Colonel Shreve to form his regiment on a hill, which was afterwards our main position, and I think, to get the two small regiments of Grayson's and Patton's there also, that the line might be formed as quick as possible."[5]

Naturally, Washington had no way of knowing just how dire the situation really was until he observed the approaching enemy for himself. This comprehension in turn initiated a sudden burst of activity, leadership, and courage in the face of the enemy that would go down in history. Private Martin watched closely as Washington surveyed the field. "After passing us, he rode on to the plain field and took an observation of the advancing enemy. He remained there some time upon his old English charger, while the shot from the British artillery were rending up the earth all around him."[6] John Laurens also describes the moment: "All this disgraceful retreating, passed without the firing of a musket, over ground which might have been disputed inch by inch. We passed a defile and arrived at an eminence beyond, which was defended on one side by an impenetrable fen [marsh], on the other by thick woods where our men would have fought to advantage. Here, fortunately for the honour of the army, and the welfare of America, Genl Washington met the troops retreating in disorder."[7]

Alexander Hamilton, a nearby observer, later wrote, "I never saw the general to so much advantage. His coolness and firmness were admirable. He instantly took measures for checking the enemy's advance, and giving time for the army, which was very near, to form and make proper disposition."[8] Washington's aide, James McHenry, was also more than a little impressed. "The enemy, who were advancing rapidly, elated by our retreat, were to be checked—the most advantageous ground to be seized—The main body of the army to be formed—The enemy's intentions and dispositions to be discovered—and a new plan of attack to be concerted—and all this too in the smallest interval of time—But it is in these moments of battle, that the genius of a general is displayed, when a very inconsiderable weight determines whether it shall be a victory or a defeat."[9] It should be noted that McHenry, Laurens, and Hamilton were all members of Washington's staff and great admirers of the general; nevertheless, many more than these three men have suggested that Washington's initial appearance on the field at Monmouth may well have been his finest moment as commander-in-chief during the course of the entire war.

It was then approximately 1 o'clock in the afternoon, and General Washington had at best fifteen minutes to fully comprehend the British advance (that is, to survey all of its elements, then deduce their intentions), locate good ground for a defense of the main body, which was still coming up, and to cobble together a rearguard action in order to buy time for all the former to materialize. It was an extraordinary task, yet Washington dove into it with stunning effect. Private John Ackerman, retreating with Maxwell's detachment, recalls how Washington rallied the vanguard's fleeing remnants. "Gen Washington halted his troops, and the retreating Regement was immediately paraded having become disordered in retreating through the [morass]. He well recollects that Gen Washington on that occasion asked the troops if they could fight and that they answered him with three cheers."[10]

Washington rode up to Wayne's troops, and ordered two units of select men out to make a stand with Wayne in a line of trees a short distance from the small bridge over which the majority of the vanguard was still crossing (to be known forever more as the Point of Woods). There General Wayne, with no more than 900 men, would be asked to fight and delay an advancing force of almost 2,500 of the King's finest troops, an assignment to which "Mad Anthony"—always up for a good fight himself—responded enthusiastically. Likewise, an infantry unit under Lt. Col. Ogden formed below Wayne's position in woods near the bridge, and there prepared to meet the British onslaught.

Riding his white charger, Washington was everywhere, extolling men to fight, slapping units together; trying desperately to position enough strength to at least slow the Redcoat juggernaut, now marching downhill in sight of the Spotswood Middle Brook. Meanwhile the main body was coming up on the road from Englishtown, and they would have to be placed with precision on dominating ground, lest they too be sacrificed in the impending action. Washington spotted Lee again, now sitting his horse at a distance, fancying himself relieved of command. There was no time to waste, nor was there time to wrangle over bruised egos. The commander-in-chief needed help *now,* and he asked if Lee would either help command the rearguard, such that it was, or retire over the bridge and help post the main body? The crestfallen Lee, much to his credit, opted to fight with the rearguard, and with that Washington dashed back across the bridge to the higher ground, hoping his meager rearguard might slow the British advance.

Henry Knox, Washington's commander of artillery, had remained behind with Lee, and the two grabbed poor artillerist Eleazer Oswald, who had been fighting his guns for most of the morning, and had him unlimber his four pieces in a field opposite Wayne's position. Oswald and his men were faint from the blistering heat and exhausted from battle, but they took their new position just the same, and prepared the guns to sweep the approaches to the bridge, now at their backs. But Oswald's guns were unsupported, so Lee dragooned Colonel Livingston's equally exhausted infantry command, insisting they take a position in defense of the guns. Livingston, almost delirious from the heat himself, eventually complied, leading his men toward a long tree lined fence (forevermore known as The Hedgerow), where sweating and faint, they began to load their muskets.

On the decline leading toward the bridge, British Grenadiers, Guardsmen, and Dragoons were sweeping inexorably toward the morass over which the bridge crossed—buckles and bayonets glistening in the noonday sun, shouted orders ringing in the suffocating air as dust trailed their footsteps, an imposing, seemingly irresistible force. Then suddenly all hell broke loose. On the right flank of the Redcoat formation, Wayne's small detachment of select Continentals—hidden in the woods—unleashed a murderous volley at almost point blank range into the right flank of the marching British. The volley had a devastating effect, but the British units wheeled and attacked almost as quickly as they had come under fire. Bayonets lowered, the British charged, as Wayne's men, prepared and waiting, received them. What ensued was a short, vicious clash as men met, bayonet-to-bayonet in the swirling smoke and confusion of the trees.[11]

Mad Anthony later described the violence in a letter to his wife, telling her that Washington "Ordered me to keep post where he met us with Stewarts…. Regiments and a Virginia Regt then under my Command with two pieces of Artillery and to keep in play until he had an [chance] of forming the Remainder of the Army and Restoring Order—We had but just taken post when the Enemy began their attack with Horse, foot, & artillery, the fire of their whole united force Obliged us after a Severe Conflict to give way."[12] Wayne's troops were routed out of the woods in short order, but they

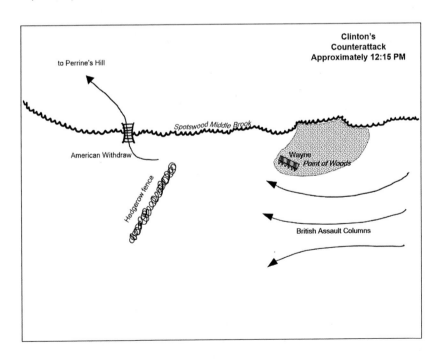

had accomplished precisely what Washington had hoped for, forcing the Redcoats to change fronts and attack, thus buying the main body precious time to deploy on the high ground just beyond the bridge.

As Wayne's men fled the woods, Colonel Matthias Ogden, commanding the 1st New Jersey, had, it can be recalled, positioned his men "on the left of the hedge-row, in a piece of wood, expecting to have had an opportunity of covering our men retreating." He did not have long to wait, for the British infantry, like a red tide, were swarming everywhere. "In a short time after this," said Ogden "there was a pretty smart firing of musquetry on the right, in my front, immediately on which, a number of our men that had been engaged, retreated towards me in a direct line from the enemy; immediately on which I saw the enemy had crossed the morass on my left, and was moving down on that quarter, on which I ordered a retreat."[13]

Not far away Lt. Col. Oswald was still blasting away with his four artillery pieces, hurling everything he could manage at the Redcoats approaching the hedgerow. "I brought up the rear with Captain Cooke's two pieces, and placed them on an eminence," he tells us, "just in rear of the hedge-row, where I found the troops formed. Through the breeches that had been made in the fence I discharged several grapes of shot at the enemy, the infantry being engaged with them." Another artillerist recalled the swirling fight. "We then unlimbered our pieces and retired a short distance, formed in the rear of a party of troops that were to cover our pieces. The enemy were then advancing; a very heavy fire began of musquetry in our front and left wing. General Knox gave us … orders to give the enemy a shot. I believe our people made a stand there about two minutes; after giving them two or three charges of grape shot, we were ordered to retire."[14]

John Laurens was now very much in the thick of things as the British approached the improvised hedgerow defense, and his account of the clash there is worth noting.

> The two regiments were formed behind a fence in front of the position. The enemy's horse advanced in full charge with admirable bravery to the distance of forty paces, when a general discharge from these regiments did great execution among them, and made them fly with the greatest precipitation. The grenadiers succeeded to the attack. At this time my horse was killed under me. In this spot the action was the hottest, and there was considerable slaughter of the British grenadiers. The General [Washington] ordered Woodford's brigade with some artillery to take possession of an eminence on the enemy's left and cannonade from thence. This produced an excellent effect. The enemy were prevented from advancing on us, and confined themselves to cannonade with a show of turning our left flank.

The British paid a heavy price for their advance, more than once being forced to regroup. Laurens continues, "The horse shewed themselves no more. The grenadiers shewed their backs and retreated every where with precipitation. They returned, however again to the charge, and were again repulsed."[15]

Private Martin had already crossed over the morass, and there his regiment took up a new position on the down slope of the hill below where the main body was forming. "When we had secured our retreat, the artillery formed a line of pieces upon a long piece of elevated ground. Our detachment formed directly in front of the artillery, as a covering party, so far below on the declivity of the hill that the pieces could play over our heads."[16] From his elevated position Martin had a direct view of the action at the hedgerow. "By this time the British had come in contact with the New England forces at the fence, when a sharp conflict ensued. These troops maintained their ground, till the whole force of the enemy that could be brought to bear had charged upon them through the fence, and after being overpowered by numbers and the platoon officers had given orders for their several to leave the fence, they had to force them to retreat, so eager were they to be revenged on the invaders of their country and rights."[17]

The meager rearguard slapped together by Washington had gained the precious minutes necessary for him to work wonders behind them. The commander-in-chief had requested that Lt. Colonel Rhea be brought to him, because, it might be recalled, Rhea had grown up in the area, so that the ground that appeared a disorienting maze of woods, streams, defiles, and hills to any visitor was for Rhea entirely familiar. If Washington's appearance at exactly the moment necessary to rescue and redirect the vanguard's retreat seemed exquisite, for the commander-in-chief, Rhea's appeared nothing less than providential. Rhea knew the ground like the back of his hand, and he was quickly able to orient General Washington to the most defensible ground—a long hill behind the morass the vanguard had just struggled through that commanded all approaches. Owned by a farming family named Perrine, it would be known ever after as Perrine's Hill. Washington, Steuben, and Stirling were all there, now placing the main body as it came up. "When fully established, the patriot line curved gently from its right, anchored just off the Englishtown Road above the ravine bridge, to a left flank on ground about a half mile away.... For infantry, it was good defensive ground."[18]

As Perrine's Hill dominated the surrounding countryside, it also provided Continental artillerists with marvelous fields of fire, which they at once took advantage of, covering the embattled rearguard. Stirling placed a battery of ten pieces in the center of the new Continental line, this soon to be augmented as more guns came up, and the rearguard withdrew across the bridge. These guns were immediately brought into line and began thumping away at the red-coated formations maneuvering below them, this, along with well delivered volleys of musketry, causing havoc in the British ranks. Lt. William Hale of the British Grenadiers, for instance, penned this description two

BATTLE-GROUND AT MONMOUTH.[1]

The pen and pencil illustration of the Monmouth Battlefield done by Benson J. Lossing. The view is toward the old Parsonage, Perrine's Hill beyond the cottage stretching from left to right along the horizon, the morass (unseen) between the cottage and Perrine's Hill.

weeks later. "I escaped unhurt in the very hot action of the 28th last month, allowed to be the severest that has happened, the Rebel's Cannon playing Grape and Case [case shot] upon us at the distance of 40 yards and the small arms within little more than half that space."[19]

As more American artillery came up and unlimbered atop Perrine's Hill, British artillery responded on the other side of the morass, going into battery about 1,200 yards from the Continental artillerists, and opening fire.[20] Thus ensued the greatest artillery duel of the entire war, as rival batteries blasted away at one another in the sweltering heat for hours on end. Colonel Dearborn, retiring up Perrine's Hill with the remnants of the vanguard, recalled the thunderous cannonade as it exploded across the fields. "We form'd about 12 pieces of Artillery being brought on the hill with us: the Enimy at the same time advancing very Rappedly finding we had form'd, they form'd in our front on a Ridge & brought up their Artilery within about 60 Rods of our front. *When the brisket Cannonade on both sides* that I Ever heard. Both Armies ware on Clear Ground & if any thing Can be call'd Musical where ther is so much Danger, I think tht ws the finest musick, I Ever heard. *however* the agreeableness of the musick was very often Lessen'd by the balls Coming too near—Our men being very much beat out with Fateague & which was very intence, we order'd them to sit Down & Rest them Selves."[21]

General Charles Lee had handled the brief rearguard action with bravery and skill, but once the last remnants of the vanguard escaped across the bridge to Perrine's Hill, his services were needed elsewhere. Washington, now firmly in command of the consolidated army, ordered Lee to return to Englishtown in order to establish a strong fallback position, should the main body suffer a reverse on their present position. To this Lee thankfully agreed, now exhausted himself, and had he simply ridden off to Englishtown and followed his orders, his fate might well have remained untarnished. But he did not because, I suspect, Lee had not the capacity to refrain from the sort of self-serving invective that had always marred his career, and which, this time around, would help bring him to ruin. Responding to failure with grace was simply beyond the general's verbal repertoire; hence his ride to Englishtown devolved very quickly into a defense of the morning's collapse and, as a natural consequence, a condemnation of Washington's aggressive tactics.

Meeting General Lee on the road to Englishtown, for instance, was Dr. Griffiths, who later testified, "From what followed in conversation, I thought his expectation was, that the day would be disgraceful to the American arms; and as sure as we did attack, we would be beat, and he went on to assign reasons for it; the superiority of the enemy in point of discipline, that they outflanked us in cavalry, and that they outmaneuvered us, were urged by General Lee."[22] This was hardly the sort of intemperate speculation generally trafficked in by officers recently rebuked on the field of battle, but then tact had never been one of General Lee's personality traits. Following his imprudent pleading with Dr. Griffiths, Lee continued his unfortunate sermonizing still further. It was at Englishtown, in fact, where James McHenry, as previously mentioned, overheard the General lecturing a gaggle of townspeople on the likelihood of an American debacle. "The general was on horseback," McHenry later testified, "observing to a number of gentlemen who were standing round, that it was mere folly or madness, or words that conveyed to me a meaning of that kind, to make attempts against the enemy when they possessed so great a superiority of cavalry, and that, under such circumstances, we could not be successful."[23] Not only were these assertions foolish, hopelessly ill-timed, and simply wrong-headed, but, given the dismal results of General Lee's morning leadership, they would rather naturally help grease the skids for his swift exit into historical oblivion, which will be addressed in a later chapter.

For hours the two sides pounded away at each other, the roar and fury of the cannonade carrying for miles in the sultry, smoke-filled air, this as infantrymen on both sides slid away into the cover of trees for protection and relief. Grenadier Hale was among them, noting that the infantry action was "followed by a most incessant and terrible cannonade of near three hours continuance; you may judge from the circumstances of our battalion

In this engraving, the apocryphal Molly Pitcher is shown servicing a field piece during the battle of Monmouth Courthouse. While the legend of Molly Pitcher is questionable, many women served in a variety of ways during battle, and Private Joseph Plumb Martin unquestionably writes of seeing a woman helping service a field piece during the battle alongside her husband. National Archives, Engraving by J.C. Armytage, from painting by Alonzo Chappel.

of guns, 6 pounders, firing 160 rounds, and then desisting only lest ammunition should be wanting for Case shot; of the roar kept up by our twelves [twelve pound cannon] and howitzers, answered by near twenty pieces from their side on a hill 600 paces from ours."[24] Joseph Plumb Martin, positioned below the American artillery, but facing the British, had a bird's eye view of the action. "The cannonade continued for some time without intermission," said he, "when the British pieces being mostly disabled, they reluctantly crawled back from the height which they had occupied and hid themselves from our sight."[25]

Curiously, during the course of this booming cannonade, Martin witnessed an incident of some novelty. "A woman whose husband belonged to the artillery and who was then attached to a piece in the engagement, attended with her husband at the piece the whole time," he explains. Then, as she was leaning over and reaching for a cartridge with which to reload the gun, "a cannon shot from the enemy passed directly between her legs without doing any other damage than carrying away all the lower part of her petticoat." Unfazed by the near miss, the woman artillerist "observed that it was lucky it did not pass a little higher, for in that chase it might have carried away something else, and continued her occupation."[26]

The ground shook and the air reverberated for hours as men ducked for cover or searched longingly for water amid the fury of shot and shell, and the heat of a sweltering afternoon sun. Then suddenly the cannonade ceased as the British pulled back their pieces, and a sudden, eerie silence took the place of artillery thunder. The men on both sides brushed the sweat from their faces and prepared again for battle, no doubt wondering: what now?

Seventeen

Martin

Come my boys, reload your pieces,
and we will give them a set-off

As smoke from the cannonade slowly drifted aloft, General Washington stood atop Perrine's Hill and took stock of the situation—there was much to be pleased with. Both the main body and the vanguard had been saved, the British advance repulsed, and the American artillerists had returned shell for shell with the Redcoats during the extended cannonade. Washington had rallied his troops and, after the morning's dismal retreat, his army had fought well. Now his Continentals were deployed atop a high, defensible hill, and he had men to spare for defending it, or perhaps even to go over to the offensive, should the situation warrant. To the east, on the ground below him, the Redcoats remained in strength along the hedgerow, and he had reports of a British turning movement on the Continentals' left that had bogged down in a nearby orchard. Those represented two immediate difficulties. But as the thick clouds of gun smoke from the afternoon's cannonade gradually cleared, the view offered from Perrine's Hill was one rife with possibilities, and for General George Washington late that June afternoon, it must have been a gratifying panorama.

Suddenly, then, there was an explosion off to his right, and as he turned about he saw another battery of American guns going into action atop a hill some 2,000 yards distant, the sudden thunder breaking the eerie calm that had just recently settled over the field. Earlier Lt. Col. Rhea had pointed that hill out to him—on the Combs Farm, known simply as Combs Hill—and suggested that a battery so placed might command the center of the battlefield. Washington grasped the point instantly, and instructed Rhea to locate General Greene's detachment—which had turned off earlier on a fork from Englishtown that led to the far right of the American line—and guide him directly to that hill. Now it was about 4:30 p.m., and Washington had reason for optimism. Greene's battery would pound the British positions in and around the hedgerow, while remaining almost impervious to attack, due to the marshy ground that Rhea explained fronted the hill.

Then Washington turned and glanced to his left, out toward the flanking threat that had been reported in that direction. To this he responded by sending an officer to reconnoiter, and the man soon returned with news that the British appeared to be withdrawing from that quarter. (To underscore an important point, before taking action Washington had the area on the American left reconnoitered. He sent Major Ogden alone to accomplish this. Lee could have easily done something similar on the British left before launching his offensive earlier that morning, but either chose not, or never thought, to do so.) We do not know if Washington smiled or frowned or showed any sign of emotion at all as this report was delivered, but we do know what he decided to do next—attack! Colonel Dearborn was there, and he recounts how promptly the commander-in-chief decided to go over to the offense. "Washington being in front of our Reg. when the Enimy began to Retire from their Right [the Orchard, on the American left] ordered Col. Cilley & me with ab. 300 men to go & attact the Enimies Right wing which then was passing thro an orchard."[1]

It would be a limited assault, however, designed to drive off those British troops on the American left who were said to be in the process of withdrawing, but no more. Two battalions of select men were chosen to make the attack, one battalion under Colonel Joseph Cilley, a capable New Hampshire veteran, the other under Colonel Richard Parker of Virginia. All told, the assault would include some 600 men and officers, Private Joseph Plumb Martin among Cilley's select Continentals. Martin recalled the moment: "Before the cannonade had commenced, a part of the right wing of the British army had advanced across a low meadow and brook and occupied an orchard on our left. The weather was almost too hot to live in, and the British troops in the orchard were forced by the heat to shelter themselves from it under the trees."

The movement of Redcoats into the orchard had been observed, however, and for a good part of the cannonade, a single artillery piece had hurled a constant stream of shot into the trees there, pinning the British under splintering limbs, injuring and killing many. "We instantly marched towards the enemy's right wing, which was in the orchard," Martin tells us, "and kept concealed from them as long as possible by keeping behind the bushes. When we could no longer keep ourselves concealed, we marched into the open field and formed our line." Unknown to Martin and his mates at the time, however, the Redcoats in the orchard were no middling bunch, but the 42nd Royal Highlanders, one of the most feared and respected fighting units in the British line—the illustrious Black Watch. The Black Watch did not fear Continental select men; thus events would soon determine—as these two elite units came face-to-face on the field at Monmouth—whether

Lee or Washington had been correct in their assessment of American fighting capabilities.

The Highlanders had been caught by surprise by the Continentals' sudden appearance on their right, but they had already received orders from Clinton to begin withdrawing, hence they moved off rapidly. "By this Time," Sir Henry later explained, "our men were so overpowered with Fatigue that I could press the Affair no farther, especially as I was confident the End was gained for which the Attack had been made."[2] Clinton had launched his attack in order to protect his baggage train by allowing Knyphausen's Division to move off unmolested, thus putting distance between themselves and the pursuing Americans with every mile trod. No doubt Sir Henry would have loved to have scored a smashing victory in the process, but the Americans had rallied on high ground and, by late afternoon, the prospect of success for British arms on the field at Monmouth appeared to be waning by the minute. With Knyphausen now on the march for over 16 hours, Clinton decided to start pulling his troops back. It was a sound, professional decision.

Meanwhile, on the British right, the Americans approached the orchard in line of battle, stewing for a fight. Martin continues: "The British immediately formed and began to retreat to the main body of their army." The Highlanders were withdrawing in good order, of course, but this was misinterpreted by Martin and his mates as a hasty retreat, and the Continentals quickly determined to press their attack. "Colonel Cilly, finding that we were not likely to overtake the enemy before they reached the main body of their army, on account of fences and other obstructions, ordered three or four platoons from the right of our corps to pursue and attack them, and thus keep them in play till the rest of the detachment could come up."

At this point our narrative shifts from that of an impersonal tactical overview to the very personal, often frightening, experience of 18th century combat. Now on the run, young, sweating, and weary Continentals like Joseph Plumb Martin began chasing down the veteran, but equally weary Highlanders, convinced the enemy was in flight, when in fact the Highlanders were moving off in good order. Martin was among those chosen to hasten forward, now on a mission to dog and harass the withdrawing enemy. "I was in this party," he tells us. "We pursued without order," racing ahead, determined to run down the foe. "As I passed through the orchard I saw a number of the enemy lying under the trees, killed by our fieldpiece, mentioned before."

The Continentals continued rushing forward until they literally stumbled upon the Highlanders directly ahead, not 30 yards distant. "We overtook the enemy just as they were entering upon the meadow," says Martin, "which was rather bushy. When within about five rods of the rear of the retreating foe, I could distinguish everything about them," he recalls vividly, the sheer passion of combat magnifying exponentially the physical senses. "They were retreating in line," Joseph continues, "though in some disorder. I singled out a man and took my aim directly between his shoulders. (They were divested of their packs.) He was a good mark, being a broad-shouldered fellow. What became of him I know not; the fire and smoke hid him from my sight. One thing I know, that is, I took as deliberate aim at him as ever I did at any game in my life. But after all, I hope I did not kill him, although I intended to at the time."

But the Highlanders were far from finished. Retreating to the southeast, they quickly formed a line of battle in that same bushy meadow along the Spotswood Middle Brook, determined there to make a stand. "Their position was strong," Martin recalled, coming upon them. "Some British light infantry, with two 3-pounder 'grass-hoppers' [thus named because the small cannons recoiled with a hop whenever fired], covered them from a bluff south of the brook."[3] By now Cilly had come up on the run with the remainder of the select men, who took their position opposite the Highlanders who "had obtained a position that suited them, as I suppose, for they returned our fire in good earnest, and we played the second part of the same tune."

Separated by no more than thirty yards, the two lines began blasting away at one another, determined to have it out. As the muskets flashed and roared, blood flew, men toppled, and burning sulfur smoke swirled into the eyes of the combatants. On the ground around them, many of the men who had fallen were screaming in pain. "The first shot they gave us from this piece cut off the thigh bone of a captain, just above the knee," says Martin, "and the whole heel of a private in the rear of him." But the select men did not waver. "We gave it to poor Sawney (for they were Scotch troops) so hot that he was forced to fall back and leave the ground they occupied."

The Highlanders turned away and withdrew back across the brook, working toward the main body of the British Army, now configured behind them—a sight that only served to further arouse the Continentals. "When our commander saw them retreating and nearly joined with their main body," Martin tells us, "he shouted, 'Come, my boys, reload your pieces, and we will give them a set-off.' We did so, and gave them a parting salute, and the firing on both sides ceased."

Whether Martin, Cilly, and the other select men realized it or not, their detachment had just gone toe-to-toe with one of the finest units in the British Army, and if their stand cannot be deemed victorious—the Black Watch had been under orders to withdraw, after all—they had surely accounted themselves as well as any British Grenadiers or Prussian infantry might have under similar circumstances. There was no denying it now, Washington's Continental Army had come of age, a fact no longer grist for debate, but evidenced clearly on the field of battle. But that evidence had required an effort far beyond anything normal or natural, inducing a sense of utter exhaustion as a result. When the balls finally stopped flying, the select men virtually collapsed to the ground where they stood, overwhelmed by the combat, heat, and effort expended. "We then laid ourselves down under the fences and bushes to take breath," Martin explains "for we had need of it. I presume everyone has heard of the heat of that day, but none can realize it that did not feel it. Fighting is hot work in cool weather, how much more so in such weather as it was on the twenty-eighth of June, 1778."[4]

As Martin and his comrades were collapsing to earth from exhaustion near the Middle Brook, high atop Perrine's Hill Washington was watching as the Black Watch made good their retreat, and the sight of the Highlanders' backs must have fed his ambition. He had come to fight, and if the British were retreating, as it now appeared, well, then he would push them as hard and as far as they could be pushed. As the fighting died out on the American left, Washington looked straight ahead toward the hedgerow where the British still maintained a heavy presence, albeit with their heads still down due to the artillery on Combs Hill. Perhaps those Redcoats could be pressed now too, and Washington had just the man on hand to give that effort a shot—General "Mad Anthony" Wayne. Typically, Wayne jumped at the opportunity, and wanted to crash the British position with a detachment of over a thousand men, but 400 Pennsylvanians were all that were available. For Mad Anthony, if he could not muster 1,000 select men for the job, then 400 hardy Pennsylvanians would do.[5]

Wayne led this new detachment down the hill and across the bridge, in search of the enemy. Over a short rise he found them soon enough, a battalion of grenadiers withdrawing from the position they had held for most of the late afternoon. Without a moment's delay—or probably a moment's thought—Wayne led his game Pennsylvania unit directly toward the retreating Redcoats. The Continentals formed at once and poured several deadly volleys into the British ranks, sending more than a few toppling to the earth. The grenadiers had been caught by surprise—following their orders to withdraw and presuming action for the day at a conclusion—and were slow to respond. But they were British grenadiers after all, so respond they soon did, falling into line and returning fire at Wayne's pesky Pennsylvanians, who seemed completely unwilling to be forced into withdrawal.

Indeed, as the Pennsylvanians pressed their attack ever harder, the grenadiers began to back away in peril, but fortunately for them, Sir Henry was near at hand, promptly taking stock of the situation. Realizing his grenadiers were in a very stiff fight, Clinton grabbed hold of the 33rd Foot, then marching toward the sound of the guns, and hurried them forward. In the meantime, Wayne's Pennsylvanians, invigorated by their initial success, were still pressing the grenadiers, but the sudden appearance of the 33rd tilted the odds decidedly against the Americans. Still, Wayne pressed ahead, undaunted by the arrival of fresh British reinforcements, and the contest became both hot and bitter, Wayne refusing to back away, despite the fact that he was now outnumbered more than two to one. Henry B. Dawson, in his 1858 description of the fight at the hedgerow, offered this stirring rendition of Wayne's Pennsylvanians:

> In this charge by General Wayne a characteristic incident occurred, which was not without its effect on the enemy. His dispositions had been made for the charge, and his men,—who were mostly without their coats,—seeing the intended character of the movement, and knowing the peculiarities of their leader, were impressed with the idea that a struggle of unusual determination was about to be commenced. For the purpose of rendering themselves as free as possible, some of the troops *rolled up their shirt-sleeves*, which was immediately imitated by their associates, and when the trying moment arrived the detachment rushed forward with a shout, and handled their weapons with so much vigor that the enemy, astonished and overpowered, hastily retired.[6]

Whether the Pennsylvanians' shirtsleeves had in fact been rolled up in a shocking display of brute determination, or had remained properly buttoned, remains a matter of conjecture but—buttoned or unbuttoned—the fighting certainly continued, swaying back and forth, at times vicious. Lender and Stone tell us that "According to traditional accounts, as the British advance gathered momentum, Wayne remained cool. Watching the developing enemy charge, he told his men, or at least those near enough to hear him, to hold their fire. He wanted the grenadiers and the 33rd to get within range of a sure kill, then have the Continentals go for the enemy officers. 'Steady, steady,' general called down this line, 'wait for the word, then pick out the King birds.'"[7]

Ultimately sheer numbers prevailed, however, and the Americans had little choice but to give ground as the British battle lines threatened to overlap both of their flanks. Sir Henry later reported the results of this second clash near the hedgerow to London, but it seems he polished the tale a bit for his superior's consumption: "I ordered the Light Infantry to rejoin me, but a strong Detachment of the Enemy having possessed themselves of a Post which would have annoyed them in their Retreat, the 33d. Regiment made a Movement towards the Enemy, which with a similar one made by the 1st Grenadiers, immediately dispersed them."[8] The grenadiers and 33rd Foot pressed the Pennsylvanians back from the hedgerow, but in doing so followed the retreating Continentals into the open where the artillerists atop Combs Hill immediately spotted their uniforms, and again jumped to their guns. Volley after volley of screaming shells and solid shot suddenly descended upon the British ranks as they advanced, instantly muting their success. Under the withering cannonade, the British had little choice but to withdraw, leaving the remainder of Wayne's plucky Pennsylvanians in command of the field; a minor success, but a success, nevertheless.

As all this was going on, Washington decided he wanted to expand the fight even further, and sent Colonel Gemat back to Englishtown with orders for the Baron—who had been sent there to help form the defenses—to bring up enough reserves so that another offensive might be launched. "Half an hour after it ceased [the cannonade]," Steuben later testified, "Colonel Gemat arrived and brought me the order from the Commander-in-Chief that the enemy was retreating in confusion, and that I should therefore bring him a reinforcement."[9] Steuben quickly complied, leading three brigades through the streets of Englishtown en route to the front. "Here he encountered the dejected Lee, who tried to stop him, challenging the veracity of the intelligence that the Baron had received from Washington. The British, Lee told Steuben, could not *possibly* be withdrawing 'in confusion'; there was no chance that the Continentals could have repulsed a determined attack by the enemy he so revered."[10] Steuben had Gemat simply repeat Washington's orders to the befuddled Lee. Then the Baron marched on, but Lee's imprudent remark would not be forgotten.

Washington's blood was still up by the time Steuben eventually reached the field, but the requisite daylight for reasonable maneuver had already faded into dusk. Grasping that Steuben's reinforcements would not arrive in time to see action, Washington hatched another plan—a pincer movement against both of Clinton's flanks, which he had already set in motion. But the pincer Washington envisioned was not a major strike capable of dislodging his enemy, but a harassing maneuver bound only to sow irritation and confusion in the fading light. For this he turned to Generals Enoch Poor of New Hampshire and Virginian William Woodford. Woodford, who had marched that morning in Nathanael Greene's detachment and taken position near Combs Hill, was to strike the British left, while Poor was to move simultaneously toward their right. Both moved off sometime after 7 o'clock that evening but, moving slowly to avoid discovery, neither had the time necessary to strike before dusk had faded into darkness.

Sensibly, Washington called off the evening attack, but it appears he had every intention of renewing the action the following morning. So, he had both Poor's and Woodford's detachments hunker down forward in sight of the British, these troops sleeping on their arms, while Stirling moved the Continentals off Perrine's Hill to a position near the hedgerow where they, too, remained overnight. Steuben then placed his reinforcements upon Perrine's Hill as they came up, serving as both a reserve and potential fallback position come morning, should the fighting be renewed with the rising sun.

Slowly the Continentals began searching for water, for friends lost in combat, or attending to the wounded who, in many areas, covered the ground. Many of the galling deficiencies that had plagued the Medical Department throughout the war had been thankfully addressed at Valley Forge, and the troops at Monmouth benefited as a result. Nathanael

Greene's efforts as Quartermaster General had the effect of filling the medicine chests before the Monmouth campaign had even been initiated, thus medicines and bandages would not be an issue. Although medical care was still horribly primitive by modern standards, there was at least an organized attempt to reach and treat the wounded. "As the British began their march across New Jersey, Dr. William Shippen, Jr., Continental director of hospitals, was aware a fight was likely, although with the rival armies on the move, he was at a loss as to where to preposition temporary hospitals. Still, the numbers and quality of medical personnel were better than previously, and when the time came, numerous New Jersey towns were close enough to accommodate temporary medical facilities."[11]

After the fighting ended, Joseph Plumb Martin wandered off in search of water. He located a well, and nearby spotted the captain who had been seriously wounded in the firefight he had just been a part of. The captain was begging a sergeant to help him, but the sergeant and a few other men were too busy plundering the dead to lend assistance. Martin asked the sergeant why he had not helped the captain, and the sergeant replied he would do so directly. "Directly!" Martin replied angrily, "why he will die directly." Finally the sergeant relented, and Martin assisted in moving the captain to the nearby hospital. "I helped him to the place, and tarried a few minutes to see the wounded and two or three limbs amputated, and then returned by my party again, where we remained the rest of the day and the following night, expecting to have another hack at them in the morning, but they gave us the slip."[12]

Little, either, did the commander-in-chief realize at the time that the last shots at Freehold had already been fired, for Sir Henry had no intention of renewing the action. He had already secured the protection of his baggage train, and any hope he had of seriously damaging the Continental Army had vanished when Washington positioned his main body atop Perrine's Hill, a location—due to the morass in front—that was essentially unassailable. So, the Redcoats rested for a few hours, then pulled out quietly around 11 o'clock that night, stealing a march on the Americans, who remained behind, exhausted from a day of marching, countermarching, and intense fighting in heat that had soared to the range of 100 degrees.

Washington rode forward to be with his troops, eventually bedding down with Lafayette on the ground under an oak tree, his men gathered likewise nearby on the field of battle. For the Americans it had been quite a day. Lafayette recalled the efforts: "During this affair, which ended so well, although begun so ill, General Washington appeared to arrest fortune by one glance, and his presence of mind, valour, and decision of character were never displayed to greater advantage. Wayne distinguished himself; Green and the Brave Stirling led forward the first line in the ablest manner.

THE BIVOUAC AT MONMOUTH.

This striking image of Washington's "Bivouac at Night" was originally created by Alonzo Chappel, later engraved by John Chester Buttre in 1856. The picture shows Washington forward on the battlefield on the night of June 28, 1778, where he, his staff, and Lafayette would encamp after the fighting had ended at Monmouth. From the Miriam and Ira D. Wallach Division of Art, Prints and Photographs, New York Public Library.

From four o'clock in the morning until night M. de Lafayette was momentarily obliged to change his occupations. The General and he passed the night lying on the same mantle, talking over the conduct of Lee."[13] When the Americans finally rose from a weary sleep the following morning, the British were gone, and the Battle of Monmouth Courthouse was over.

EIGHTEEN

Hamilton

The behaviour of the officers and men in general
was such as could not easily be surpassed.

Monday morning, the 29th, came on hot and steamy, shrouds of warm mist hanging over the creeks and meandering lowlands that surrounded Monmouth Courthouse. As the red sun inaugurating another sweltering summer day crested the eastern horizon, the men of the Continental Army stirred from a night of restless sleep. Already much had taken place. Scouts from the advanced elements had discovered the British missing in the early hours and reported that fact back to Washington.[1] In fact, Clinton had allowed his men to rest only for a number of hours after the fighting had died off, then around midnight silently slipped away east leaving campfires burning behind to cover his withdrawal. The exhausted Americans would not discover the British absent until hours later, too late to mount an effective pursuit, but it really didn't matter.[2] The British were moving off onto high ground, cut with steep defiles where an aggressive pursuit might prove dangerous indeed, and Washington had not the fresh troops capable of moving at the requisite speed to run down the retreating British column, so pursuit appeared fruitless. Besides, the commander-in-chief had already achieved essentially what he had taken the field to accomplish in the first place—a successful strike at the British withdrawal.

Indeed, as the Americans stirred from their sleep that Monday morning, they found themselves in sole possession of the field of battle as the British marched away, a circumstance they had rarely had opportunity to relish in the past. According to the generally accepted rules of 18th century warfare, the army that held the field after combat ended had the right to declare victory, no matter how close that combat had been. For instance, the British had been happy to declare victory at Bunker Hill when the Americans eventually withdrew due to a declining supply of ammunition, despite having been savaged in their uphill assault upon the American lines. Likewise, Lord Charles Cornwallis would declare victory at Guilford Court House in North

175

Carolina in 1781 for the very same reason, despite almost destroying his army in combat against Nathanael Greene's American force, which had moved off slightly to reorganize and redeploy. So, the Americans had every right to fancy themselves victorious that Monday morning at Monmouth, and this they most assuredly did, many offering up visions of a fabulous victory. General Washington, however, maintained a far more guarded view of the affair, penning a factual report to Congress on July 1, explaining his reasons for not pursuing Clinton on the morning of the 29th, and praising his men's efforts. In part it read:

> The extreme heat of the Weather—the fatigue of the Men from their march thro' a deep sandy Country almost entirely destitute of Water, and the distance the Enemy had gained by marching in the Night, made a pursuit impracticable and fruitless. It would have answered no valuable purpose, and would have been fatal to numbers of our Men, several of whom died the preceding day with Heat.
>
> Were I to conclude my account of this days transactions without expressing my obligations to the Officers of the Army in general, I should do injustice to their merit, and violence to my own feelings. They seemed to vie with each other in manifesting their Zeal and Bravery. The Catalouge of those who distinguished themselves is too long to admit of particularizing individuals: I cannot however forbear mentioning Brigadier General Wayne whose good conduct and bravery thro' the whole action deserves particular commendation.
>
> The Behaviour of the troops in general, after they recovered from the first surprize occasioned by the Retreat of the advanced Corps, was such as could not be surpassed.
>
> All the Artillery both Officers and Men that were engaged, distinguished themselves in a remarkable manner.[3]

While Washington's account praised his troops and stuck to the facts, a far more ominous version of the battle had seemingly circulated throughout the army, this apparently in the blink of an eye. This rendering insisted that the British would have surely been soundly thrashed, had not it been for Lee's poor performance during the morning's action. Elijah Fisher, for instance, added this note to his journal on Sunday, 28 June, just after the fighting subsided.

> The 28th. On Sunday our army had the Engagement with the British at Monmouth Court-house where Gen. Lee went Contrary to orders but our army Drove them and if that he had managed according to his orders it was likely in all probability we should have taken the howl [whole] or the bigar Part of there army. It was a vary hot Day and a grate many died a drinking water.[4]

If Fisher, whose unit had not seen combat, and therefore could not have had any real grasp of the day's events beyond what rumor had circulated, fancied General Lee the prime suspect for the day's adversity, then it is probably safe to assume that this was the general understanding throughout the army. Lee, of course, would have his defenders, but it appears that quickly—indeed, very quickly—his reputation had tumbled into serious decline. Meanwhile, many others waxed euphoric: "The enemy 'had retired in a great hurry in the Night,' Chaplain David Griffith wrote to his wife, leaving the field and their wounded to the victorious Americans. 'It is Glorious for America,' Colonel Israel Shreve exulted, 'the Glory of the Day was Doubtful,' but at last 'the Enemy was Drove off the Ground.'"[5]

While the Americans painted events with their own happy brush, from a strictly military perspective, the actual outcome on the field appeared to represent something far more akin a tactical draw, than any substantial American triumph of arms. Clinton's task and overall objective, after all, had been to move his monstrous column safely to New York, and there is little question that in this he had been successful. The Americans had done precious little damage to the British column, and on the morning of the 29th it appeared beyond question that Sir Henry had placed his troops and wagons beyond reach of the Americans. Still, he had doubled back to try to inflict a serious blow to Washington's vanguard—catching them on difficult ground in front of the deep ravines—but Washington had arrived literally in the nick of time, and masterfully fashioned an almost impenetrable defense. Sir Henry had been ultimately forced to withdraw, leaving the field and many of his wounded behind, thus offering the delighted Americans an opportunity to crow. That their claims at times appeared a bit hyperbolic did not alter the fact that on Monday morning Clinton was gone, and the Americans in sole command of the field of battle.

For General George Washington, however, the extent of victory took a back seat to the ever-present realities of war. There were wounded to be promptly gathered and treated, dead to be buried, and the British, even if they could not be successfully attacked, had to be trailed and accounted for, lest Clinton double back again and catch the Continentals napping. As far as pursuit was concerned, as Washington had reported to Congress, he had virtually no fresh troops to dispatch in that effort. Only Morgan's riflemen, who by error had been left sitting idle by Lee's aides, were fresh and capable of such a task, but Morgan's manpower was naturally limited, thus great diligence would be required on his part, lest this crack unit be caught in a trap. Morgan's biographer, Don Higginbotham, explains the Virginian's activities in pursuit of the British: "Had he tried, Morgan could have gleaned some satisfaction from his part in this New Jersey campaign. He took approximately 30 prisoners and 100 deserters. These statistics include the week following the battle, during which Morgan and Maxwell tried to prevent enemy foraging parties from ravaging the countryside along Clinton's line of retreat. On July 1, the rifle corps skirmished briskly with part of the British rear guard, then withdrew on the appearance of two redcoat reinforcing columns. Four days after that Clinton's army, having boarded transports at Sandy Hook, sailed for New York City."[6]

With Morgan off in pursuit of the British, the next issue became the wounded, dead, and dying of both armies. Moving the wounded to field hospitals began almost immediately after the last shots were fired. Burying, and compiling a list of the dead, took a bit longer, and the numbers, due to the nature of the fighting, were far from precise. In Washington's letter to Congress dated July 1 he attached a list of the American dead and wounded, at least as it had been so far compiled. It indicated eight officers, one sergeant, and sixty infantrymen killed; eighteen officers, one adjutant, and one hundred and thirty-two infantrymen wounded; five sergeants and one hundred and twenty-seven men missing, noting that many of the missing had simply fallen out due to heat and exhaustion and were expected to return to duty.[7] As far as British casualties were concerned, Washington reported: "The Enemy's slain left on the field and buried by us, according to the Return of the persons assigned to that duty were four Officers and Two hundred and forty five privates. In the former number was the Honble Colo. Monckton. Exclusive of these they buried some themselves, as there were several new Graves near the field of Battle. How many Men they may have had wounded cannot be determined; but from the usual proportion the number must have been considerable. There were a few prisoners taken."[8]

These numbers were to prove preliminary, and far better figures, in terms of accurate casualty numbers, have over time have been tabulated. Today's best estimates of American casualties put the number at somewhere between 450 and 500 dead and wounded (90 killed, 360 wounded). The British, on the other hand, fighting on the offensive, often on open ground where they were subject to severe artillery fire, suffered far more grievously. Today's best estimates put the British dead and wounded in combat at 890, (250 killed, 640 wounded) a figure that does not include desertions, stragglers, and prisoners taken on the field. "Thus if we include deserters, it is safe to assume the British army paid a toll in the neighborhood of 2,000 men (including wounded) for their march through New Jersey."[9]

These figures suggest the British were roughly handled at Monmouth Courthouse. Moreover, in that those casualties were incurred by some of their most elite units, they could not easily be made good, and it is not hard to imagine losses like these having a particularly galling effect on overall morale. These were precisely the type of losses the British Army could not well suffer at the time—now engaged in a global contest with France. Sir Henry had intended to deliver a sharp, overwhelming blow to the American vanguard on ground he had seen and liked, but in the end, he paid a very heavy price for his decision. He left a good number of his finest soldiers behind—dead, wounded, captured—and the field of battle in the hands of the Americans. This may all have been a product of sheer good fortune for the Americans (that Washington had shown up precisely when he did, taking forward command of his army), but in the end the Americans' good luck hardly diminished the impact of the British losses.

From a strictly strategic point of view, in the end the Battle of Monmouth Courthouse meant very little. Clinton continued along on his way to Sandy Hook, and Washington, grasping the lay of the land, declined to follow. For the British Monmouth had been little more than a rearguard action, professionally executed. For the Americans, however, it meant a great deal more. They had marched from Valley Forge with the singular intent of delivering a blow to the British column, and they had managed to achieve just that. For them it did not matter that the British had moved on; only that their enemy had been bloodied in the process. The Continentals had stood toe-to-toe against Grenadiers, Highlanders, and the Queen's Guards, to name just a few of the elite units that had been hurled at them, and they had acquitted themselves admirably. *That* is the lesson the American infantryman took away from Monmouth, and they did not have to have it read aloud to them by their officers to grasp its importance. They had experienced it first-hand. Paul Lockhart captures this vital point:

> Monmouth was not a turning point in the war. It was, however, a turning point in the history of the Continental Army. Even with an uncertain chain of command and lackluster leadership, the rebels had performed magnificently. At Bunker Hill, Trenton, Princeton, and even Germantown, they had displayed great fortitude and bravery, but at Monmouth they showed *discipline* for the first time.... The Continentals held firm as musket balls and solid shot slammed into their ranks, as fabled regiments like the Highlanders of the Black Watch advanced on their lines with bayonets leveled. They held their ground through all of these things, mounted a furious counterattack, and drove the Redcoats from the field. The British had retreated, not they.[10]

This new-found confidence was reflected in the comments of many participants. For instance, the General Orders for the 29th read: "The Commander in Chief congratulates the army on the victory obtained over the arms of his Britannic Majesty yesterday and thanks most sincerely the gallant officers and men who distinguished themselves upon the occasion."[11] Alexander Hamilton, generally a harsh critic of the army, writing to Elias Boudinot on 5 July, could barely contain his newfound sense of enthusiasm. "Lt Col: Parker were particularly useful on the left—Col Craig, with General Wayne, on the right. The Artillery acquitted themselves most charmingly. I was spectator to Lt Col: Oswalds behaviour, who kept up a gallant fire from some pieces commanded by him, uncovered and unsupported. In short one can hardly name particulars without doing injustice to the rest. The behaviour of the officers and men in general was such as could not easily be surpassed. Our troops, after the first impulse from mismanagement, behaved with more spirit & moved with greater order than the British troops. You know my way of thinking about our army, and that I am not apt to flatter it. I assure you I never was pleased with them before this day."[12]

For those who had fought and survived unscathed (like Hamilton), battle at Monmouth no doubt proved an affirmation of their abilities and recent training under Steuben; in short, an enormous psychological plus. For those who had been shot down in the fray, however, the experience proved far less cheerful. A field hospital was established in the courthouse and, once the firing died down, teams spread out to try and locate the wounded, dead, and dying. This was not an easy task. Many of the wounded had crawled under bushes or into any form of shade they could find in order to try and find water, or at least get out of the unforgiving sun. As a result, they were often difficult to find, and more than a few went initially undiscovered. Eventually, however, the wounded were brought in for care at the courthouse, and from there shipped off to various regional hospitals or homes where individuals could be cared for on a long-term basis. The majority of wounded were ultimately transferred to a hospital at Princeton, the largest in the area, but even here space was limited. By any modern standard, medicines were inadequate, care primitive, hospital diseases often rampant, hence recovery a very dicey proposition. It is now presumed that many of the long-term wounded wound up in private homes, these ranging from Eastern Pennsylvania all the way to Northern New Jersey.

As General Washington digested the reports on the morning of the 29th, the strategic situation resolved rather rapidly into focus. The British were gone and beyond his grasp, now bound for New York City. A move north was thus called for, but his army was exhausted, the heat still insufferable, the ground around Monmouth difficult and sandy, good drinking water hard to come by. He would have to give his troops time to rest and recover, then move north to a suitable defensive position outside New York City, all this at a cautious pace. Late on the 29th, Washington shifted his army back to Englishtown, where they could consolidate once again, rest, and draw rations from the supply train. Then on July 1, the army began a slow movement north, ultimately bound for White Plains, New York. "The next day after the action each man received a gill of rum, but nothing to eat," Martin tells us. "We then joined our regiments in the line and marched for Hudson's River. We marched by what was called 'easy marches,' that is, we struck our tents at three o'clock in the morning, marched ten miles and then encamped, which would be about one or two o'clock in the afternoon. Every third day we rested all day."[13]

Suffering mightily from the heat, the army limped slowly into New Brunswick, where the commander-in-chief decided to rest his troops for a few days, allowing the men to swim, wash themselves, fish, and dally along the banks of the Raritan River. For many it seemed as through the Continental Army had at long last arrived in a region of milk and honey. Then, once the troops had recovered from the heat and exhaustion, Washington decided to stage a stunning 4th of July celebration along the banks of the river, very much reminiscent of the grand review staged earlier that spring at Valley Forge. The general orders of the day were specific. "After the Army is formed upon a signal by order of the Commander in Chief, thirteen Pieces of Cannon will be discharged, after which a single Cannon which will be a signal for a running fire to begin on the right of the Army and be continued to the left with Musquetry and Cannon. At the Conclusion of which, on a signal three Cheers will be given, 'Perputual and undisturbed Independence to the United States of America.'"[14] It proved a stunning exhibition. "At 5:00 P.M. the entire army formed on the New Brunswick side of the Raritan, the troops wearing 'Green-Boughs' in their hats 'to make the best appearance possible.' Henry Knox thought the double line of infantry and gun crews stretched for two miles."[15] It was a display surely meant to put an exclamation point on the Continentals' victory at Monmouth, and broadcast Washington's triumph to the country at large. Elijah Fisher paints the scene: "July 4ath. We Selebrated the Independence of America the howl army paraded and at the Right of Every Brigade there was a field peace placed, then was the signal given for the howl army to fire and they fired one round apiece and the artillery Discharged thirteen Cannon we gave three Chears &c. At Night his Excelency and the gentlemen and Ladys had a Bawl at Head Quarters."[16] The display of musketry and cannon fire were impressive, loud enough to be heard by the British not terribly far off at Sandy Hook, a sure sign of just what the Americans believed they had accomplished at Monmouth Courthouse. A few days later the army marched from New Brunswick, bound for Scotch Plains, New Jersey, along the route to White Plains, New York.[17]

The lessons learned from the Battle of Monmouth Courthouse appeared clear. The fighting units of the Continental Army had now come of age, but leadership at the division level still appeared glaringly deficient. General Charles Lee had demanded—and been given—operational command of the vanguard units, but his handling of the advance on the morning of the 28th had somehow disintegrated into utter confusion, a withdrawal in the face of the enemy that at the time almost no one could understand. Lee had his defenders, of course, but already the long knives had come out and were circling, adamant that Lee was either incompetent or perhaps even a traitor. Alexander Hamilton, in his letter to Elias Boudinot, lays the groundwork for the charge many at the time were convinced was true. "The advanced corps came up with the enemys rear a mile or two beyond the court House; I saw the enemy drawn up, and am persuaded there were not a thousand men; their front from different accounts was then ten miles off. However favourable this situation may seem for an attack it was not made; but after changing their position two or three times by retrograde movements our advanced corps got into a general confused retreat and even route would hardly be too strong an expression." What, precisely, had taken place that morning? No one could say for sure at the time, but a trial was about to explore in some depth General Lee's actions, creating in its wake a controversy that would ultimately take on a life of its own. Hamilton, now convinced that Lee had to go, made his feelings clear to Boudinot: "What think you now of General Lee? You will be ready to join me in condemning him: And yet, I fear a Court Martial will not do it. A certain preconceived and preposterous opinion of his being a very great man will operate much in his favour. Some people are very industrious in making interest for him. Whatever a court Martial may decide, I shall continue to believe and say—his conduct was monstrous and unpardonable."[18] General George Washington now had a serious problem on his hands in the person of Charles Lee, and it was a problem Lee would force him very soon to address.

Nineteen

Lee

To these maneuvers the success of the day was entirely owing

It is no small wonder that General Lee's handling of the American vanguard on the morning of July 28, its confused withdrawal, and the court-martial that resulted have befuddled military historians ever since. The situation was, without question, a mess. To begin with, orders issued that morning were confused. Secondly, the withdrawal of the individual vanguard units was predicated upon a welter of disparate views of the battlefield, ultimately the precarious positions the commanders of those units suddenly discovered themselves in. These issues were in turn aggravated by conflicting memories and testimony, raw emotions—martial, political, personal—and lastly a profound sense of animosity for General Lee (by many, but not all), coupled with a deep sense of appreciation and loyalty for General Washington. To tease all these interwoven threads apart over the years has proven a Herculean task, at the time a job so confused that many simply threw up their hands in futility. For some emotion, not reason, reigned supreme. Fortunately, with the advantage of a great deal of study, we can today bypass much of the confusion, and focus our inquiry instead on a few basic, essential facts that will turn confusion into clarity

Importantly, it should be noted that General Lee was not placed under arrest on the field of battle or immediately thereafter by General Washington, this despite what was viewed at the time as an inexplicable withdrawal of the American vanguard before the advancing British. Washington had simply demanded an explanation (quite possibly, a *very* heated demand), and once Lee had stammered his way through some sort of excuse, the commander-in-chief had given him the option of bringing up and placing the main body or assisting with the rearguard. As we know, to his credit, Lee chose the rearguard, and went on to handle these duties with courage and skill. Nothing regarding this issue arose late on the 28th or all day on the 29th, so it can be assumed that Washington may have had no further interest in the matter and was even possibly willing to let it drop. After all, heated verbal confrontations often take place on the field of battle, where life and death issues are at stake, and placed in this light, the meeting between Lee and Washington had been intense but hardly tumultuous. But Lee had heard the rumors of his declining prestige; that he had failed miserably, in fact, and for someone as grounded in personal vanity as was General Lee, this devolving situation soon proved intolerable. Rather than deal with the problem sensibly—say, by asking for a private meeting with Washington and hashing the matter out—he responded with an absurd, intemperate letter that in turn set off a flurry of correspondence between the two generals on June 30. Initiating the evolving hostility was Lee's first letter, the essentials of which read as follows:

> From the knowledge I have of your Excellency's character, I must conclude, that nothing but misinformation of some very stupid, or misrepresentation of some very wicked persons, could have occasioned your making use of such very singular expressions as you did, on my, coming up to the ground where you had taken post; they imply'd that I was guilty of either **disobedience** of orders, of want of conduct, or want of courage. Your Excellency will therefore infinitely oblige me, by letting me know, on which of these three articles you ground your charge, that I may prepare for my justification, which I have the happiness to be confident I can do, to the army, to the Congress, To America, and to the World in general.... And to speak with a becoming pride, I can assert, that to these maneuvers the success of the day was entirely owing—I can boldly say that had we remained on the first ground, or had we advanced, or had the retreat been conducted in a manner different from what it was, this whole army, and the interest of America, would have risked being sacrificed. I ever had (and hope ever shall have the greatest respect and veneration for General Washington) I think him endowed with many great and good qualities, but in this instance I must pronounce that he has been guilty of an act of cruel injustice towards a man who certainly has some pretensions to the regard of every servant of this country—and, I think, sir, I have the right to demand some reparation for the injury committed—and unless I can obtain it, I must in justice to myself, when this campaign is closed, which I believe will close this war retire from a service at the head of which is placed a man capable of offering such injuries. But at the same time in justice to you I must repeat that I from my soul believe, that it was not a motion of your own breast, but instigated by some of those dirty earwigs who will for ever insinuate themselves near persons in high office.[1]

Set aside for a moment—if at all possible—the utterly insufferable tone of this correspondence, and focus instead on Lee's demands. He insists that the commander-in-chief detail charges against him—which Lee has conveniently listed for Washington—when in fact no charges existed at the time. Lee then demands that Washington explain the nature of these charges (again, which didn't yet exist), these, he insists, taken from the conversation the two had while meeting on the field of battle. Of course, the letter's tone is impossible to ignore—pompous, insulting, hopelessly self-congratulatory. Washington replied both promptly and obligingly as follows:

I received your letter, (dated thro' mistake, the 1st of July) expressed, as I conceive, in terms highly improper. I am not conscious of having made use of any very singular expressions at the time of my meeting you, as you intimate. What I recollect to have said was dictated by duty and warranted by the occasion. As soon as circumstances will permit, you shall have an opportunity either of justifying yourself to the army, to Congress, to America, and to the world in general; Or of convincing them that you were guilty of a breach of orders and of misbehavior before the enemy, on the 28th inst. In not attacking them as you had been directed and in making an unnecessary, disorderly, and shameful retreat.[2]

At this point it appears Washington had had enough of General Charles Lee. One might conclude that Lee, now getting what he had demanded, would have ceased in his imperious invective, but this was apparently beyond him. He would dispatch two more foolish, insulting letters before receiving Washington's final response. Lee's next note read as follows:

I beg your Excellency's pardon for the inaccuracy in misdating my letter—you cannot afford me greater pleasure than in giving me the opportunity of shewing to America the sufficiency of her respective servants—I trust that the temporary power of office and the tinsel dignity attending it will not be able by all the mists they raise can offuscte the bright rays of truth.[3]

And, as if this were not enough, Lee promptly followed with this:

Since I had the honor of addressing my letter by Col. Fitzgerald to your Excellency I have reflected on both your situation and mine, and beg leave to observe, that It will be for our mutual convenience, that a court of inquiry should immediately ordered— but I could wish it might be a court martial—for if the affair is drawn into it may be difficult to collect the necessary evidences, and perhaps might bring on a paper war betwixt the adherents to both parties which may occasion some disagreeable feuds on the Continent—for all are not my friends nor all your admirers—I must intreat therefore from your love of justice that you will immediately exhibit your charge—and that on the first halt I may be brought to tryal.[4]

Washington responded with this simple, terse reply:

Your letter by Colo. Fitzgerald and also one of this date have been duly received. I have sent Colo. Scammel, the Adjutant General to put you under arrest, who will deliver you a copy of the charges on which you will be tried.[5]

With this string of imprudent letters, General Lee had launched himself headfirst into a confrontation with General Washington, the man who had, by any objective standard, saved the army at Monmouth Courthouse and, in a stunning performance on the field of battle, snatched victory from the jaws of imminent defeat. Not only that but, according to Lee's tortured logic, it was he, not Washington, who deserved credit for the Continentals' victory at Monmouth, for it had been his own actions on the field that morning for which (in his own words) "the success of the day was entirely owing." Given the facts, this was simply an astonishing assertion, as foolish as it was objectively incorrect, and an assertion for which General Lee would pay a heavy price.

To be fair, before we look at the charges leveled against him, or the facts relating to the trial, it might be best to briefly review General Lee's performance as a combat leader in order to give him his due. At the time, and to this day, Lee has had his defenders, so let's take a close look at his conduct after being given command of the vanguard units, his actions on the field, and the results those actions produced.

It can be recalled that Charles Lee insisted he be inserted into the leadership role of the vanguard units (after previously turning this position down) literally at the last moment. Washington acquiesced to Lee's demand in a letter dated June 26, just two days before American and British units finally clashed at Monmouth. Given the circumstances, knowing that battle was imminent, one would expect of any professional combat leader a flurry of specific activities: to take firm command of the far-flung units, to review all intelligence reports regarding enemy strength, positions, movements, etc., to learn the lay of the land and network of roads, check on ammunition and supplies, beef-up his staff to meet combat expectations, locate and have on hand local guides, and to place his units into position for the attack he had been *ordered* to deliver. In short, to prepare a plan, and execute that plan, in relation to impending combat. This involves a great many activities, many not mentioned here. Did Charles Lee do any of this? No, he did not. In fact, he did not do any of them, and although he did meet with several of his unit commanders, but nothing of substance came of that meeting. Indeed, on the evening of the 27th Charles Lee gave no preparatory orders and simply went to bed. It was not until roused from sleep by Washington's early morning rider with fresh orders, reaffirming his orders to attack early on the 28th, that Lee began to prepare for an offensive movement.

Perhaps, it might be argued, General Charles Lee was such a superb combat leader that preliminary details such as these were unnecessary for a man of his experience and ability. That come first light, Charles Lee would simply wheel into action, bringing the advanced units under his unified command, marching them forward under a coherent plan, with determination and skill. Did he do this? Hardly. As can be recalled, he did order Colonel William Grayson forward with some 700 men to find, fix, and attack the enemy if possible (in compliance with Washington's latest order), but that was about the size of it. So, if we are to grade General Lee in terms of his *preparation* for battle, that grade would of necessity be one of complete failure. If General Lee was, in fact, a fine combat leader, he certainly failed to demonstrate those skills during the lead-up to Monmouth, and there appears to be no serious argument to the contrary, once his lack of preliminary activity is closely examined.

There is one other plausible explanation for General Lee's lack of preparation prior to battle at Monmouth, but that explanation places the general in an even harsher light. This is that he had absolutely no intention of fighting in the first place, which, of course, if true, would have made preparation entirely unnecessary. That course of action, after all, was precisely what Lee had been urging all along. The general was sound asleep, it might be recalled, until the dragoon sent by Hamilton galloped into his headquarters in the early hours of the 28th with fresh orders from Washington, forcing him to rise and take action. Did he intend to ignore his orders once again, sleeping until dawn, then feigning activity as the British slipped away unmolested in complete disregard of Washington's orders, oft repeated? This is an unknowable hypothetical, of course, but Lee's utter lack of activity suggests either gross incompetence or gross insubordination, between which readers may judge for themselves. But either would warrant his removal.

What we do know is that Grayson would not reach the main battlefield until almost 8 o'clock that morning, and that Lee was well behind him with the rest of the vanguard, even though Lee had received intelligence from Steuben earlier that morning that the British were breaking camp and moving off. All this fumbling about was avoidable, had Lee made the proper arrangements the night before, but, of course, he had not. Lee finally reached the area around the courthouse around 9 o'clock, and at this point the situation ahead appeared confused. Lee subsequently ordered Wayne to take the lead, and then followed Wayne out to reconnoiter the situation around the courthouse around 10 o'clock that morning.

This is where General Lee made his most critical mistake, a mistake from which virtually all the subsequent confusion, mistakes, and withdrawals that morning would emanate. It was here where both Lee and Wayne put their glasses to their eyes and observed the British formed ahead. Lee observed what he presumed to be a British rearguard consisting of cavalry and infantry, ultimately estimated by him at no more than perhaps 1,500 to 2,000 men (although initially less). He then decided almost immediately upon a plan of action. The critical error Lee had made, of course, was mistaking his initial opinion of British strength and intentions for absolute fact. He then concocted an elaborate plan to "bag" the entire British rearguard, but his plan was based entirely upon a fiction, an illusion he had accepted as fact and had taken no steps to verify. This is when he decided to move off in strength toward the British right, while having Wayne demonstrate across their front, all of this apparently without explaining clearly his intentions to his own subordinates.

So confident of success was General Lee at the time, it can be recalled he exclaimed to Lafayette, "My dear Marquis, I think those people are ours."

Unfortunately, it might also be recalled that soon after Lee departed, Wayne and Colonel Jackson saw the opposing British force in a far different light. Jackson later stated that he could see the Redcoats from his left to his right, as far as the eye could see. "I should have supposed the apparent number," said Jackson, "to be at least three thousand men, but I saw no end to them, I had reason to suppose there were more." Had Lee taken the time to properly reconnoiter the situation ahead, he would have discovered a growing number of British troops across the front but, utterly confident of his initial assessment, he had not. Arguments that he had not enough cavalry or other means to accomplish this reconnaissance are groundless. Multiple means were available to him for a quick reconnaissance, and it was Lee's *job* to employ them. A competent commander would have done so. Had he not sent an officer off to reconnoiter the British right? Why not the left?

Meanwhile, reality was fast approaching. Hearing the gunfire behind him, Sir Henry had decided to double back, bringing with him some of the finest units in the British Army. In all Clinton would counterattack in three columns, eventually with a force of some 10,000 troops, the main thrust headed toward the vulnerable American right flank near the courthouse. It would not be until Lee emerged from the woods on the British right, however, that the Redcoat assault—then already in midcareer—would be spotted by him, and by then it was already too late.

Chasing a chimera, a fiction, Lee had ignored the reality fast building across his front, and now the entire American vanguard would pay a price for his negligence. Convinced the visible British force was nothing more than a meager rearguard, he had left the forward American units in scattered, indefensible positions. At once he tried to cobble together a response by having Lafayette (now commanding Wayne's former unit of selectmen) race toward the courthouse to cut the British off, but that was a hopeless solution even before it had been conceived. Taking heavy fire, Lafayette never got to the courthouse, and was ultimately forced to withdraw. Meanwhile, the commanders of the forward units on the American left, now being pressed by overwhelming British numbers, and in danger of being overrun or cut off entirely, grasped the predicament they were in, and soon began to withdraw individually, a piecemeal movement devoid of any controlling hand. Some of these withdrawals were accomplished in good order, others less so. Meanwhile, Lee watched the battlefield collapse before his eyes as the British columns advanced upon the fleeing Americans. The general finally ordered the withdrawal of those few units not already in retreat, but that was a necessity imposed by the chaos already swirling on the field of battle, hardly the tactical ingenuity he would later claim for himself. Of course, it can be recalled that General Lee had failed to designate a fallback position, so the American retreat proceeded in confusion, as many American officers later testified.

The Americans continued withdrawing in confusion until General Washington appeared on the scene and, in a flurry of activity, took command of the situation, ordering a brief rearguard action to buy time for the arriving units of the main body to be placed on high ground nearby. Had he not appeared when he did, there is every chance the vanguard units would have been savaged by the closing British columns, and Monmouth Courthouse would be remembered today as another incompetent disaster for American arms.

This then, in a nutshell, is what happened at Monmouth during those confused morning hours. The notion, advanced by some, that Lee "conducted" a withdrawal is not supported by fact. The advanced American units withdrew by and large on their own, and by the time General Lee ordered a general retreat, that retreat was already a fact, well beyond his orders or control. The supplementary proposition that Lee somehow "assisted" Washington by withdrawing the vanguard units to a point where the advancing British columns might come under withering artillery fire from Perrine's Hill is equally unfounded. When Washington encountered Lee on the field, Perrine's Hill was yet to be occupied, and there had been no tactical considerations inherent in the American withdrawal beyond sheer survival. Those, therefore, who have suggested that Lee is owed some degree of credit for the American success at Monmouth are engaging in fantasy.

General Charles Lee was supposedly a man of prodigious military knowledge and accomplishment, but if he was, his actions prior to and during the morning hours at Monmouth hardly support that assessment, and Monmouth is the only sustained action of any consequence we have to judge him by. Lee was a well-educated man, of course, had been in the military for most of his life, and no doubt had absorbed a great deal of military history and knowhow along the way. But understanding Alexander the Great's tactical genius at Gaugamela, for instance, does not make one an Alexander, any more than grasping Hannibal's utter destruction of the Roman legions at Cannae makes one a Hannibal. Knowledge, and the ability to employ it, are two different things and, given the facts, it is impossible to view General Lee's preparation and handling of his troops at Monmouth Courthouse except in the harshest light. Lee's performance at Monmouth fails in so many ways and on so many levels, that to call it amateurish serves only as an insult to amateurs. Perhaps it was only, for him, a bad day, but if so, it was a *very* bad day.

All that said, two of the three charges that were ultimately brought against General Lee were not only unfair, but factually untrue. The three charges were:

1. For disobedience of orders, in not attacking the enemy on 28th of June, agreeable to repeated instructions.

2. For misbehavior before the enemy on the same day, by making unnecessary, disorderly, and shameful retreat.

3. For disrespect to the Commander-in-Chief, in two letters dated 1st of July and the 28th June.[6]

Of course, at the time these charges were filed, Washington really had no clear understanding exactly what had happened that morning at Monmouth, and frankly, that *clear* understanding remained a bit fuzzy for quite some time. So, the charges made sense at the time they were filed, for it certainly appeared as though the vanguard units had been deliberately ordered into a retreat (just as Hamilton suggested in his letter to Boudinot), and Washington's order to attack simply disregarded by an officer who had an established penchant for disobeying direct orders and had argued forcefully against the very attack he had been ordered to make. But, in fairness, that was only an initial assessment, and an assessment that was to prove incorrect. The truth was, Lee was very much in the process of engaging in an offensive maneuver against the British that morning (no matter how ill-conceived), and the vanguard's withdrawal had been undertaken by the various unit commanders as a function of necessity, not Lee's orders, in response to an overwhelming British counterattack. The third charge, however, that of having disrespected the commander-in-chief, was the true dagger, for it was the absurd chain of General Lee's insulting, insolent letters that had apparently triggered all three charges in the first place. In other words, Washington, digesting Lee's disrespectful letters, appears to have concluded that he would give General Lee the trial he had demanded.

By means of his poor showing at Monmouth, and his subsequent string of foolish letters, Lee had demonstrated once and for all—surely to Washington's satisfaction—that he had no place in the upper echelons of leadership in the Continental Army. Those ridiculous letters, that continued to erupt from Lee's pen for weeks on end, hurled indiscriminately like hot blasts of literary shrapnel, in the end hardly helped his cause. Indeed, they doomed him, but typically, Lee was the last to grasp this obvious point, if indeed he ever actually came to grips with it. All of Lee's prior faults and failings—the attempts at usurpation, the flagrant disobedience of orders, his foolish capture by the British, his underhanded attempts at undermining Steuben's efforts; his prior unseemly comments about Washington (and others), his endlessly imperious attitude, his unfortunate after action statements regarding British military superiority—began to settle into clear focus. As a result, it became obvious that Lee could no longer be conceived as potential help to General Washington, but rather an unrelenting hindrance. Thus had he become persona non grata, a troublesome irritant that had to be removed from command. His trial would see to his removal.

In today's world, General Lee's troubling personality characteristics might be suggestive of what modern psychologists call Narcissistic Personality Disorder. But it requires no elaborate historical psychoanalysis to come to grips with General Charles Lee. His long track record of self-inflation, backbiting, slander, deceit, and repeated devious shenanigans, like footprints in the snow, paint a portrait of a man of decidedly low character, and vastly overshadow whatever military acumen he might have possessed. By virtually any measure, he was a painfully flawed human being, a man who had been given every opportunity to prove himself a worthy officer in the American cause yet had used many of those opportunities to injure others while attempting to promote himself. Now he had failed on the field of battle (rather miserably, in fact), but rather than accept that failure with a dose of humility and learn from it, he tried to spin that failure into success, and paint Washington's success as his own. Sadly, that this upside-down assertion was a flagrant, even *obvious* lie seemed beyond his capacity to digest, even though he was the one who had spun it.

Lee's trial began on July 4 as the army began its encampment at New Brunswick. The trial dragged on until August 12, meeting in various locations in New Jersey along the army's march route north to White Plains, finally convening in Peekskill, New York, where the final verdict was rendered. Lee pled not guilty to all charges and defended himself, at times sensibly and articulately, while at others sarcastically cross-examining witnesses, or lecturing at length on military arts and history. In all, some 39 witnesses were called to testify. Lord Stirling presided over the trial, while four generals and eight colonels formed the jury.[7] In that the charges against Lee had been brought by Washington himself, members of the jury did not require a weathervane to understand in which direction the storm was blowing, and those winds did not suggest good tidings for General Lee. As pointed out above, the first two charges against Lee were neither true nor fair, but by then it really didn't matter. Charles Lee seems never to have understood that the trial really wasn't technically about his conduct at Monmouth Courthouse; it was a referendum on Charles Lee the officer, his fitness to command. In that Lee had foolishly decided, essentially, to pit himself against General George Washington, the much-admired leader of the Continental Army, and the very man who most officers and men *knew* had saved the day at Monmouth, the outcome, regardless of testimony, was virtually assured. Washington kept his distance from the trial, allowing his officers to do the dirty work, but in fairness to the commander-in-chief, he had given Lee every opportunity to prove himself, only to be repeatedly slapped in the face for his efforts.

The final verdict was read on August 12, much to Lee's surprise and subsequent rage. He was found guilty on all three counts, although the term "shameful" was removed from the second charge. His penalty was to be removed from command for one year, this sent to Congress for confirmation. Congress voted to affirm the verdict on December 5, 1778. It would not be overstatement to suggest that Lee went ballistic.

Author Jeff Dacus, writing for *The Journal of the American Revolution,* writes: "After the trial Lee tried to exonerate himself through letters to Congress and newspapers, the 'paper war' he had wanted to avoid by court martial. The only results were the alienation of many supporters and of Congress. His personal attacks on Washington, and those close to him, resulted in a duel with one of the men he had referred to as an 'earwig,' John Laurens, the young son of the president of Congress. At the time appointed, Laurens wounded Lee in the side. Lee's wound was serious enough to persuade him to forgo fighting an additional duel with another of Washington's favorites, Anthony Wayne. In addition to Wayne, six other officers were waiting for their turn to duel the wounded major general, but his injury and placating letters ended his dueling career."[8]

Charles Lee continued haranguing friend and foe alike, until even Congress had had enough of him, voting to permanently cashier him from the army on January 10, 1780. For Washington it had been the simple expedient of addition by means of subtraction. Some in the Continental Army lamented the trial, the verdict, and Lee's departure, for sure. Many of the rank and file—not privy to the facts—had no informed opinion, while for most officers in the know, it was good riddance.

Twenty

Greenwood

After a while it rained, hailed, snowed, and froze

The Battle of Monmouth Courthouse, along with the testimony at Lee's trial, demonstrated the basic fact—oft repeated in this narrative—that the Continental Army lacked capable leadership at the division level. Yes, Steuben had taught the rank and file to march and fight almost like a professional army, but decision making at the army's highest levels remained suspect. Indeed, Washington's own management of the Monmouth Campaign—before his stunning performance on the field during the early afternoon hours of the 28th, that is—was far from credible, in that he had created the very command problem he later sought to solve with the elevation of Lafayette, then later Lee. Looking back now, it is easy to see that the colonial era in America had been a vibrant incubator for democratic thought, not the science of war. That would not change until the establishment of the United States Military Academy at West Point in 1802, an invaluable addition for the nation's continued viability.

Lee's morning failure at Monmouth has led some to speculate that the commander-in-chief might well have been better served had he left the Marquis in command of the vanguard units, but this, of course, remains speculation. Considering the Marquis' prior performances, however, both at Barren Hill and his few days immediately prior to Monmouth, that suggestion seems overly optimistic. At Barren Hill Lafayette had ignored Washington's specific orders, only to see his entire command virtually enveloped and swept up by the British, while preceding Monmouth he promptly marched well beyond the main body's support, exhausting his troops to the point that entire units began to physically break down. Simply put, at the time, the Marquis appears to have been too young and inexperienced to have handled an assignment of such magnitude, and that analysis suggests disaster rather than success. We will never know, of course, but had Lafayette been in charge of the American vanguard on the morning of the 28th, he may well have jubilantly marched the advanced units into the jaws of Clinton's counter attack, with no more reconnaissance or sensible preparation than Lee himself had taken.

There was one other officer in the field during the Monmouth Campaign, however, worth mentioning. He would, given time, prove to be one of the finest field officers in American combat history, but in June 1778, the full extent of his talent remained unclear. That officer was Colonel Daniel Morgan, then in command of a forward unit of sharpshooting select men, and well-known to Washington as an able commander of frontier style, hit-and-run tactics. At Saratoga Morgan's Riflemen had been an invaluable asset in forcing the British surrender, and he had done nothing to diminish his image as a capable officer since returning. Unfortunately, it would not be until 1781 that Morgan would be promoted to Brigadier General. Then, in the wilds of South Carolina during the Southern Campaign, Morgan's corps ran roughshod over an elite contingent of British infantry and cavalry sent to run him down in a brilliant display of leadership and tactical ingenuity.[1] Unfortunately, at Monmouth Morgan's military genius was either unknown or not yet fully developed, and he and his entire unit remained regrettably out of action due to Lee's staff errors, previously mentioned.

In the end, however, Lee's bumbling failure was in all probability the most fortunate thing that could have happened to the Americans that morning, although it was *entirely* fortuitous! The clumsy withdrawal inadvertently brought the vanguard back to defensible ground just as the commander-in-chief was approaching the field where, in a burst of fury and activity, he took firm command of the battle, just one more example of how luck, or Providence, or simple good fortune saved the American cause—and there were many such examples during the course of the war.

Those fortuitous examples of success have led some over the years to suggest that Providence had a firm hand in directing the American cause, a theory that remains far beyond the scope of this narrative to resolve. Theology aside, however, the American Revolution *was* a far different war than those that had ravaged the world since warfare had first reared its ugly head, approximately twelve thousand years earlier.[2] It was not, for instance, a predatory conflict, instigated to conquer bordering countries, or lands useful for a vast array of strategic purposes. Nor was it a war predicated upon tribal, regional, ethnic, or religious hostilities, the sorts of conflicts that had raged globally for generations. Rarely indeed, in the long history of human warfare, had a conflict been instigated over *ideas*, yet the American War for Independence was just such a confrontation. As such, it was a contest the British military mind had a difficult time coming to grips with, for none of the old rules of warfare seemed to apply.

The British conquered American ports, suffocating the rebels' supply of imports, and making export almost impossible, but this seemed only to spur the Americans on all the more. Regions were occupied, but Washington's army simply moved off to fight again, while local rebels took their turn at guerrilla warfare. Even when Howe had thumped Washington at Brandywine Creek, then marched north to occupy Philadelphia, the American capital—a triumph of arms that would surely have ended virtually any European conflict—the Continental Army simply slipped away to Valley Forge. Meanwhile, Congress departed for York, Pennsylvania, where it conducted business as usual, as if nothing of significance had occurred. For British generals this posed a perplexing question: how, exactly, were these Americans to be conquered, after all, if they refused to play by the rules? Classic British military strategies had failed, one after the other, because they seemed never to understand that they were fighting against ideas, and ideas had no front or rear, no flanks or lines of supply. Ideas existed in individual minds, and those minds were *everywhere*. As military historian Robert L. O'Connell notes, "Boston, New York, Philadelphia, and Charleston—all key colonial cities had been occupied, but always without decisive results. And still the countryside remained rebellious, a dangerous morass where every tree hid a potential rebel sharpshooter."[3]

Because the American Revolution was fundamentally about a new way of conceiving the individual in relation to his or her government, it represented a sea change, not only in terms of the psychology of the individual, but also regarding the very purpose and authority of government itself. Monarchy—or its cultural equivalents around the world—had prevailed across the globe for eons, and the American Revolution represented one of the first serious threats to that long-established tradition. O' Connell: "The ancien régime was a bulwark against change in a time of transition, a delicately balanced mechanism poised on a volcano. Given the forces to which it was subject, it proved remarkably tenacious. Yet in the end all would be swept away."[4] The volcanic forces O'Connell refers to were, of course, the seismic disruptions that democratic principles inherently represented to the age-old order, and a volcano that tyrannical regimes to this day (secular and religious alike) struggle mightily to suppress.

Unsurprisingly, news of the American victory at Monmouth was hailed often in the most grandiose terms, sometimes with great exaggeration, but this was hardly surprising for such a struggling enterprise. Indeed, for the American cause, the winter of 1777–1778 at Valley Forge had surely seen some of its darkest days, making the news of victory—any victory!—electrifying for its supporters. Ideas of independence, individual freedom and rights, were powerful incentives to fight for in a world dominated by warlords, tyrants, and monarchs, and Monmouth Courthouse most certainly gave those who believed in the Revolution an enormous shot in the arm. Some even fancied Washington's success proof positive that the war was on a short road to victory for the Americans, but they were quickly disappointed.

Monmouth may have been a wonderful propaganda coup for the

American cause but, on the ground, it changed very little. The Continental Army marched for White Plains, a town just north of New York City, where it settled in, while the British enjoyed the comforts and defenses of the city itself for the next two years. In the North the war settled into a standoff, neither side strong enough to overpower the other, so for the next two years the war remained in a sort of uncomfortable impasse, each side eyeballing the other, to no event. A strong French force finally arrived to reinforce Washington's Continental Army, but the staredown around New York would not resolve until late summer, 1781. It was then when Washington received urgent news from Lafayette—who by then was in command of a significant cavalry force in Virginia—that General Cornwallis, then in charge of the British Southern Campaign, had moved to a location on the Chesapeake Bay at Yorktown where he might be quickly enveloped and pinned against the shores of the Bay. Washington responded at once—leaving a covering force around New York to deceive Clinton—then headed south, leading both the Continentals and French troops toward Yorktown.

The lead elements of the American force arrived at Yorktown in late September, and immediately initiated siege operations. It was around this time when another remarkably fortuitous event occurred. The French Fleet under Comte de Grasse was, by a stroke of good luck, just then returning from operations in the Caribbean and ran headfirst into a British Fleet sent to relieve Cornwallis at Yorktown. The French soundly defeated the British in what came to be called the Battle of the Chesapeake, and with that Cornwallis became entirely cut off, by land and sea alike. At Yorktown, Washington immediately began tightening his grip around the British troops.

Not surprisingly, Joseph Plumb Martin was near at hand, now in an elite unit of miners and sappers, charged with the duties of siege operations. This consisted of digging a series of parallel trenches, each trench moving ever closer to the enemy. "We now began to make preparations for laying close siege to the enemy," Martin tells us. "We had holed him and nothing remained but to dig him out. Accordingly, after every precaution to prevent his escape, [we] settled our guards, provided facines [bundles of wood or brush over which dirt is placed to form parapets] and gabions [containers of stone or sand], made platforms for the batteries, to be laid down when needed, brought on our battering pieces, ammunition, &c. On the fifth of October we began to put our plans into execution."[5] During one dark night in the trenches, Martin had the good fortune of coming across the commander-in-chief himself, when a stranger, asking questions, suddenly appeared in the trenches nearby. "The stranger inquired what troops we were, talked familiarly with us a few minutes, when, being informed which way the officers had gone, he went off in the same direction.... In a short time the engineers returned and the afore-mentioned stranger with them. They discoursed together some time when, by the officers often calling him 'Your Excellency,' we discovered that it was General Washington. Had we dared, we might have cautioned him for exposing himself too carelessly to danger at such a time, and doubtless he would have taken it in good part if we had."[6]

The American parallels crept ever closer. Faced with a hopeless situation, on October 17 Cornwallis requested terms, and on the 19th he surrendered, for all intents and purposes ending the War for American Independence. According to many accounts of the surrender, the British band played the old English ballad *The World Turned Upside Down* as the red-coated troops marched out and stacked their arms. If true, it was surely appropriate for the moment, for many then standing at attention in the American ranks were the same who had endured the cold and misery of Valley Forge, Steuben's endless drills, and finally the march and battle at Monmouth Courthouse. For them, and for the British who surrendered, it surely must have seemed as if the world had indeed been turned upside down.

Fortunately, Joseph Martin, now waiting anxiously in the ranks, provides a bird's eye view of the momentous event. According to Martin, the Americans had waited quite some time for the British to finally show themselves for the official surrender, but "they were compelled at last, by necessity, to appear, all armed, with bayonets fixed, drums beating, and faces lengthening. They were led by General O'Hara [Cornwallis having feigned illness], with the American General Lincoln on his right, the Americans and French beating a march as they passed out between them. It was a noble sight to us, and the more so, as it seemed to promise a speedy conclusion to the contest.... The British paid the Americans, seemingly, but little attention as they passed them, but they eyed the French with considerable malice depicted in their countenances. They marched to the place appointed and stacked their arms."[7] It would take two more years to finalize the treaty of peace in Paris, finally officially ending the war, and granting British recognition for the United States of America.

Martin remained in the army for most of those two long, additional years, before finally returning to New England. For him, the war had been an extraordinary experience, an epic tale of hardship, fatigue, and valor. He had joined the army as a boy and departed as a man. Martin's story seems quite remarkable, but in many ways, it was typical of the young men who fought for the American cause. In Europe young men generally had to be dragged into the ranks, but boys were very often quite motivated to fight on the American side. Elijah Fisher, often quoted in this narrative, was only seventeen when he took part in the Battle of Bunker Hill. He went on to serve a total of six years in the Continental Army, and his was not an unusual story. Indeed, in many ways the fighting in the ranks was done by young men, and some of their individual stories are breathtaking. These

young men were not only witness to some of America's most iconic historical events but helped create much of that history themselves. In so doing,
many of them lived lives of adventure, deprivation, and violence far beyond
anything most of us can even imagine today.

John Greenwood, for instance, was born in Boston in 1760. One of his
best friends was killed in the "Boston Massacre" of 1770, and he witnessed
first-hand the Boston Tea Party of 1773. He later joined the Massachusetts
militia, and endured the brutal hardships of the Canadian Campaign. He
then fought with General Washington on his famous Trenton raid of 1776.
One of the first across the frozen Delaware River that freezing night, upon
reaching the New Jersey shore he recalled, "After a while it rained, hailed,
snowed, and froze." Surviving the attack on Trenton, Greenwood was so
consumed by the itch that ill health forced his return home. Once cured,
however, he signed on as a seaman on an American warship and finished
the Revolution fighting at sea.[8]

The tale of Ebenezer Fox is even more intriguing. Born into a poor
Massachusetts farming family, at the age of only twelve he ran away from
home and signed on as a cabin boy on a merchant ship. When war broke out,
however, that ship had to be beached and Ebenezer was forced to jump overboard and swim for his life as British bullets stung the water all around him.
He then signed on with the American warship *Protector* and fought the British at sea, only later to be taken prisoner and tossed into the infamous *Jersey*,
the worst prison ship in the waters surrounding New York City. Attempting
escape, he was captured and immediately impressed into the British Army.
Fox was then shipped off to Jamaica in the Caribbean, where soon thereafter he escaped with some mates. Wandering across the island for days, they
finally found the north shore, stole a boat, and frantically sailed for Cuba as
a band of angry Jamaicans followed in pursuit, firing muskets and cannons
most of the way. In Cuba Fox signed on as a seaman with the American warship *Flora* but was grabbed onshore and impressed into service on a French
vessel. That night he jumped overboard and swam through shark-infested
waters all the way back to the *Flora*. The ship then sailed for France but had
to wait out the war in the port of Bordeaux due to the British coastal block-
ade. When the war finally ended in 1783, Fox returned home to Boston and
the serene life—of all things—of a barber.[9]

From Bunker Hill, to Valley Forge, from Monmouth to victory at
Yorktown, the American Revolution required a rare blend of guts, determination, and fighting spirit. Ebenezer Fox, Joseph Plumb Martin, Elijah
Fisher, and John Greenwood were just a few examples of individuals who
entered the American service as boys, but departed after years of adventure, hardship, and battle as mature young men. That they all survived
their varied experiences is remarkable but, in a larger sense, their trials

were emblematic of the young nation they served, a nation that was still very much in its infancy. Of course, there were also thousands of mature men who served in the ranks and officer corps of the Continental Army (and many women who assisted the cause in one way or another) during those six long years, not to mention those who contributed to the militias of the various states. These soldiers—from General George Washington on down to the youngest drummer—all played varying roles in an extraordinary tale, and roles they would never forget. Together they defeated the greatest military power of the age, and in so doing established a new, independent nation. Equally as important, however, these were the same men and women who returned home as citizens, to seed the character and future of the nation they had just labored to create. As a result, they collectively helped lead the world into a new era of democratic government, freedom, and individual rights, fundamental achievements that today we all take for granted. In that sense, their efforts were simply the first chapter in what today remains the most consequential legal, social, and political revolution in history. That's why their stories are worth remembering.

Appendix:
Selected Biographies

Sir Henry Clinton: Born April 16, 1730 (?), into the aristocratic Clinton family in Cornwall, England. His family left for North America due to his father's military assignment, and Henry was educated in New York City. In 1745 he joined the New York militia as a lieutenant, and in 1749 returned home to London where he was commissioned in the British Army. In 1762 he was wounded at the Battle of Nauheim during the Seven Years' War and later promoted to the rank of general in 1772. In 1767 he married Harriet Carter, and the couple had five children. Unfortunately, Harriet died in August 1772, sending Henry into a deep depression. In 1775 he accompanied Sir William Howe to the United States as second in command of British forces in North America. Knighted in 1778, Sir Henry took supreme command in 1778 after Howe's retirement. In 1781, after the British defeat at Yorktown, Henry resigned his commission and returned to England, where he was shocked to discover popular opinion decidedly against him for the British defeat in North America. In 1783, and in his defense, he wrote a *Narrative of the Campaign of 1781,* and in 1790 was elected to Parliament. In 1793 he was promoted Governor of Gibraltar but died before he could take post. He is buried in St. George Chapel, Windsor Castle, U.K.

Elijah Fisher: Born June 18, 1758, in Norton, Massachusetts, he first volunteered his service to the American cause in 1775. Fisher was at the Battle of Bunker Hill and saw action at Saratoga. He was appointed to General Washington's "Life Guard" and served for the duration of the war. After hostilities ended, Fisher moved to northern Maine where he purchased land, built a cabin, and began life as a farmer. He later married Jerusha Keen of Turner, Maine, and the two settled down near Livermore. Their marriage produced eight children. Elijah died in 1841 at the age of 83, and is buried near Livermore, Maine.

Nathanael Greene: Born August 7, 1742, in Potowomat, Rhode Island, into a prosperous Quaker family. As a youngster, Greene was widely read, and essentially educated himself before imploring his father to hire a tutor to expand his education. Prior to the Revolution, Greene was instrumental in the founding of the Kentish Guards. He was promoted to the rank of general and given command of the unit when it marched to join the rebellion at Boston. Greene quickly fell under the eye of General George Washington, and over time became Washington's virtual right-hand man. In 1778 he was given the job of Quartermaster General, which he handled superbly. In 1780 Greene was sent south to command the Southern Army after Horatio Gates's disastrous defeat at Camden, and divided his army as the British, then under Cornwallis, went into winter quarters. One half of Greene's army was then under command of General Daniel Morgan, and in January 1781 Morgan delivered a serious blow to Cornwallis by defeating Banastre Tarleton at Cowpens, South Carolina. The Southern Campaign then moved into North Carolina, where Greene met Cornwallis at Guilford Courthouse, a tactical draw for both sides. Greene then returned to South Carolina where he handled the Southern Army until war's end. After the war he moved to Georgia with his wife Caty and children, and built a plantation known as Mulberry Hill. Unfortunately, in 1786 while inspecting crops at a nearby plantation, Greene suffered heat stroke, and died a few days thereafter at the age of forty-three. He is buried at Johnson Square, Savannah, Georgia.

Alexander Hamilton: Born January 11, 1757, in Charleston, capital of the island of Nevis, located in the Leeward Islands. His parents were Rachael Faucette and James Hamilton, a Scotsman. Alexander and his brother James were denied an ordinary education on the island in that their parents were not properly married, and his mother later moved to the island of St. Croix in order to avoid legal complications. His mother died of yellow fever in 1758 when Alexander was only eleven, leaving him and his brother alone as orphans. Alexander found a job as a clerk at the import-export firm of Beekman & Cruger which had contacts in London and New York City. He remained in that capacity for four years. He impressed many locals with his intelligence, and in 1772 enough money was raised to send him off to Boston to be formally educated. He arrived in Boston that year, then traveled to New York City. Alexander began taking classes at the Elizabethtown Academy in Elizabeth, New Jersey, and entered King's College (modern Columbia University) in 1774. There he excelled as a student, began writing political pieces, and became a strong advocate for revolution. (British troops occupied the city before Hamilton could graduate, but he returned after the war and passed the New York bar exam.) After the clashes at Lexington and Concord Hamilton turned his attention to military matters. He raised an artillery unit, and was involved in the battles of White Plains, Trenton, and Princeton. Ultimately, due to his intelligence and education, Hamilton found his way into Washington's inner circle as an aide de camp, and later as chief staff aide. He served in that capacity until the end of the war, when Washington finally consented to give him a field command. That unit fought with distinction at Yorktown. After the war Hamilton won election to Congress from New York. He became a delegate to the Constitutional Convention and urged ratification of the Constitution through a series of articles written with John Jay and James Madison known as *The Federalist Papers,* urging a strong central government. Hamilton then became the first Secretary of the Treasury in the Washington administration, and is remembered for his ideas regarding payment of the national debt and empowering a national bank, among others. He resigned from that position in 1795, and for a period practiced law in New York. He later returned to Congress and was hotly involved in the presidential election of 1800. When the electoral votes in Congress became tied between Thomas Jefferson and Aaron Burr, Hamilton eventually broke the tie by voting for Jefferson. Four years later, Hamilton worked tirelessly to defeat Burr in the New York governor's campaign, and when Burr lost, he challenged Hamilton to a duel for disparaging remarks Hamilton had allegedly made. The duel took place in Weehawken, New Jersey, across the Hudson River from Manhattan on July 12, 1804. Hamilton was mortally wounded in the duel and died the next day. He is buried in Trinity Churchyard, Manhattan, New York.

Lafayette: Marie-Joseph Paul Yves Roch Gilbert du Motier de Lafayette was born on September 6, 1757, at his family's estate in Auvergne, France. His family's lineage was one of the most respected and venerable in the history of the country. When his father was killed in battle in 1759, his grief-stricken mother fled for Paris, and the young Lafayette was left to be raised by his grandmother. At the age of eleven he was summoned to live with his mother in Paris and later enrolled in the University of Paris along with a school for Musketeers. Both his mother and grandmother died in 1770, leaving Lafayette an enormous inheritance. In 1773 he was commissioned a lieutenant in the Dragoons, and at the age of sixteen he married Marie Adrienne Francoise (age fourteen). They remained happily married until her death in 1807. The affairs in North America began then to draw his attention, and he soon became convinced that Republican virtues and the American cause were at one with his own ideals. His family was desperate to keep him from leaving, but he avoided their intrigues, and purchased the sailing vessel *Victoire.* He arrived off the South Carolina coast on June 13, 1777. He then made the long trip north to Philadelphia, and later was presented to General Washington. The two formed a natural bond, and Congress accepted Lafayette's offer to serve as a volunteer with no pay. His early command functions at both Barren Hill and Monmouth were questionable, but by war's end he had developed into a reasonably capable officer. He was instrumental in following and then trapping General Cornwallis at Yorktown. After the war he returned to France, now a hero on two continents. He was hailed in France and worked to negotiate trade agreements between France and the U.S., as well as helping to reduce American debt. He also became active in the cause of abolition and wrote Washington, urging him to free his slaves. In 1784 Lafayette returned to the United States to revisit many of his old friends and comrades. His arrival was celebrated wherever he went, and the states of Maryland, Virginia, Connecticut, and Massachusetts all granted him citizenship. Lafayette then returned to France where political trouble was brewing. A fiscal crisis had the government and common people in an uproar. The king was unable and unwilling to cede power to a more unified government, and on July 14, 1786, the Bastille was stormed by a raging mob. Lafayette was appointed leader of the National Guard, and attempted to maintain order, but revolution had run riot, and order became impossible. A new constitution was finally put into place in 1791, and France then declared war against Austria the following year. Lafayette, a general in the French forces, attempted to lead his troops into battle, but many of the French troops were influenced by the political views of the radical Jacobins, and refused to fight. Lafayette returned to Paris where he spoke forcefully against the radical elements of the French Revolution, but this put him at odds with the Jacobins, who were then ascendant. Hoping to flee to America, Lafayette was captured by the Austrians, and he—along with his family—would remain imprisoned until 1797. In the following years, with the rise of Napoleon, Lafayette declined to return to French politics. In 1825 President Monroe and Congress invited him back to the U.S. to celebrate the country's fiftieth anniversary. Lafayette responded with a tour of all the states and was virtually swarmed along the way by well-wishers. He returned to France in 1825, survived yet another revolution, and died on May 20, 1834. He was laid to rest next to his wife in the Picpus Cemetery, Paris, where his son, Georges Washington Lafayette, sprinkled soil Lafayette had secured from Bunker Hill atop his grave.

John Laurens: Born October 28, 1754, in Charleston, South Carolina, into the wealthy Laurens family. He lived at home and was tutored until the age of sixteen, at which time his family moved to Great Britain, where John was educated in private schools in London, and later Geneva, Switzerland. He returned to England and entered Middle Temple to study law. On October 26, 1776, he married Martha Manning—apparently a marriage of necessity—but left his pregnant wife behind in December of that year to return to the United States and fight for the American cause. His father, then President of Congress, was able to secure a position for him on Washington's staff, but Laurens had an unnecessarily reckless streak which he often displayed in battle. He fought wildly at Brandywine and was wounded at Germantown. He was also heavily involved during the most intense fighting at Monmouth Courthouse. Laurens, a son of some privilege from the South, was nevertheless an early advocate for the abolition of slavery and argued for a Continental brigade to be formed of freed slaves. His ideas, unfortunately, were not widely supported. After the British defeat at Yorktown, Laurens returned to South Carolina, where he was involved in the ongoing Southern Campaign waged by Nathanael Greene. On August 27, 1782, he rose from a sickbed to lead a foolish charge against a strong British position on the Combahee River, not far from Charleston. His command was decimated, and Laurens shot dead during the assault, only weeks before the British evacuated Charleston. He is buried at Mepkin Abbey, South Carolina.

Charles Lee: Born February 6, 1732, into the aristocratic Lee family in Darnhall, Cheshire, England. He was educated at the King Edward VI school and Bury St. Edmunds, until being sent off to private school in Switzerland. His father, John, then colonel of the 55th Foot, purchased an ensign's commission for him in April 1747. Charles was then stationed in Ireland, and later purchased a lieutenant's commission after the death of his father. In 1754 he was redeployed to North America and saw action during the French and Indian War (called the Seven Years' War in Europe). He took part in General Braddock's disastrous march west, and later married the daughter of a Mohawk chief, who bore him twins. In 1756 he purchased a captain's commission, took part in the assault on Louisbourg, and was wounded during the attack on Fort Ticonderoga. He also participated in the taking of Fort Niagara and the capture of Montreal. Lee then returned to Europe where he served as a lieutenant colonel in the Portuguese Army. His unit fought with some distinction at Vila Velha. He then returned to England and was retired at half-pay. Moving on to Poland, he worked as an aide de camp for King Stanislaus II but returned to England after the Seven Years' War ended in Europe. Finding himself sympathetic to the colonies' dispute with the English crown, he moved to North America in 1773 and purchased property in present day West Virginia. For a short period he traveled the colonies, then, when war erupted at Boston, expected to be offered command of the American forces. He bristled when this command was not forthcoming and held a grudge against Washington thereafter. Lee accepted a general's commission in the Continental Army and served in South Carolina and later New York without distinction. He was captured in 1776 at a tavern in New Jersey and held by the British until exchanged in 1778. Restored to a ranking position in the Continental Army, he performed poorly at Monmouth Courthouse, and was tried and removed from the army as a result. Having verbally attacked Washington and many of his officers, Lee became the target of much animosity, and was challenged to numerous duels. John Laurens shot Lee during one such duel, and the wounded Lee begged off the others. Cashiered from the army by Congress in 1780, he returned to his home and dogs in the Shenandoah Valley until October 2, 1782, when he fell ill in a tavern in Philadelphia and died, essentially a forgotten man. Lee's legacy was further tarnished when George Moore, working for the New York Historical Society in 1850, uncovered and published a document written by Lee in March 1777—while in British custody—offering a detailed plan for the defeat of the Continental Army. While Lee's precise motives for penning the plan remain debatable, the discovery hardly enhanced his image. Lee was buried in Christ Church graveyard, Philadelphia.

Joseph Plumb Martin: Born November 21, 1760, to the Rev. Ebenezer Martin and Susannah Plumb in Becket, Massachusetts. At the age of seven, due to financial problems, he was sent to live with his grandparents in Milford, Connecticut. At the age of 15 he joined the Connecticut militia, and later reenlisted in the Continental Army in April 1777. He fought during the New York Campaign, and his unit later rejoined the main army near Philadelphia after the battle of Germantown. He wintered in Downingtown, Pennsylvania, during the Valley Forge encampment of 1777–1778 as a forager and later took part in the battle of Monmouth Courthouse. Martin was promoted to sergeant, and took part in the siege at Yorktown, where as a sapper he helped dig the parallel lines that led to the British surrender. After the war he moved to northern Maine, purchased land, and worked as a farmer. In 1794 he married Lucy Clewley, and the couple had five children. In his later years Martin penned *A Narrative of Some of the Adventures, Dangers and Sufferings of a Revolutionary Soldier, Interspersed with Anecdotes of Incidents That Occurred Within His Own Observation,* a work that is now considered a classic of the Revolutionary period for its breadth, insight, and dry humor. Interestingly, it is recorded that in 1836 a platoon of U.S. infantry, while marching through nearby Prospect, got word of Martin's Revolutionary War escapades, and marched promptly to his home and fired a salute to honor his service. Martin died on May 2, 1850, at the age of eighty-nine. He and his wife are buried in Sandy Point Cemetery, Stockton Springs, Maine.

Baron von Steuben: Friedrich Wilhelm von Steuben was born in September 1730 in Magdeburg, Germany, to Baron Wilhelm Von Steuben and the former Elizabeth von Jagvadin. His father served as an engineer in posts throughout Russia and Prussia, and Friedrich was educated in small garrison towns in those countries. At the age of sixteen he entered the Prussian service as an officer cadet, and at the age of twenty-two was commissioned a lieutenant. He served in the Seven Years' War and was wounded at the Battle of Prague, and again at Kunersdorf. Promoted captain, he served as an aide de camp to Frederick the Great and was later selected for a special officer training course taught by the king himself, from which Steuben was later dropped. Leaving the army due to downsizing in 1763, he moved on to a minor governmental post which he held until 1777, at which time, desperate for employment, he sailed for the United States as a volunteer. General Washington found Steuben's unique qualifications of use, and almost immediately charged the baron with the task of training the Continental Army. In this Steuben proved remarkably successful, transforming what had been a brave and dedicated group of amateurs into something approaching a professional fighting force in a matter of months. For this he was given the position of Inspector General and promoted to the rank of major general. After Monmouth Courthouse, Steuben prepared a manual of uniform drill, known thereafter as the *Blue Book*, which remained the official infantry manual for decades. Steuben then assisted Nathanael Greene during the Southern Campaign, and after Yorktown was discharged from the army in 1784. The state of Pennsylvania granted him citizenship, and Congress voted him a substantial pension. He died at his northern New York property on November 28, 1794, in Oneida County, and is buried on the grounds

Albegence Waldo: Born February 27, 1749, in Pomfret, Connecticut, to Zacharia and Abigail Waldo. He was married on November 19, 1772, in Windham, Connecticut, to Lydia Hurlbutt and the couple had seven children. He was later married to Lucy Cargill in 1787, presumably because his first wife had passed on. He first appears in the Revolutionary record as a clerk in Samuel McClellan's company, and later as a surgeon's mate in the Eighth Connecticut Regiment. He next appears as surgeon on the American ship *Oliver Cromwell*, then again as a full surgeon attached to Huntington's Brigade, First Connecticut Infantry. Much of his life remains a mystery, particularly his post-war years. His diary of the first few months of the Valley Forge encampment has been much appreciated for its insight and pathos. He died 29 January 1794; location unknown.

George Washington: Born February 22, 1732, in Westmorland County, Virginia, to Augustine and Mary Ball Washington, a landowning family of reasonable means. George did not receive a formal education, but was schooled in English, mathematics, and surveying, and in 1748 he was contracted by William Fairfax to survey the Fairfax family's Shenandoah Valley holdings. He inherited Mount Vernon from his brother Lawrence in 1761 when Lawrence passed away. In 1752 Washington was put in command of one of Virginia's militia districts, with the rank of major. The following year Governor Dinwiddie charged him with the special mission of taking a message to the French authorities in the Ohio Territory. This involved a trip through wilderness of some two and a half months, and Washington's successful return brought him notoriety when his report was printed in the colonies and London. In 1754 he was promoted to command of the Virginia Regiment, but his actions in the Ohio Territory ignited the French and Indian War when, in charge of regulars and Indian allies, they fell upon a group of French officers and men, who were mistakenly slaughtered. The French became enraged. Washington fell back to a fort he had constructed earlier called Fort Necessity, but the French followed and forced a disgraceful surrender. In 1775 Washington accompanied Braddock's expedition into the Ohio Territory, and was credited with a skillful performance for forming a rearguard and allowing what remained of the expedition to escape, after being attacked by the French and their Indian allies. This action revived confidence in Washington's military abilities, and in 1759 he was promoted to the command of the Virginia Regiment. Tiring of military life, in 1759 he married Martha Dandridge Custis, a widower and owner of a substantial estate. He immediately adopted the life of a Virginia planter, and soon entered politics. He was elected to Virginia's House of Burgesses from Frederick Country in 1758, and soon became an acknowledged force in Virginia's social and political aristocracy. Over the next decade and a half, he became increasingly distressed over British policy toward the colonies, and openly opposed many of the acts imposed by the crown. In 1775 the Continental Congress established the Continental Army in response to the fighting around Boston, and Washington was chosen as the army's commander over John Hancock and Charles Lee. From 1775 until victory in 1783 Washington served as commander of the American forces and, more than any other individual, is today credited with the final American triumph. Historically, such a victory often led to the seizing of power by the victor, but Washington made it known that he had no such designs. King George, upon hearing of Washington's disinterest in power, remarked that, if true, Washington would be "The greatest man in the world." After the Revolution, Washington promptly delivered his commission to Congress, and returned to civilian life. In 1787 he was called out of retirement and unanimously elected to preside over the Constitutional Convention as President General. Upon adoption of the new constitution, Washington was elected the first President of the United States, then reelected in 1791. He served two full terms and retired from public life in 1797. By means of his military career he secured the freedom and sovereignty of the United States and developed the structure of its armed forces. Through his role as President General he helped guide the Constitutional Convention toward an organizational format that has endured for centuries. By means of his two presidential administrations, Washington established the scope of the presidency itself, its style and parameters, helped guide the nation through a raft of early difficulties—foreign and domestic—and lastly exited gracefully in a peaceful exchange of power that even today remains the envy of the world. While Washington can certainly be criticized for his lagging views on slavery, he was nonetheless—as historian James Thomas Flexner styled him—*The Indispensable Man*, the one individual without whom the Revolution, the early government, and the infant nation would never have come into being, or long survived. George Washington died on December 14, 1799. He is buried along with his wife Martha at Mount Vernon.

Chapter Notes

Prologue

1. Martin, Joseph Plumb. *A Narrative of Some of the Adventures, Dangers and Sufferings of a Revolutionary Soldier*, ed. George E. Scheer (Boston: Little, Brown and Co., 1962) 99.

2. Waldo, Albigence. "Valley Forge, 1777-1778. Diary of Surgeon Albigence Waldo, of the Connecticut Line." *The Pennsylvania Magazine of History and Biography* (1897) 21, no. 3: 303–304.

3. Martin, 98.

4. Waldo, 304.

5. Martin, 99.

6. Stoudt, John, Joseph, *Ordeal At Valley Forge* (Philadelphia: University of Pennsylvania Press, 1963) 20.

7. Waldo, 305.

8. Ibid, 305.

9. Ibid, 306.

10. Martin, 99.

11. Dearborn, Henry, *Revolutionary War Journals of Henry Dearborn*, ed. Lloyd A. Brown and Howard H. Peckham (Chicago: The Caxton Club, 1939) December 18.

12. Martin, 100.

13. McCullough, David, *1776* (New York: Simon & Schuster, 2005) 25.

14. Stoudt, 22.

15. Martin, 101.

16. George Washington to John Parke Custis, February 1, 1778, *The Papers of George Washington, Revolutionary War Series*, W.W Abbott, Dorothy Twohig, Philander D. Chase, Edward G. Lengel, Theodore J. Crackel, and David R. Hoth, eds. (Charlottesville: University of Virginia Press, 1998-1999).

17. Stoudt, 25.

18. Elijah Fisher, *Elijah Fisher's Journal While in the War for Independence, and Continued Two Years After He Came to Maine, 1775-1784* (Augusta, Press of Badger and Manley, 1880) 7.

19. (Trussell, John B. B., Jr., *Epic on the Schuylkill* (Harrisburg: Pennsylvania Historical and Museum Commission, 1992) 1.

Chapter One

1. (1909) Bureau, United States Census. Population in the Colonial and Continental Periods. In a Century of Population Growth from the First Census of the U.S. to the Twelfth (Section 1). Retrieved from arachive.org/stream/centuryofpopulat00unite#page/2.

2. Martin, 103.

3. Waldo, 309.

4. "From George Washington to Henry Laurens, 23 December 1777," *Founders Online*, National Archives, last modified June 13, 2018, http://founders.archives.gov/documents/Washington/03-12-02-0628. [Original source: *The Papers of George Washington*, Revolutionary War Series, vol. 12, *26 October 1777–25 December 1777*, ed. Frank E. Grizzard, Jr., and David R. Hoth. Charlottesville: University of Virginia Press, 2002, pp. 683–687.]

5. Ellis, Joseph, *His Excellency, George Washington* (New York: Vintage Books, 2004) 11–12.

6. "From George Washington to Samuel Washington, 18 December 1776," *Founders Online*, National Archives, last modified June 13, 2018, http://founders.archives.gov/documents/Washington/03-07-02-0299. [Original source: *The Papers of George Washington*, Revolutionary War Series, vol.

7, *21 October 1776–5 January 1777*, ed. Philander D. Chase. Charlottesville: University of Virginia Press, 1997, pp. 369–372.]

7. Numerous texts and sources have been used to produce the biographical information regarding George Washington in this book, but the most prominent were two highly recommended modern biographies. The first is Joseph J. Ellis' *His Excellency, George Washington* (New York: Vintage Books, 2004), and the second is Ron Chernow's *Washington; A Life* (New York: Penguin Books, 2010).

8. "General Orders, 20 December 1777," *Founders Online*, National Archives, last modified June 13, 2018, http://founders.archives.gov/documents/Washington/03-12-02-0584. [Original source: *The Papers of George Washington*, Revolutionary War Series, vol. 12, *26 October 1777–25 December 1777*, ed. Frank E. Grizzard, Jr., and David R. Hoth. Charlottesville: University of Virginia Press, 2002, pp. 641–644.]

9. Martin, 103.

10. Waldo, 309–310.

11. Stoudt, 31.

12. Trussell, Jr., 5.

13. Dearborn, 25th.

14. Waldo, 312.

15. Stoudt, 39.

16. Dearborn, 26th.

Chapter Two

1. Stoudt, 45–47.

2. "General Orders, 18 December 1777," *Founders Online*, National Archives, last modified June 13, 2018, http://founders.archives.gov/documents/Washington/03-12-02-0573. [Original source: *The Papers of George Washington*, Revolutionary War Series, vol. 12, *26 October 1777–25 December 1777*, ed. Frank E. Grizzard, Jr., and David R. Hoth. Charlottesville: University of Virginia Press, 2002, pp. 626–628.]

3. Brier, Marc, A., "*Tollerably Comfortable*": *A Field Trial of a Recreated Soldier Cabin at Valley Forge* (Valley Forge Historical Park: National Park Service, U.S. Department of the Interior, 2004) 5.

4. Trussell, Jr., 313.

5. Brier, 3.

6. Waldo, 316.

7. *Pennsylvania Magazine of History and Biography* (Philadelphia, Vol. XVIII, 1897) 494.

8. Martin, x–xv.

9. *Ibid.*, 103–106.

10. Waldo, 316.

11. Lafayette, *Memoirs and Manuscripts of General Lafayette, Vol. 1* (New York: Saunders & Otley, MDCCCXXXVII) 2.

12. *Ibid.*, 2.

13. *Ibid.*, 3.

14. *Ibid.*, 8.

15. *Ibid.*, 19.

16. *Ibid.*, 14.

17. George Washington to Richard Henry Lee, July 17,1777, *The Papers of George Washington; Revolutionary War Series*, Charlottesville: University of Virginia Press, 2003).

18. Lafayette, 16.

19. *Ibid.*, 17.

20. *Ibid.*, 20.

21. *Ibid.*, 19.

22. Chernow, 331–332.

23. *Ibid.*, 331–332.

24. Buchanan, John, *The Road to Valley Forge* (New York: John Wiley & Sons, 2004) 229.

25. Chernow, 304.

26. Lafayette, 24.

27. *Ibid.*, 27.

28. *Ibid.*, 32–33.

29. *Ibid.*, 36.

30. *Ibid.*, 35.

31. *Ibid.*, 142.

32. Waldo, 317.

Chapter Three

1. Trussell, Jr, 8.

2. *Ibid.*, 8.

3. *Ibid.*, 30.

4. Waldo, 318–319.

5. Trussell, Jr., 34.

6. Waldo, 315.

7. *Ibid.*, 314–315.

8. Trussell, Jr., 35.

9. "From George Washington to Brigadier General George Weedon, 10 February 1778," *Founders Online*, National Archives, last modified June 13, 2018, http://founders.archives.gov/documents/Washington/03-13-02-0422. [Original source: *The Papers of George Washington*, Revolutionary War Series, vol. 13, *26 Decem-*

ber *1777–28 February 1778*, ed. Edward G. Lengel. Charlottesville: University of Virginia Press, 2003, pp. 505–506.]

10. George Weeden (1902). *Valley Forge Orderly Book of General George Weedon of the Continental Army Under Command of Genl. George Washington: In the Campaign of 1777–8, Describing the Events of the Battles of Brandywine, Warren Tavern, Germantown, and Whitemarsh, and of the Camps at Neshaminy, Wilmington, Pennypacker's Mills, Skippack, Whitemarsh, & Valley Forge.* (New York: Dodd, Mead and Company, 1902) 174–175.

11. Lafayette, 36.

12. "From George Washington to Brigadier General Thomas Conway, 5 November 1777," *Founders Online*, National Archives, last modified June 13, 2018, http://founders.archives.gov/documents/Washington/03-12-02-0118. [Original source: *The Papers of George Washington*, Revolutionary War Series, vol. 12, *26 October 1777–25 December 1777*, ed. Frank E. Grizzard, Jr., and David R. Hoth. Charlottesville: University of Virginia Press, 2002, pp. 129–130.]

13. Chernow, 316.

14. "To George Washington from Brigadier General Thomas Conway, 5 November 1777," *Founders Online*, National Archives, last modified June 13, 2018, http://founders.archives.gov/documents/Washington/03-12-02-0119. [Original source: *The Papers of George Washington*, Revolutionary War Series, vol. 12, *26 October 1777–25 December 1777*, ed. Frank E. Grizzard, Jr., and David R. Hoth. Charlottesville: University of Virginia Press, 2002, pp. 130–131.]

15. Lafayette, 37.

16. Buchanan, 296.

17. "From George Washington to William Gordon, 23 January 1778," *Founders Online*, National Archives, last modified June 13, 2018, http://founders.archives.gov/documents/Washington/03-13-02-0281. [Original source: *The Papers of George Washington*, Revolutionary War Series, vol. 13, *26 December 1777–28 February 1778*, ed. Edward G. Lengel. Charlottesville: University of Virginia Press, 2003, pp. 322–323.]

18. "From George Washington to Patrick Henry, 28 March 1778," *Founders Online*, National Archives, last modified June 13, 2018, http://founders.archives.gov/documents/

Washington/03-14-02-0310. [Original source: *The Papers of George Washington*, Revolutionary War Series, vol. 14, *1 March 1778–30 April 1778*, ed. David R. Hoth. Charlottesville: University of Virginia Press, 2004, pp. 336–337.]

19. Trussell, Jr., 14.

20. Stoudt, 53.

21. Lee, Henry, *The Revolutionary War Memoirs of General Henry Lee*, Robert E. Lee, editor (New York: Da Capo Press, 1998) 107.

22. Charles Royster, *Light-Horse Harry Lee; and the Legacy of the American Revolution* (Baton Rouge: Louisiana State University Press, 1981) 26.

23. Weeden, 200–201.

24. Waldo, 319–320.

Chapter Four

1. Stoudt, 77.

2. George Washington, *The Writings of George Washington, Vol. VI, 1777–1778*, Worthington Chauncey Ford, editor (New York: G.P. Putnam's Sons, 1890) 281.

3. *Ibid.*, 288.

4. Trussell, Jr., 35.

5. Waldo, 320 -321.

6. Weeden, 186.

7. Wood, Rich, "For To Cure For The Etch," *Journal of the American Revolution*, https://allthingsliberty.com/author/richwood/, August 19, 2015, 1–6.

8. Martin, 110–111.

9. Stoudt, 99.

10. *Ibid.*, 106–107.

11. Mark M. Boatner, III, *Encyclopedia of the American Revolution*, Alexander Hamilton to James Duane, September 6, 1780 (Mechanicsburg, PA: Stackpole Books, 1994) 415.

12. Lafayette, 38.

13. *Ibid.*, 39.

14. "To George Washington from Major General Lafayette, 9 February 1778," *Founders Online*, National Archives, last modified June 13, 2018, http://founders.archives.gov/documents/Washington/03-13-02-0407. [Original source: *The Papers of George Washington*, Revolutionary War Series, vol. 13, *26 December 1777–28 February 1778*, ed. Edward G. Lengel. Charlottesville: University of Virginia Press, 2003, pp. 488–489.]

15. Lafayette, 39–40.

16. *Ibid.*, 40.

17. "To George Washington from Major General Lafayette, 23 February 1778," *Founders Online*, National Archives, last modified June 13, 2018, http://founders. archives.gov/documents/Washington/ 03-13-02-0552. [Original source: *The Papers of George Washington*, Revolutionary War Series, vol. 13, *26 December 1777–28 February 1778*, ed. Edward G. Lengel. Charlottesville: University of Virginia Press, 2003, pp. 648–650.]

18. Stoudt, 110–111.

19. Waldo, 322.

20. Lafayette, 42.

21. *Ibid.*, 43–44.

Chapter Five

1. George Washington, *The Writings of George Washington, Vol. VI, 1777–1778,* Worthington Chauncey Ford, editor (New York: G.P. Putnam's Sons, 1890) 355 -356.

2. Stoudt, 129.

3. Chernow, 330.

4. George Washington, *The Writings of George Washington, Vol. VI, 1777–1778,* Worthington Chauncey Ford, editor (New York: G.P. Putnam's Sons 1890) 358.

5. Stoudt, 132.

6. Thomas Paine, *The Crisis.*

7. Stoudt, 151.

8. Paul Lockhart, *The Drillmaster of Valley Forge* (New York: HarperCollins, 2008) 68.

9. *Ibid.*, 77.

10. Stoudt, 158–159.

11. "From George Washington to Henry Laurens, 27 February 1778," *Founders Online*, National Archives, last modified June 13, 2018, http://founders.archives.gov/ documents/Washington/03-13-02-0585. [Original source: *The Papers of George Washington*, Revolutionary War Series, vol. 13, *26 December 1777–28 February 1778*, ed. Edward G. Lengel. Charlottesville: University of Virginia Press, 2003, pp. 686–688.]

12. Lockhart, 1–2.

13. *Ibid.*, 4.

14. *Ibid.*, 5.

15. *Ibid.*, 6.

16. Buchanan, 302.

17. Lockhart, 44–45.

18. William North, General, *Baron Von Steuben; Major General, Inspector General & Drill Master, Continental Army* (Utica: North County Books, 1990) 11.

19. Stoudt, 157–158.

Chapter Six

1. Curtis F. Morgan, Jr., "Nathanael Greene as Quartermaster General," *Journal of the American Revolution*, November 18, 2013, 6.

2. Valley Forge Legacy, *The Muster Roll Project*, http://valleyforgemusterroll.org/ army_divisions.asp 9/12/2018.

3. "From George Washington to Major General Nathanael Greene, 12 February 1778," *Founders Online*, National Archives, last modified June 13, 2018, http://founders.archives.gov/documents/ Washington/03-13-02-0430. [Original source: *The Papers of George Washington*, Revolutionary War Series, vol. 13, *26 December 1777–28 February 1778*, ed. Edward G. Lengel. Charlottesville: University of Virginia Press, 2003, pp. 514–517.]

4. "To George Washington from Major General Nathanael Greene, 16 February 1778," *Founders Online*, National Archives, last modified June 13, 2018, http://founders. archives.gov/documents/Washington/ 03-13-02-0470. [Original source: *The Papers of George Washington*, Revolutionary War Series, vol. 13, *26 December 1777–28 February 1778*, ed. Edward G. Lengel. Charlottesville: University of Virginia Press, 2003, pp. 557–558.]

5. Stoudt, 134.

6. Francis Vinton Greene, *General Greene* (New York: D. Appleton & Company, 1893) 97.

7. Nathanael Greene to Samuel Ward, Jr., October 9,1772. Rhode Island Historical Society, *Major Nathanael Greene Collection,* Military official, Rhode Island, Papers 1768–1786, Processed by Elizabeth Delmage, September, 2005, Box 1, Folder, 11.

8. John Buchanan, *The Road to Guilford Courthouse* (New York: John Wiley & Sons, 1997) 262.

9. *Ibid.*, 264.

10. William Johnson, *Sketches of the Life and Correspondence of Nathanael Greene, Major General of the Armies of the United States, in the War of the Revolution* (Charleston, SC: A. E. Miller, 1822) 101.

11. Morgan, Jr., 3–4.
12. Johnson, 101.
13. Morgan, Jr., 7–8.
14. *Ibid.*, 7–8.
15. Johnson, 102.
16. Martin, 111–113.

Chapter Seven

1. Stoudt, 181.
2. *Ibid.*, 186.
3. *Ibid.*, 186.
4. Lockhart, 96.
5. *Ibid.*, 98.
6. Stoudt, 192–193.
7. Frederick William Baron von Steuben, *Baron von Steuben's Revolutionary War Drill Manual* (New York: Dover Publications, Inc., 1985) 11.
8. *Ibid.*, 11–12.
9. *Ibid.*, 12–13.
10. Lockhart, 101.
11. *Ibid.*, 104.
12. Stoudt, 198.
13. *Ibid.*, 210.
14. Trussell, Jr. 22.

Chapter Eight

1. Stoudt, 205–244.
2. Valley Forge Legacy, *The Muster Roll Project*, http://valleyforgemusterroll.org/army_divisions.asp 9/12/2018.
3. Stoudt, 217.
4. *Ibid.*, 219.
5. James Thomas Flexner, *Washington; The Indispensable Man* (New York: Little, Brown, 1979) 120.
6. Buchanan, *The Road to Guilford Courthouse*, 30.
7. *Dictionary of National Biography*, ed. Leslie Stephen (London: Smith, Elder & Co. 1885) 344–347.
8. Jacques, Tony, *Dictionary of Battles and Sieges* (Santa Barbara: Greenwood Press, 2007) 1075.
9. Chernow, 175.
10. Buchanan, *The Road to Guilford Courthouse*, 16.
11. George Washington, *The Writings of George Washington, Vol. VI, 1777–1778*, Worthington Chauncey Ford, Editor (New York: G.P. Putnam's Sons, 1890) 31.
12. *Ibid.*, 48.

13. Chernow, 264.
14. Charles Lee to George Washington, 12/4/1776, George Washington, *The Papers of George Washington: Colonial Series*, 10 Vols., ed. W.W. Abbot et al. (Charlottesville: University of Virginia Press, 1985).
15. "To George Washington from Major General Charles Lee, 8 December 1776," *Founders Online*, National Archives, last modified June 13, 2018, http://founders.archives.gov/documents/Washington/03-07-02-0216. [Original source: *The Papers of George Washington*, Revolutionary War Series, vol. 7, *21 October 1776–5 January 1777*, ed. Philander D. Chase. Charlottesville: University of Virginia Press, 1997, p. 277.]
16. Lockhart, 130.
17. Stoudt, 244.

Chapter Nine

1. Brier, 3.
2. Trussell, Jr., 13.
3. Fisher, 7.
4. Martin, 117.
5. *Ibid.*, 118.
6. General Orders, April 30, 1778, Stoudt, 259.
7. Chernow, 335.
8. Lockhart, 114–115.
9. Stoudt, 260–261.
10. *Ibid.*, 260–266.
11. Don Higginbotham, *Daniel Morgan: Revolutionary Rifleman* (Chapel Hill: University of North Carolina Press, 1961) 86.
12. Stoudt, 269.
13. General Orders, May 6, 1778, Stoudt, 271–272.
14. Lockhart, 115.
15. Fisher, 7–8.
16. Stoudt, 273–274.

Chapter Ten

1. Stoudt, 277.
2. Ellis, 85.
3. Stoudt, 278–279.
4. *Ibid.*, 295.
5. *Ibid.*, 295.
6. George Washington, Washington to Major General Lafayette, May 18, 1778, *The Writings of George Washington, Vol. VII*

(1778–1779) [1890] edited by Worthington Chauncey Ford, 16.

7. Martin, 118.

8. Lafayette, 46–47.

9. Martin, 118.

10. *Ibid.*, 118–120.

11. Fisher, 8.

12. Lockhart, 122.

13. Lafayette, 47.

14. Stoudt, 299.

15. Lafayette, 48.

16. Fisher, 8.

17. Lafayette, 48.

18. Fisher, 8.

19. Martin, 119–121.

20. Lafayette, 48.

21. Dearborn, 121.

Chapter Eleven

1. George Washington, Washington to Landon Carter, May 30, 1778, *The Writings of George Washington, Vol. VII (1778–1779)* [1890] edited by Worthington Chauncey Ford, 43.

2. General Orders, May 27, 1778, Stoudt, 311.

3. George Washington, Washington to Gouverneur Morris, May 29, 1778, *The Writings of George Washington, Vol. VII (1778–1779)* [1890] edited by Worthington Chauncey Ford, 31.

4. Stoudt, 312.

5. Lockhart, 127.

6. *Ibid.*, 132–133.

7. Stoudt, 318.

8. Fisher, 8.

9. Stoudt, 342.

10. Higginbotham, 85–86.

11. Stoudt, 321.

12. George Washington, Washington to Major General Dickinson, June 5, 1778, *The Writings of George Washington, Vol. VII (1778–1779)* [1890] Editor: Worthington Chauncey Ford, 54.

13. Fisher, 9.

14. Higginbotham, 86.

15. George Washington, Washington to The President of Congress, June 18, 1778, *The Writings of George Washington, Vol. VII (1778–1779)* [1890] Editor: Worthington Chauncey Ford, 67.

16. George Washington, Washington to Major General Lee, May 30, 1778, *The Writings of George Washington, Vol. VII*

(1778–1779) [1890] edited by Worthington Chauncey Ford, 43.

17. Fisher, 9.

Chapter Twelve

1. Mark Edward Lender and Garry Wheeler Stone, *Fatal Sunday* (Norman: University of Oklahoma Press, 2016) 126.

2. John Watts De Peyster, *The Engagement at Freehold, Known as the Battle of Monmouth, N.J., More Properly of Monmouth Courthouse, 28th June, 1778* (New York: A.S. Barnes & Co., 1878) 2.

3. Lender and Stone, 143.

4. Johnson, 102.

5. Henry Clinton, General Clinton to Lord Germain, July 5, 1778, Gilder Lehrman Collection # GlC04283.

6. Watts De Peyster, 3.

7. Lockhart, 144.

8. Lender and Stone, 130.

9. Buchanan, *The Road to Guilford Courthouse*, 29–33.

10. George Washington, *General Orders, 22 June 1778, The Writings of George Washington, Vol. XII*, Editor: John C. Fitzpatrick [1931–1934].

11. Fisher, 9.

12. George Washington, Washington to the President of Congress, June 22, 1778, *The Writings of George Washington, Vol. VI, 1777–1778*, Worthington Chauncey Ford, editor (New York: G.P. Putnam's Sons, 1890) 73.

13. Lender and Stone, 135–138.

14. Clinton to Germain.

Chapter Thirteen

1. Lafayette, 51.

2. *Ibid.*, 51.

3. Lender and Stone, 174.

4. Martin, 122–123.

5. Lafayette, 51.

6. Washington to the Marquis De Lafayette, Instructions, June 25, 1778, *The Writings of George Washington, 1732–1799, Vol. XII*, edited by John C. Fitzpatrick [1931–1934], 74.

7. Lockhart, 149.

8. Fisher, 9.

9. Martin, 123–124.

10. "From Alexander Hamilton to Mar-

quis de Lafayette [25 June 1778]," *Founders Online*, National Archives, last modified June 13, 2018, http://founders.archives. gov/documents/Hamilton/01-01-02-0492. [Original source: *The Papers of Alexander Hamilton*, vol. 1, *1768–1778*, ed. Harold C. Syrett. New York: Columbia University Press, 1961, pp. 503–504.]

11. Dearborn, June 26.

12. "From Alexander Hamilton to George Washington, [26 June 1778]," *Founders Online*, National Archives, last modified June 13, 2018, http://founders.archives. gov/documents/Hamilton/01-01-02-0493. [Original source: *The Papers of Alexander Hamilton*, vol. 1, *1768–1778*, ed. Harold C. Syrett. New York: Columbia University Press, 1961, pp. 504–505.]

13. Henry Lee, *The Revolutionary War Memoirs of General Henry Lee*, ed. Robert E. Lee (New York: Da Capo Press, 1998) 113.

14. Dearborn, June 27.

15. Martin, 125.

16. "To George Washington from Major General Charles Lee, 25 June 1778," *Founders Online*, National Archives, last modified June 13, 2018, http://founders.archives.gov/ documents/Washington/03-15-02-0574. [Original source: *The Papers of George Washington*, Revolutionary War Series, vol. 15, *May–June 1778*, ed. Edward G. Lengel. Charlottesville: University of Virginia Press, 2006.]

17. "From George Washington to Major General Charles Lee, 26 June 1778," *Founders Online*, National Archives, last modified June 13, 2018, http://founders.archives.gov/ documents/Washington/03-15-02-0593. [Original source: *The Papers of George Washington*, Revolutionary War Series, vol. 15, *May–June 1778*, ed. Edward G. Lengel. Charlottesville: University of Virginia Press, 2006, p. 556.]

Chapter Fourteen

1. "General Orders, 27 June 1778," *Founders Online*, National Archives, last modified June 13, 2018, http://founders.archives.gov/ documents/Washington/03-15-02-0600. [Original source: *The Papers of George Washington*, Revolutionary War Series, vol. 15, *May–June 1778*, ed. Edward G. Lengel. Charlottesville: University of Virginia Press, 2006, pp. 559–560.]

2. Washington, Washington to the President of Congress, June 28, 1778, *The Writings of George Washington, 1732–1799, Vol. XII*, edited by John C. Fitzpatrick [1931–1934] 127.

3. Lender and Stone, 193.

4. *Ibid.*, 194.

5. "Proceedings of a General Court-Martial for the Trial of Major General Charles Lee [4 July 1778]," *Founders Online*, National Archives, last modified June 13, 2018, http://founders.archives. gov/documents/Hamilton/01-01-02-0498. [Original source: *The Papers of Alexander Hamilton*, vol. 1, *1768–1778*, ed. Harold C. Syrett. New York: Columbia University Press, 1961, pp. 507–509.]

6. Higginbotham, 89.

7. *Ibid.*, 89.

8. Henry Clinton, General Clinton to Lord Germain, July 5, 1778, Gilder Lehrman Collection # GlC04283.

9. Lockhart, 153.

10. "To George Washington from Major General Philemon Dickinson, 28 June 1778," *Founders Online*, National Archives, last modified June 13, 2018, http://founders.archives.gov/documents/ Washington/03-15-02-0615. [Original source: *The Papers of George Washington*, Revolutionary War Series, vol. 15, *May–June 1778*, ed. Edward G. Lengel. Charlottesville: University of Virginia Press, 2006, pp. 573–576.]

11. Lender and Stone, 194.

Chapter Fifteen

1. Proceedings of the General Court-Martial of Major General Lee, July 4, 1778 (New York: Privately Reprinted, 1864), Library of Congress, hereinafter referred to as the Lee Court-Martial, 14.

2. Lockhart, 155.

3. Martin, 125–126.

4. Lee Court-Martial, 10.

5. *Ibid.*, 23.

6. *Ibid.*, 176.

7. *Ibid.*, 188.

8. *Ibid.*, 140–144.

9. *Ibid.*, 17.

10. *Ibid.*, 30.

11. *Ibid.*, 17.

12. Lender and Stone, 256.

13. *Ibid.*, 256.

14. Martin, 126–127.
15. Lockhart, 158.
16. Lee Court-Martial, 15.
17. *Ibid.*, 16.
18. Martin, 127.
19. Dearborn, June, 28.
20. Henry Clinton, General Clinton to Lord Germain, July 5, 1778, Gilder Lehrman Collection # GlC04283.
21. Lender and Stone, 174.
22. Lee Court-Martial, 82.
23. *Ibid.*, 84–85.
24. *Ibid.*, 79.
25. *Ibid.*, 72–73.
26. *Ibid.*, 63–65.

Chapter Sixteen

1. Martin, 127.
2. Henry B. Dawson, *Battles of the United States: Sea and Land* (New York: Fry and Company, 1858) 407–408.
3. George F. Scheer and Hugh F. Rankin, *Rebels and Redcoats* (New York: The World Publishing Co., 1957) 330–331.
4. Bernardus Swartout, *Bernardus Swartout Diary* (New York: New York Historical Society), 4–6.
5. Lee Court-Martial, 79–82.
6. Martin, 127.
7. John Laurens to Henry Laurens, 30 June, 1778, *Lee Papers, Vol. 5* (New York: New-York Historical Society, 1871–74) 433.
8. Alexander Hamilton to Elias Boudinot, 5 July, 1778, Syrett, *The Papers of Alexander Hamilton*, 512.
9. Lender and Stone, 291–292.
10. John Ackerman pension deposition S16028, Revolutionary War Pension Applications, National Archives.
11. Lender and Stone, 292.
12. Anthony Wayne to his wife, 1 July, 1778, Lee Papers, *Collections of the New-York Historical Society*, 448–449.
13. Lee Court-Martial, 63–67.
14. *Ibid.*, 136–139.
15. John Laurens to Henry Laurens, 30 June, 1778, Lee Papers, Vol. II, *Collections of the New-York Historical Society*, 431–434.
16. Martin, 128.
17. *Ibid.*, 128.
18. Lender and Stone, 297.
19. William Hale letter, 14 July, 1778, Wilkin, *British Soldiers in America*, 262–263.
20. Lender and Stone, 322.

21. Dearborn, June 28th.
22. Lee Court-Martial, 95.
23. *Ibid.*, 90–91.
24. Hale letter.
25. Martin, 128–129.
26. *Ibid.*, 132–133.

Chapter Seventeen

1. Dearborn, 28th.
2. Henry Clinton, General Clinton to Lord Germain, July 5, 1778, Gilder Lehrman Collection # GlC04283.
3. Lender and Stone, 338.
4. Martin, 129–131.
5. Lender and Stone, 342.
6. Dawson, 409.
7. Lender and Stone, 345.
8. Henry Clinton, General Clinton to Lord Germain, July 5, 1778, Gilder Lehrman Collection # GlC04283.
9. Lee Court-Martial, 110–111.
10. Lockhart, 163–164.
11. Lender and Stone, 359–360.
12. Martin, 131.
13. Lafayette, 54.

Chapter Eighteen

1. Lockhart, 164.
2. Martin, 132, n.11.
3. "From George Washington to a Continental Congress Camp Committee, 29 January 1778," *Founders Online*, National Archives, accessed September 29, 2019, https://founders.archives.gov/documents/Washington/03-13-02-0335. [Original source: *The Papers of George Washington*, Revolutionary War Series, vol. 13, *26 December 1777–28 February 1778*, ed. Edward G. Lengel. Charlottesville: University of Virginia Press, 2003, pp. 376–409.]
4. Fisher, 9.
5. Lender & Stone, 353.
6. Higginbotham, 91.
7. "From George Washington to a Continental Congress Camp Committee, 29 January 1778," *Founders Online*, National Archives, accessed September 29, 2019, https://founders.archives.gov/documents/Washington/03-13-02-0335. [Original source: *The Papers of George Washington*, Revolutionary War Series, vol. 13, *26 December 1777–28 February 1778*, ed. Edward G.

Lengel. Charlottesville: University of Virginia Press, 2003, pp. 376–409.] n.12.

8. *Ibid.*

9. Lender & Stone, 367–369.

10. Lockhart, 165–166.

11. William S. Baker, *Itinerary of General Washington, From June 15, 1775, to December 23, 1783* (Philadelphia: J.B. Lippincott Company, 1892) 135.

12. "From Alexander Hamilton to Elias Boudinot, [5 July 1778]," *Founders Online,* National Archives, accessed September 29, 2019, https://founders.archives.gov/documents/Hamilton/01-01-02-0499. [Original source: *The Papers of Alexander Hamilton,* vol. 1, *1768–1778,* ed. Harold C. Syrett. New York: Columbia University Press, 1961, pp. 510–514.]

13. Martin, 133.

14. "General Orders, 4 July 1778," *Founders Online,* National Archives, accessed September 29, 2019, https://founders.archives.gov/documents/Washington/03-16-02-0020. [Original source: *The Papers of George Washington,* Revolutionary War Series, vol. 16, *1 July–14 September 1778,* ed. David R. Hoth. Charlottesville: University of Virginia Press, 2006, pp. 19–20.]

15. Lender & Stone, 370.

16. Fisher, 9.

17. *Ibid.,* 9.

18. "From Alexander Hamilton to Elias Boudinot, [5 July 1778]," *Founders Online,* National Archives, accessed September 29, 2019, https://founders.archives.gov/documents/Hamilton/01-01-02-0499. [Original source: *The Papers of Alexander Hamilton,* vol. 1, *1768–1778,* ed. Harold C. Syrett. New York: Columbia University Press, 1961, pp. 510–514.]

Chapter Nineteen

1. Edward Lengel et al., *The Papers of George Washington: Revolutionary War Series, Vol. 15* (Charlottesville: University of Virginia Press, 2006) 594–596.

2. *Ibid.,* 594–596.

3. *Ibid.,* 594–596.

4. *Ibid.,* 594–596.

5. "From George Washington to Major General Charles Lee, 30 June 1778," *Founders Online,* National Archives, accessed September 29, 2019, https://founders.archives.gov/documents/Washington/03-15-02-0655. [Original source: *The Papers of George Washington,* Revolutionary War Series, vol. 15, *May–June 1778,* ed. Edward G. Lengel. Charlottesville: University of Virginia Press, 2006, pp. 597–598.]

6. *The Lee Papers, Vol. III* (New York: New-York Historical Society, 1872) 2.

7. "General Orders, 22 December 1778," *Founders Online,* National Archives, accessed September 29, 2019, https://founders.archives.gov/documents/Washington/03-18-02-0550. [Original source: *The Papers of George Washington,* Revolutionary War Series, vol. 18, *1 November 1778–14 January 1779,* ed. Edward G. Lengel. Charlottesville: University of Virginia Press, 2008, pp. 486–489.]

8. Jeff Dacus, "Lee's Defeat … In Court," *Journal of the American Revolution,* November, 2016.

Chapter Twenty

1. Jim Stempel, *American Hannibal* (Penmore Press, Tucson, 2017) XXV.

2. Jim Stempel, *The Nature of War: Origins and Evolution of Violent Conflict* (Jefferson, NC: McFarland, 2012) 4–6.

3. Robert L. O'Connell, *Of Arms and Men: A History of War, Weapons, and Aggression* (New York: Oxford University Press, 1989) 172.

4. *Ibid.,* 167.

5. Martin, 230.

6. *Ibid.,* 231.

7. *Ibid.,* 240–241.

8. Greenwood, John, *The Revolutionary Services of John Greenwood of Boston and New York, 1775–1783* (New York: Mrs. Joseph Rudd Greenwood, 1922).

9. Fox, Ebenezer, *The Adventures of Ebenezer Fox, in the Revolutionary War* (Boston: Fox, 1848).

Bibliography

Ackerman, John. Pension deposition S16028 Revolutionary War Pension Applications, National Archives.

Alden, John Richard. *General Charles Lee, Traitor or Patriot?* Baton Route: Louisiana State University Press, 1951.

Baker, William S. *The Itinerary of General Washington, from June 15, 1775, to December 23, 1783.* Philadelphia: J. B. Lippincott Company, 1892.

Billias, George. *George Washington's Opponents.* New York: Morrow, 1969.

Black, Jeremy. *War for America: The Fight for Independence, 1775–1783.* New York: St. Martin's Press, 1991.

Boatner, Mark. M., III. *Encyclopedia of the American Revolution.* Mechanicsburg, PA: Stackpole Books, 1994.

Brier, Marc, A. *"Tollerably Comfortable": A Field Trial of a Recreated Soldier Cabin at Valley Forge.* Valley Forge Historical Park: National Park Service, U.S. Department of the Interior, 2004.

Buchannan, John. *The Road to Guilford Courthouse.* New York: John Wiley & Sons, 1997.

_____. *The Road to Valley Forge.* New York: John Wiley & Sons, Inc., 2004.

Burrows, Edwin G. *Forgotten Patriots.* New York: Basic Books, 2008.

Calhoon, Robert M. *The Loyalists in Revolutionary America: 1760–1781.* New York: Harcourt Brace Jovanovich, 1965.

Carrington, Henry B. *Battles of the American Revolution, 1775–1781.* New York: Barnes, 1876.

Chernow, Ron. *Washington: A Life.* New York: Penguin Books, 2010.

Clinton, Henry. Gilder Lehrman Collection # GIC04283.

Coggins, Jack, ed. *Boys in the Revolution:* *Young Americans Tell Their Stories in the War for Independence.* Harrisburg, PA: Stackpole Books, 1967.

Cohen, Lester H. *The Revolutionary Histories: Contemporary Narratives of the American Revolution.* Ithaca, NY: Cornell University Press, 1980.

Collins, James. *Autobiography of a Revolutionary Soldier, Sixty Years in the Nueces Valley: 1870–1930.* San Antonio: Naylor Printing Co., 1930.

Constable, George, ed. *Winds of Revolution.* Alexandria, VA: Time-Life Books, 1989.

Cummings, William P., and Hugh Rankin, eds. *The Fate of a Nation: The American Revolution Through Contemporary Eyes.* London: Phaidon Press, 1975.

Dacus, Jeff. "Lee's Defeat.... In Court." *Journal of the American Revolution:* November, 2016.

Dann, John C., ed. *The Revolution Remembered.* Chicago: University of Chicago Press, 1980.

Davie, William Richardson. *The Revolutionary War Sketches of William R. Davie.* Ed. Blackwell P. Robinson. Raleigh: North Carolina Division of Archives & History, 1976.

Dawson, Henry. *Battles of the United States: Sea and Land.* New York: Fry & Company, 1858.

Dearborn, Henry. *Revolutionary War Journals of Henry Dearborn.* Ed. Lloyd A. Brown and Howard H. Peckham. Chicago: The Caxton Club, 1939.

De Peyster, John Watts. *The Engagement at Freehold, Known as the Battle of Monmouth N.J., More Properly Monmouth Courthouse, 28th June, 1778.* New York: A. S. Barnes & Co., 1878.

Dictionary of National Biography. Ed. Leslie

Stephen. London: Smith, Elder & Company, 1885.

Dimmock, Martha McHutchinson. *A Chronicle of the Revolutionary War.* New York: Perennial Library, 1976.

Dupuy, Trevor N. *The Evolution of Weapons and Warfare.* New York: Da Capo Press, 1984.

Ellis, Joseph. *His Excellency, George Washington.* New York, Vintage Books, 2004.

Everhart, Lawrence, Pension Application S25068, 1834, Transcribed and annotated by C. Leon Harris.

Ewald, Johann. *Diary of the American War: A Hessian Journal.* Ed., Joseph P. Trustin, New Haven: Yale University Press, 1979.

Ferling, John. *Almost a Miracle: The American Victory in the War of Independence.* New York: Oxford University Press, 2007.

Fisher, Elijah. *Elijah Fisher's Journal While in the War for Independence, and Continued Two Years After He Came to Maine, 1775–1784.* Augusta, ME: Press of Badger and Manley, 1880.

Flexner, James Thomas. *Washington: The Indispensable Man.* New York: Little, Brown, 1979.

Flood, Charles Bracelen. *Rise, and Fight Again: Perilous Times Along the Road to Independence.* New York: Dodd, Mead & Co., 1976.

Fox, Ebenezer. *The Adventures of Ebenezer Fox In the Revolutionary War.* Boston: Fox, 1848.

Gaines, James R. *For Liberty and Glory: Washington, Lafayette, and Their Revolutions.* New York: W. W. Norton & Co., 2007.

Gavin, John R. *The Minute Men: The First Fight: Myths and Realities of the American Revolution.* Washington, D.C.: Brassey's, 1996.

Graham, James. *The Life of General Daniel Morgan of the Virginia Line of the Army of the United States.* New York: Derby & Jackson, 1856.

Green, Charles E. *The Story of Delaware in the Revolution.* Wilmington: Press of William N. Cann, 1975.

Green, Peter. *Alexander of Macedon.* Berkeley: University of California Press, 1989.

Greene, Francis Vinton. *General Greene.* New York: D. Appleton & Company, 1893.

Greene, Nathanael. *Major Nathanael Greene Collection.* Rhode Island Historical Society, Military Official, Rhode Island, Papers 1768–1786. Processed by Elizabeth Delmage, September, 2005, Box 1, Folder 11.

Greenwood, John. *The Revolutionary Services of John Greenwood of Boston and New York, 1775–1783.* New York: Mrs. Joseph Rudd Greenwood, 1922.

Hamilton, Alexander. *The Papers of Alexander Hamilton.* Vol. 1, 1768–1778. Ed. Harold C. Syrett. New York: Columbia University Press, 1961.

Hammond, Samuel, Pension Application S21807, 1832, transcribed by Will Graves.

Hibbert, Christopher. *Redcoats and Rebels: The American Revolution Through British Eyes.* New York: Avon Books, 1991.

Higginbotham, Don. *Daniel Morgan: Revolutionary Rifleman.* Chapel Hill: University of North Carolina Press, 1961.

_____. *The War of Independence: Military Attitudes, Policies, and Practice 1763–1789.* New York: Macmillan, 1971.

Jacques, Tony. *Dictionary of Battles & Sieges.* Santa Barbara, CA: Greenwood, 2007.

Johnson, William. *Sketches of the Life and Correspondence of Nathanael Greene, Major General of the Armies of the United States, in the War of the Revolution.* Charleston, SC: A. E. Miller, 1822.

Jones, W. T. *Masters of Political Thought.* Boston: Houghton Mifflin, 1969.

Keegan, John. *A History of Warfare.* New York: Vintage, 1993.

Kirkwood, Robert. *The Journal and Order Book of Captain Robert Kirkwood of the Delaware Regiment of the Continental Line.* Dover: Press of the Delawarean, 1910.

Kwasny, Mark V. *Washington's Partisan War, 1775–1783.* Kent, OH: Kent State University Press, 1996.

Lafayette. *Memoirs and Manuscripts of General Lafayette, Vol. 1.* New York: Saunders & Otley, 1837.

Lagemann, Robert, and Albert Mauncy. *The Long Rifle.* New York: Eastern Acorn Press, 1993.

Lee, Charles. *The Lee Papers, 1754–1811.* 4 Vols. Collections of the New-York Historical Society. New York: New-York Historical Society, 1871–74.

Lee, Henry. *The Revolutionary War Memoirs of General Henry Lee.* Ed. Robert E. Lee. New York: Da Capo Press, 1998.

Lender, Mark Edward, and Garry Wheeler Stone. *Fatal Sunday: George Washington, the Monmouth Campaign, and the Politics of Battle*. Norman: University of Oklahoma Press, 2016.

Lockhart, Paul. *The Drillmaster of Valley Forge*. New York: HarperCollins, 2008.

Mackenzie, Roderick. *Strictures on Lt. Col. Tarleton's History "Of the Campaigns of 1780 and 1781, in the Southern Provinces of North America."* London: R. Raulder, New Bond Street; T. and J. Egerton, Charing-Cross, R. Jameson, Strand; and T. Swell, Cornhill, 1787.

Mackesy, Piers. *The War for America, 1775–1783*. Lincoln: University of Nebraska Press, 1993.

Martin, Joseph Plumb. *A Narrative of Some of the Adventures, Dangers and Sufferings of a Revolutionary Soldier*. Ed. George Scheer. New York: Eastern National, 1962.

May, Robin. *The British Army in North America: 1775–1783*. London: Osprey, 1997.

McCullough, David. *1776*. New York: Simon & Schuster, 2005.

McGuire, Thomas J. *The Philadelphia Campaign: Germantown and the Roads to Valley Forge*. Mechanicsburg, PA: Stackpole Books, 2007.

McJunkin, Joseph. *Memoirs of Major Joseph McJunkin—Revolutionary Patriot*. Reverend James Dodge Saye, originally appearing as a series of articles in *Watchman and Observer*. Richmond, Virginia: 1847–49.

Morgan, Curtis, Jr. "Nathanael Greene as Quartermaster General. *Journal of the American Revolution*, November 18, 2013, 6.

Myers, Theodorus Bailey. *Cowpens Papers*. Charleston, SC: The News and Courier, 1881.

Nelson, Paul David. *General Horatio Gates: A Biography*. Baton Rouge: Louisiana State University Press, 1976.

North, William, General. *Baron Von Steuben, Inspector General & Drill Master, Continental Army*. Utica: North County Books, 1990.

O'Connell, Robert, L. *Of Arms and Men: A History of War, Weapons, and Aggression*. New York: Oxford University Press, 1989.

Palmer, Dave A. *George Washington's Military Genius*. Washington, D.C: Regnery History, 2012.

Peckham, Howard H. *The War for Independence: A Military History*. Chicago: University of Chicago Press, 1958.

Peden, Henry C. *Revolutionary War Patriots of Baltimore Town and Baltimore County, 1775–1783*. Silver Spring, MD: Family Line Publications, 1988.

Pennsylvania Magazine of History and Biography. Philadelphia, Vol. XVIII, 1897.

Piecuch, Jim, and John Beakes. *John Eager Howard in the American Revolution*. Charleston, SC: The Nautical and Aviation Publishing Co. of America, 2009.

Proceedings of a General Court-Martial for the Trial of Major General Charles Lee.

Papers of Alexander Hamilton, Vol. 1, 1768–1778. Ed. Harold C. Syrett. New York: Columbia University Press, 1961.

Raphael, Ray. *A People's History of the American Revolution*. New York: The New Press, 2001.

Robinson, Blackwell P. *William R. Davie*. Chapel Hill: University of North Carolina Press, 1957.

Rossie, Jonathan Gregory. *The Politics of Command in the American Revolution*. Syracuse: Syracuse University Press, 1975.

Royster, Charles. *Light-Horse Harry Lee and the Legacy of the American Revolution*. Baton Rouge: Louisiana State University Press, 1981.

_____. *A Revolutionary People at War: The Continental Army and American Character, 1775–1783*. New York: W.W. Norton, 1979.

Sabine, George, H. *A History of Political Theory*. New York: Holt, Rinehart, and Winston, 1961.

Schaun, George, and Virginia Schaun. *Everyday Life in Colonial Maryland*. Lanham: Maryland Historical Press, 1996.

Scheer, George F., and Hugh F. Rankin, *Rebels and Redcoats*. New York: The World Publishing Company, 1957.

Smith, Samuel S.. *The Battle of Monmouth*. Trenton: New Jersey Historical Commission, 1975.

Steadman, Charles. *The History of the Origin, Progress, and Termination of the American War*. Two Volumes. London: N.p., 1794.

Stempel, Jim. *American Hannibal: The Extraordinary Account of Revolutionary War Hero Daniel Morgan at the Battle of Cowpens*. Tucson: Penmore Press, 2017.

_____. "Cowpens; A Miracle in the Wilderness." *Drumbeat, Publication of the General Society, Sons of the Revolution*, Vol. 35, Number 2–3. Fall, 2018.

_____. *The Nature of War: Origins and Evo-*

lution of Violent Conflict. Jefferson, NC: McFarland, 2012.

_____. "You Remember the American Victory at Cowpens, Don't You?" History News Network. April 1, 2018.

Stephenson, Michael. Patriot Battles: How the War of Independence Was Fought. New York, HarperCollins, 2007.

Steuart, Rieman. A History of the Maryland Line in the Revolutionary War, 1775–1783. Baltimore: Society of the Cincinnati of Maryland, 1972.

Steuben, Frederick William, Baron von. Baron von Steuben's Revolutionary War Drill Manual. New York: Dover Publications, Inc., 1985.

Stoudt, Joseph John. Ordeal at Valley Forge. Philadelphia: University of Pennsylvania Press, 1963.

Swartout, Bernardus. Bernardus Swartout Diary. New-York Historical Society, n.d..

Swearinger, Richard. Pension Application S31402, 1832. Transcribed by Will Graves.

Tarleton, Banastre. A History of the Campaigns of 1780 and 1781, in the Southern Provinces of North America. A Reproduction. Manchester, UK, John Rylands University, 1787.

Trussell, John B.B., Jr. Epic on the Schuylkill. Harrisburg: Pennsylvania Historical and Museum Commission, 1992.

Valley Forge Legacy. Muster Roll Project. http://valleyforgemusterroll.org/army__divisions9/12/2018.

Volo, Dorothy Denneen, and James M. Volo. Daily Life During the American Revolution. Westport, CT: Greenwood Press, 2003.

Waldo, Albigence. Valley Forge, 1777–1778. Diary of Surgeon Albigence Waldo, of the Connecticut Line. The Pennsylvania Magazine of History and Biography (1897) 21, no. 3.

Washington, George. The Papers of George

Washington. Revolutionary War Series, Vol. 7, 21 October 1776–January 1777. Ed. Philander D. Chase. Charlottesville: University of Virginia Press, 1997.

_____. The Papers of George Washington. Revolutionary War Series. W.W. Abbott, Dorothy Twohig, Philander D. Chase, Edward G. Langel, Theodore J. Crackel, and David R. Hoth, eds. Charlottesville: University of Virginia Press, 1998–1999.

_____. The Papers of George Washington. Revolutionary War Series, Vol. 14, March 1776–30 April 1778. Ed. David R. Hoth, Charlottesville: University of Virginia Press, 2004.

_____. The Papers of George Washington. Revolutionary War Series, Vol. 15, May–June 1778. Ed. Edward Lengel. Charlottesville: University of Virginia Press, 2006.

_____. The Writings of George Washington. Vol. VI, 1777–1778. Worthington Chauncey Ford, editor. New York: G.P. Putnam's Sons, 1890.

Weeden, George. Valley Forge Orderly Book of General George Weeden of the Continental Army Under Command of Genl. George Washington: In the Campaign of 1777–1778, Describing the Events of the Battles of Brandywine, Warren Tavern, Germantown, and Whitemarsh, and of the Camps at Neshaminy, Wilmington, Pennypacker's Mill, Skippack, Whitemarsh, & Valley Forge. New York: Dodd, Mead and Company, 1902.

Wickshire, Franklin, and Mary Wickshire. Cornwallis: The American Adventure. New York: Houghton Mifflin, 1970.

Wood, Rich. "For to Cure the Etch." Journal of the American Revolution. August 19, 2015.

Young, Thomas. Memoirs of Major Thomas Young; A Revolutionary Patriot of South Carolina. Orion Magazine: October, 1834.

Index